Homes and Libraries
of
the Presidents

For Donald, Lynne, and Amy

They keep me going

Homes and Libraries

of

the Presidents

An Interpretive Guide

by

William G. Clotworthy

The McDonald & Woodward Publishing Company
Blacksburg, Virginia
1995

The McDonald & Woodward Publishing Company
P. O. Box 10308, Blacksburg, Virginia 24062-0308

A McDonald & Woodward Guide to the American Landscape

**Homes and Libraries of the Presidents
An Interpretive Guide**

All rights reserved
Printed in the United States of America
by McNaughton & Gunn, Inc., Saline, Michigan

01 00 99 98 97   10 9 8 7 6 5 4 3 2

First Printing May 1995
Second Printing March 1997

Library of Congress Cataloging-in-Publication Data

Clotworthy, William G., 1926–
  Homes and libraries of the presidents : an interpretive guide /
by William G. Clotworthy.
    p. cm. -- (McDonald & Woodward guide to the American land-
scape)
  Includes bibliographical references (p.) and index.
  ISBN 0–939923–32–7 : $19.95
  1. Presidents--United States--Homes and haunts--Guidebooks.
2. Presidents--United States--Museums--Guidebooks. #. Presidential libraries--United States--Guidebooks. 4. United States--
Guidebooks. I. Title. II. Series.
E176.1.C66 1995
   973'.099--dc20   94–44390
                                                        CIP

Contents

Section I
Introduction

Section II
**Homes, Libraries, and Museums of
the Presidents**

Franklin D. Roosevelt (continued)

Section III
Additional Information about Presidential Sites

Acknowledgements

I would like to express my thanks to those who were of such great assistance in preparing this book: the publishers, Jerry McDonald and Susan Woodward, whose vision and gentle prodding made it a pleasant experience; editor Kathie Dickenson, whose valiant attempts to turn an organizer into a writer almost succeeded; Karl Decker, the king of punctuation, especially commas; and Tina Stoll, interpreter of scribbles and scrawls, secretary par excellence.

Most credit for any success, however, lies with the hundreds of devoted park rangers, archivists, docents, senior citizen volunteers, and staffers, who dedicate themselves to the preservation and maintenance of Presidential homes and sites, thus perpetuating the heritage contained within their walls. It has been my privilege to meet many of these fine Americans, and I am honored to salute them.

Credits for Color Plates

Ash Lawn–Highland: 5; Berkeley Plantation: 8; Capital Area Preservation, Inc.: 15; William G. Clotworthy: 12, 14, 16, 22, 26, 30, 31, 37; Richard Frear, National Park Service: 23, 32; Gerald R. Ford Library: 35; Greg Hadley Photography: 9; The Ladies' Hermitage Association: 6; James Buchanan Foundation: 13; Rix Jennings: 11; Jennie Jones: 18; Jerry N. McDonald: 33; Montpelier, a museum property of the National Trust for Historic Preservation: front cover, 4; Mount Vernon Ladies' Association: 1; National Park Service: 2, 28, 36; New Jersey Department of Environmental Protection: 20; New York State Department of Economic Development: 7; James K. Polk Ancestral Home: 10; President Benjamin Harrison Home: 21; Richard Nixon Library & Birthplace: 34; R. Lautman/Monticello: 3; Roosevelt Campobello International Park Commission: 29; Rutherford B. Hayes Presidential Center: 17; Vermont Division for Historic Preservation: 19, 27; William Howard Taft National Historic Site: 24; Woodrow Wilson House, National Trust: 25.

Ann Pamela Cunningham, c. 1866.
Photograph courtesy Mount Vernon Ladies' Association.

Dedication

This book is dedicated to Miss Ann Pamela Cunningham (1816 – 1875), founder and first Regent of the Mount Vernon Ladies' Association. Her vision, tireless effort, and personal dedication inspired thousands of private citizens to organize and contribute to the purchase, restoration, renovation, and maintenance of homes and other places associated with America's great leaders, thereby preserving forever an important part of our precious national heritage.

Scope and Purpose

There is a three-fold purpose to this book. It is, first of all, a traveler's guide to almost one hundred Presidential homes, libraries, and museums that are open to the public in the United States and Canada. As such, it provides basic information on access, admission fees, restaurants, tours, and facilities for the disabled. Included are pictures of the sites, as well as maps showing how to reach them.

Second, the book attempts to put each Presidential life and home into personal and historical context — the colonial gentry lifestyle of Thomas Jefferson at Monticello, the hardscrabble farm life of Abraham Lincoln, the all-American, small-town background of Ronald Reagan — and to describe not only the homes in which they lived, but the era, their families, their communities, and their education — some of the influences that helped to shape the forty-one men who have become President of the United States.

Third, the book serves as a tribute to the local, state, and national historic preservation societies and organizations that have resurrected, restored, reconstructed, replicated, and maintained these American treasures. It describes the efforts they have made to preserve an important part of our national heritage, efforts that enable us to visit these places and to observe, learn, and honor the great Americans who once lived in them. The book also traces the federal government's role, carried out by the National Park Service and the National Archives, in administering and maintaining humble cabins, splendid mansions, ordinary houses, and great modern libraries.

The book is divided into three sections. The first presents an overview of the historical significance of the homes, libraries, and museums, discusses restoration and preservation efforts, and eulogizes the woman who, in the mid-nineteenth century, organized the first restoration project, that of George Washington's Mount Vernon.

Section II contains a short biography of each President, followed by a description of each home, museum, or library site associated with him. The biographies are not full, but anecdotal, serving primarily to associate the President with the site descriptions that follow. Each site description is accompanied by a map, visitor information, and suggestions for additional reading material.

Section III provides additional sources for information and provides a brief description of other attractions associated with the Presidents. These include monuments, such as the Lincoln Memorial; battlefields, such as Gettysburg; and Presidential homes that are privately owned and closed to the public. In addition, there is a roster of birthplace and burial sites. Section III also includes a list of important historical societies and a list of recommended publications.

A visit to any Presidential site is a rich and rewarding experience. The host personnel, whether Park Service rangers, professional curators, teen-age docents, or senior citizen volunteers, are friendly, knowledgeable, and anxious to enhance everyone's enjoyment of the facility. Most important, they want visitors to leave with a deeper awareness and appreciation of the men who have led our nation, through the past two centuries, to its preeminence in the world.

Every effort has been made to ensure the accuracy of the information in this book. However, some information — such as visiting hours, admission fees, and facilities for the disabled — is subject to change. When planning a visit to one of the sites identified in this book, it would be prudent to call or write the site to obtain current information.

Caveat on Architecture

This book is not a text on architecture. Nevertheless, there are references to eras and styles of architecture that should be defined, if only to delineate time frames of architectural popularity.

The earliest American homes are called Colonial (1600-1700). They were utilitarian in design, their construction influenced by weather conditions, the availability of building materials, and familiarity with construction methods rather than by artistry. New England Colonial homes, for example, were characterized by a box-like look: two stories of small rooms built around a central chimney; tiny casement windows; a steeply-pitched roof; and exterior siding of clapboard or shingles. In the Virginia Colony to the south, "Colonial" more often describes brick houses of a story or story and a half, with two end chimneys and a sloped roof. The southern houses usually featured more extensive decorative touches as well.

The eighteenth century brought the Georgian style (1700-1800) from England. The style was named for the four Kings George who ruled from 1714 to 1830. England at that time was becoming urbanized, and its architecture began to reflect a balanced view of life, with the accent on towns and neighborhoods. Georgian styling was marked by a symmetry in both the interior floor plan and the exterior facade, with gabled roofs and a central chimney. The period was noteworthy, also, for the introduction of landscape gardening as part of home design, its purpose being to display the house and grounds in aesthetic harmony. The Georgian style was in no small measure influenced by the Palladian style, a style developed by the sixteenth-century Italian designer Andrea Palladio, who discovered connections between nature and architecture and consequently linked his buildings with the countryside.

In the latter part of the century, Thomas Jefferson returned from his European diplomatic endeavors, bringing back ideas about Neo-classic architecture, which was influenced by the architecture of Ancient Greece and Ancient Rome; the style was free, open, columned, and symmetrical — the columns not merely decorative, but intrinsic to the geometry of the design and the practicality of construction.

At the same time, America was starting to develop its own unique style, called Federal, named in honor of the newly federated republic. Federal paralleled Georgian by using delicate classical parts to define entrances and practical gambrel roofs with dormer windows to minimize heat loss. The style was sometimes called Adam Federal, after the brothers Adam, Scottish-English architects known in this country primarily for interior design — low-relief plaster decorations on ceilings, elaborate door trim, decorated cornices, and slender end chimneys.

Other styles followed in time, including Gothic Revival (1830-1880), which borrowed from castles and vaulted churches in its use of arched windows and extensive carved woodwork; Greek Revival (1825-1860); Italianate (1840-1880), characterized by multiple stories, a low-pitched roof, cupolas, towers, decorative window treatments, and narrow doors; and Folk Victorian, with an overall simplicity of form and decorative treatment in porch and gable trim.

Architectural styles are, of course, mere reference points. Exteriors may reflect the aspirations of the people who built the houses, but what is important is what went on inside the house, what kind of people lived there: hardworking people trying to bring up their children in secure surroundings — people never dreaming that the values being nurtured in their homes would one day manifest in social, moral, and political success as one of their own achieved the ultimate goal of becoming President of the United States.

There are a few other terms appearing throughout the text that seem interchangeable, but which have nuances of meaning:

Restoration, according to decorating expert Martha Stewart, means "putting things back the way they were," not to be confused with **Renovation,** or "making something new again . . . making an old house more livable for today," as when indoor plumbing or air conditioning is added. **Replication** is copying or reproducing, as when a house that has been destroyed by fire or time is rebuilt. **Redecorate,** according to language maven William Safire, means "to redo the style of interior furnishings," lying somewhere between the old-fashioned *Refurbish* and *spruce up.*

Section I
Introduction

Introduction

History is but the prologue to the future.

John F. Kennedy

All too often the study of history, which most of us recall from high school, leaves in our minds a mixture of dates and events; we really learn little about people. But George Washington, John Adams, Thomas Jefferson, and the Presidents who followed them were people with frailties, foibles, and problems not unlike those with which the rest of us live every day.

Those high school textbooks may have recounted accomplishments in the halls of Congress, on the battlefield, or in the White House, but visits to Presidential birthplaces and homes might help us complete a picture of the whole man; for these men, like us, experienced disappointment and satisfaction, economic hardship and success, tragedy and joy.

Some of the houses in which our former Presidents once lived have been razed, some destroyed by fire, others sold to private citizens (Figures 1 and 2), but many have been preserved or restored as sites of historical significance and opened to public visitation. The houses and other buildings commemorating past Presidents are numerous and diverse.

Some, such as Washington's Mount Vernon, have been restored to their former grandeur, whereas others, such as Coolidge's Plymouth Notch, are maintained in their original simplicity. Some are rough log cabins, some imposing mansions filled with priceless antiques and fine furniture. There are estates designed and

Figure 1. The birthplace of James Monroe, in Westmoreland County, Virginia, is representative of the many buildings affiliated with American Presidents that have been lost. Figure courtesy of James Monroe Museum.

built by the owners, and there are ordinary houses bequeathed by parents or in-laws. Some are on farms, others in large cities. Some reflect inherited wealth; others reflect occupancy by members of the working middle class. All display something of the personality and work of the different but accomplished men who lived in them. The dignified Monticello, reflecting the genius of Thomas Jefferson, and the simple one-room cabin where Abraham Lincoln lived and studied represent extremes, both, perhaps, touching us deeply, but doing so in profoundly different ways.

As we walk about Sagamore Hill today, we can still sense the joy of Teddy Roosevelt romping with his children over its spacious grounds. But we might feel a different emotion as we visit the tiny tailor shop where Andrew Johnson toiled with needle and thread while his wife and, later, local men sat teaching and helping him to read and write.

Summer twilight in Canton, Ohio, would find William McKinley on the porch of his simple frame home, relaxing with an after-supper cigar. Smoking indoors would have bothered his invalid wife, a courageous lady whom he tended with life-long solicitude.

4

Figure 2. Greenway, birthplace of John Tyler, at Charles City, Virginia, is representative of those buildings affiliated with American Presidents that are in private ownership and not managed for public visitation. Photograph courtesy of Virginia Department of Historic Resources.

And as we walk on the veranda of The Hermitage, set amid the fragrant pines of Tennessee, we can visualize tough "Old Hickory," Andrew Jackson, with his beloved Rachel, rocking in their chairs and puffing on their pipes as they shared a rare and tender moment, far from the cares of the day.

The ramps built to accommodate Franklin Roosevelt's wheelchair at Hyde Park are a poignant reminder that, while some men became President after overcoming disadvantages of birth, poverty, or educational opportunity, Roosevelt overcame a severe physical disability to become one of the greatest leaders this nation and the world have ever known.

America's heritage is embodied in the forty-one men who have been Chief Executive but who came from different places and diverse backgrounds. Each gave part of himself to our national character; each added to the strength of our constitutional system. A search for a pattern reveals the absence of one, for these forty-one men represent the diversity of thought and political principle that has propelled our nation forward and made our form and expression of government the envy of countries around the world.

The places whence these men came must remain as they were, for to know the men is to know ourselves. "After all," said John F. Kennedy, "history is people, and particularly, in great periods of history, Presidents." Fortunately we have come to realize the importance not only of preserving Presidential homes but also of preserving Presidential history by building Presidential libraries — sometimes while a President is still in office — and stocking them with historical displays, gifts, souvenirs, mementos, and millions of important — as well as trivial — papers and documents. It was not always so.

Mount Vernon, the first of our historic homes to be preserved, remained in the Washington family for many years, but by the mid-1800s it had fallen into decline. It had become agriculturally unproductive and was dangerously close to bankruptcy. The owner, John Augustine Washington, Jr., appealed to the federal government and then to the Commonwealth of Virginia, but neither was interested in assuming responsibility for preserving the property.

An unlikely savior appeared in the person of Miss Ann Pamela Cunningham of South Carolina. As a girl she had been injured in a fall from a horse, and the accident had caused a painful and debilitating spinal injury. In constant pain and discomfort, she remained a semi-invalid and spent most of her time in South Carolina resting and reading; she made frequent trips to Philadelphia for treatment from a specialist, who provided relief but not a cure.

One day in 1853, her mother left Ann Pamela in Philadelphia and returned to Charleston by boat; the journey took Mrs. Cunningham past the forlorn and dilapidated Mount Vernon. In a now-historic letter, she wrote to her daughter:

> I was painfully distressed at the ruin and desolation of the home of Washington, and the thought passed through my mind; why was it that the women of his country did not try to keep it in repair, if the men could not do it? It does seem such a blot on our country!

Her mother's rhetorical question ignited a spark in the frail young woman lying in a rented room in Philadelphia. Surely, she reasoned, this was an urgent, important and — yes — noble cause in which she could lead the women of America. This, she felt, was her destiny.

From the perspective of today's age of instant communication it is difficult to grasp the enormity of the task facing Miss Cunningham, whose only tools were her pen and a fervent dedication to the cause of preserving the home, memory, and heritage of George Washington. After many years of emotional struggle, physical hardship, political manipulation, fundraising, ingenious organization, and gentle and not-so-gentle persuasion, her goal was attained. In 1860, on the very eve of the Civil War, the Mount Vernon Ladies' Association took possession of Mount Vernon.

Still, many trials lay ahead. Efforts to raise funds to finance the urgently needed repairs continued. Mount Vernon was threatened because it lay in a no-man's-land between the opposing forces of the North and South. With communications disrupted by the war, the leading figures of the Ladies' Association were frustrated in their attempts to communicate with each other. It was not until 1866, thirteen years after the idea was first suggested, that the first national meeting of the Association took place at Mount Vernon. Miss Cunningham announced final success:

> Ladies of the Mount Vernon Association, it is with feelings whose particular depth and intensity I must fail to clothe in fitting words, that I greet you, sister guardians, on this proud, long-hoped-for day. Looking back from our present assured stand-point of an accomplished fact, my memory cannot fail to recall the early vicissitudes, the oft-discouraging progress of our labor of love, in redeeming from oblivion and sure decay the home and the grave of the immortal Washington! Then we lived on hope! We would not yield to despair! Now we rejoice, with intense satisfaction, to know that Mount Vernon is ours . . . the Nation's! And well may I feel almost overpowered to find myself, at this moment, in the midst of ladies representing the varied sections of our country, pledged to guard that sacred spot forever!

She was the instigator, but Miss Cunningham was not alone. Ordinary citizens, women from every state, and sympathetic politicians — for whom women could not vote — had contributed money, effort, and influence. The most dramatic contribution was made by Miss Cunningham's secretary, Sarah Tracy, and Upton Herbert, Mount Vernon's first superintendent. Attended by a chaperone — this was 1861, after all — they resided at Mount Vernon throughout the four years of the Civil War. Always at the mercy of the surrounding military forces and often cut off from food supplies, they protected the ramshackle estate from man and nature.

The most active and successful fundraiser was a retired minister and college president, the Reverend Edward Everett. He was well known for his oratorical prolixity and, in particular, for a two-hour discourse on the life of Washington in which he dwelt on the need for national unity — certainly pertinent in that troublesome time. Everett became interested in Miss Cunningham's efforts and delivered his speech all over the country, contributing all gate receipts to the Mount Vernon cause.

Without Everett's unique contribution and the attendant publicity, the restoration effort might not have succeeded; thus Edward Everett stands tall in the annals of the Mount Vernon Ladies' Association. Ironically, Everett is not remembered for his work on behalf of Mount Vernon, but for the long-winded two-hour speech he delivered at the dedication of the Gettysburg National Cemetery preceding Lincoln's famous address.

The Mount Vernon Ladies' Association was the first national historic preservation society and still functions as the caring guardian-owner of America's most cherished historic home. The Association's stewardship and its activities in education, archaeology, and expansion have continued for more than a century. It has served as a model for other preservation organizations, which have followed its inspiring example of enlightened volunteerism.

The charter of the Mount Vernon Ladies' Association includes old-fashioned but simple and fervent words articulating its objective — words paraphrased by Presidential home charters everywhere:

> *To perpetuate the sacred memory of "The Father of His Country" and, with loving hands, to guard and protect the hallowed spot where rest his mortal remains. To forever hold, manage and preserve the estate, properties and relics at Mount Vernon, belonging to the Association, and, under*

proper regulations, to open the same to the inspection of all who love the cause of liberty and revere the name of George Washington.

Twenty-nine similar non-profit historical organizations have been formed since 1858, initiated by hometown or homestate friends and political constituents of the Presidents. Like the Mount Vernon Ladies' Association, they have raised money, bought properties, collected artifacts, and refurbished or reconstructed buildings appropriate to the period of the Presidential occupancy. Many continue to maintain and administer their facilities under state charters as educational foundations staffed by dedicated volunteers.

Prominent among historical organizations is the National Trust for Historic Preservation, a non-profit organization chartered by Congress in 1949 and now consisting of over 250,000 members. Its mission is to:

encourage preservation of significant American buildings, sites and historic districts. . . . as the leader of the national preservation movement, it is committed to saving America's diverse historic environments and to preserving and revitalizing the livability of communities nationwide.

Headquartered in Washington, DC, the National Trust works with over 2,000 local historic preservation organizations throughout the country. It directly owns and operates eighteen house museums, including three Presidential sites described in this book: Montpelier (Madison), Decatur House (Van Buren), and the Woodrow Wilson House Museum in Washington, DC.

All of the organizations, indeed all of us, owe a debt of gratitude to Ann Pamela Cunningham and every past and present member of the Mount Vernon Ladies' Association for their devotion and for their decades of responsible, practical, and inspirational leadership.

Some preservation societies have chosen to present Presidential homes to the federal government for maintenance, and a few houses have been donated in the form of family bequests. Once accepted by the government, the homes are placed under the aegis of the National Park Service, which currently serves as administrator of over twenty Presidential birthplaces or homes in the United States and one — Franklin Roosevelt's Campobello — in affiliation with the government of Canada.

The National Park Service was conceived and authorized by Congress in 1916, its mandate to administer the parks, monuments, and other preserves under the jurisdiction of the Department of the Interior. In 1933 a large number of facilities run by the Forest Service and the War Department were transferred to the Park Service, a significant step in the development of the truly coordinated system currently responsible for the management of more than 350 natural, scenic, scientific, and historical places.

We may think of the National Park Service simply as the overseer of the great National Parks — Yellowstone, Grand Canyon, or Sequoia — but more than half of the sites maintained by the Park Service are places associated with events and activities important to the nation's history. These sites range from archaeological finds associated with early Indian civilizations to houses and museums memorializing individual Americans who have made significant contributions to our society.

On December 10, 1938, President Franklin D. Roosevelt announced plans for an institution for preserving his Presidential papers and other historical materials. He proposed that a building financed by private subscription be erected on land donated from the Roosevelt Hyde Park estate. When completed it would be turned over to the National Archivist, to be administered and maintained at government expense. A joint resolution of Congress formalizing such a plan was approved by the President shortly afterward. He and Mrs. Roosevelt deeded sixteen acres of property to the United States, and the cornerstone of the Franklin D. Roosevelt Library was laid on November 19, 1939. On July 4, 1940, the government accepted the completed building (Figure 3). Since that time the trend has been to follow Roosevelt's example by building Presidential libraries and museums with private funds, then trans-

Figure 3. The Franklin D. Roosevelt Library in Hyde Park, New York. Completed in 1940, this was the first structure built specifically to house the personal papers and related materials of an American President. Figure courtesy of The Franklin D. Roosevelt Library; Daisy De Puthod, artist.

ferring them to the American people, often with the still-living President in attendance at the dedication. The facilities usually consist of separate library and museum areas, although they may be under the same roof.

The Presidential libraries are not public libraries in the traditional sense. Each is an archive of the valuable documents of an individual Presidency. For each administration there are millions of pages, including records created or received by the White House staff. Before material can be made available to the public, it must be reviewed for access by an archivist, according to the Presidential Records Act of 1978. That act, among other stipulations, distinguishes between Presidential records, which are the property of the federal government, and Presidential papers (personal records), which are the property of the President.

The National Archives and Records Administration, Office of Presidential Libraries, currently supervises the archival work of nine Presidential Libraries, those of Presidents Hoover, Roosevelt, Truman, Eisenhower, Kennedy, Johnson, Ford, Carter, and Reagan. The Nixon Library is administered privately. While the libraries are usually reserved for the exclusive use of scholars and historians, the museum sections are open to the public and chronicle Presidential history through exhibits and audio-visual presentations.

It is not surprising that our first five Presidents were active in the War for Independence and that the sixth, John Quincy Adams, was reported to have witnessed the Battle of Bunker Hill from his back yard when he was a lad. Six of the first ten Presidents were manor-born Virginians, members of what was called the planter aristocracy. Their estates, still open, are a reminder of the vast plantations and tobacco farms whose products were so important to the financial well-being and vitality of the Virginia colony and the fledgling nation.

Several of the manor houses are on the shores of the James and Potomac rivers, whose shipping terminals were essential to trade with England and the world. The farmers and planters who cultivated these vast acres were mostly descendants of English settlers, who brought to the colonies not only their agricultural skills but an inherited sense of responsibility for public service—an implied duty to their fellow citizens.

Roaming the halls and rooms of the mansions, standing on the docks overlooking the mighty rivers, wandering the fields and woods, one may conjure up thoughts of the hard work, dedication, and tenacity of our ancestors as they cleared the forests and developed the land into rich farms and lush plantations. We can understand their desire to enjoy the fruits of their new life without arbitrary direction and taxation being impressed upon them by an unresponsive government far across the sea. A visit to Mount Vernon's slave graveyard reminds us of the underside of these elegant estates: the success of the plantation was due, in great measure, to the efforts of slave labor. Washington, Jefferson, and other patriots were landowners whose products and profits depended on the enslavement of others.

Slavery in the early days of our republic was legal until the sixteenth President, a man born in a log cabin, wrote and signed the Emancipation Proclamation in the midst of a bloody civil war.

Figure 4. The Old Hermitage, Nashville, Tennessee, the original log cabin home of Andrew Jackson, has been destroyed. Photograph courtesy of The Ladies' Hermitage Association.

A century later another President, one born on a hardscrabble Texas farm, would sign into law the most comprehensive civil rights legislation since Lincoln's time.

There has been progress in our two hundred years of existence, from slavery to civil rights, from horseback to jet planes, from outhouses to indoor plumbing, from dispatch riders to television news, from periwigs to hair transplants. It's a long way from Andrew Jackson's duels in defense of his wife's honor to Harry Truman's letter to a music critic who had dared to write a negative review of daughter Margaret's Washington singing debut.

Progress has also meant expansion of our borders and has brought increased population and diversity. Six of the Presidents who followed the Virginians were born in log cabins. They were poorly educated but possessed native intelligence and ambition and, to a man, were imbued with the principle of hard work and a belief in goodness and opportunity.

The log cabin in which Andrew Jackson, the first "western" President, was born (Figure 4) has been lost, but his home, The

Hermitage, near Nashville, Tennessee, has been restored to its original beauty. Jackson's journey from log cabin to the White House and back to The Hermitage as his final resting place is a shining example of the American dream coming full circle.

When we visit the places identified in this book (Figure 5), then, we will be inspecting the Presidents from the perspective of their origins, and sometimes we may well discover a different person from the one in the history books.

A. Cranston Jones, in his *Homes of the American Presidents*, has written:

> *These homes are a historic bequest providing us with an eloquent link to the past . . . it was in homes very much like these across the nation that men and women met to discuss the issues of the day. This grass-roots fact the Presidents bore in mind as they mapped their political strategy. And it was to these front porches that their cheering fellow citizens came in torchlight procession with bands playing to hail the victor, or, more quietly, to console the loser. As such, these Presidents' homes have all known the limelight of history. For us today they can also be beacons, guiding us to the hearthstone of our great national heritage, quickening our awareness of the great personalities of the past, and vividly recreating our own history.*

Figure 5. The distribution of homes, libraries, and museums commemorating American Presidents that are described in this book. The sites identified on this map are listed below.

1. George Washington Birthplace National Monument
2. Mount Vernon
3. Adams National Historic Site
4. Tuckahoe Plantation
5. Monticello
6. Poplar Forest
7. Montpelier
8. James Madison Museum
9. Octagon House
10. Ash Lawn-Highland
11. James Monroe Museum
12. The Hermitage
13. Martin Van Buren National Historic Site
14. Decatur House
15. Berkeley Plantation
16. Grouseland
17. Sherwood Forest
18. James K. Polk Memorial

19. Polk Ancestral Home
20. Millard Fillmore Log Cabin
21. Fillmore House Museum
22. Franklin Pierce Homestead
23. The Pierce Manse
24. Buchanan Historic Site
25. Wheatland
26. Abraham Lincoln Birthplace National Historic Site
27. The Lincoln Museum (Hodgenville, Kentucky)
28. Abraham Lincoln's Boyhood Home, Knob Creek Farm
29. Lincoln Boyhood National Memorial
30. The Lincoln Museum (Fort Wayne, Indiana)
31. Lincoln's New Salem
32. The Abraham Lincoln Museum
33. Lincoln Home National Historic Site
34. Lincoln Memorial Shrine

continued next page . . .

15

35. Lincoln College Museum
36. Ford's Theatre National Historic Site
37. Andrew Johnson Birthplace
38. Andrew Johnson National Historic Site
39. Andrew Johnson Presidential Library and Museum
40. Grant's Birthplace
41. U. S. Grant Boyhood Home
42. Ulysses S. Grant National Historic Site and Grant's Farm
43. Ulysses S. Grant Home State Historic Site
44. Grant Cottage State Historic Site
45. Rutherford B. Hayes Presidential Center
46. James A. Garfield National Historic Site, "Lawnfield"
47. Chester A. Arthur Historic Site
48. Grover Cleveland Birthplace Historic Site
49. Benjamin Harrison Home
50. McKinley National Memorial
51. National McKinley Birthplace Memorial
52. Theodore Roosevelt Birthplace National Historic Site
53. Sagamore Hill National Historic Site
54. Maltese Cross Cabin
55. William Howard Taft National Historic Site
56. Woodrow Wilson Birthplace and Museum
57. Woodrow Wilson Boyhood Home (Augusta, Georgia)
58. Woodrow Wilson Boyhood Home (Columbia, South Carolina)
59. Woodrow Wilson House Museum
60. President Harding's Home
61. Plymouth Notch Historic District
62. Herbert Hoover National Historic Site
63. Hoover-Minthorn House
64. Franklin D. Roosevelt National Historic Site
65. Roosevelt Campobello International Park
66. FDR's Little White House
67. Harry S Truman Birthplace State Historic Site
68. Truman Farm Home
69. Harry S Truman National Historic Site
70. Harry S. Truman Library
71. Little White House Museum
72. Eisenhower Birthplace State Historic Park
73. The Eisenhower Center
74. Eisenhower National Historic Site
75. John F. Kennedy National Historic Site
76. John Fitzgerald Kennedy Library and Museum
77. The John F. Kennedy Hyannis Museum
78. Lyndon B. Johnson State and National Historic Parks
79. Lyndon B. Johnson Library and Museum
80. The Richard Nixon Library & Birthplace
81. Gerald R. Ford Library
82. Gerald R. Ford Museum
83. Jimmy Carter National Historic Site
84. Carter Presidential Center
85. Ronald Reagan Birthplace
86. Ronald Reagan Boyhood Home
87. Ronald Reagan Presidential Library
88. The White House

Section II

Homes, Libraries, and Museums of the Presidents

George Washington

First President
1789 – 1797

Born February 22, 1732, Popes Creek Plantation, Virginia
Died December 14, 1799, Mount Vernon, Virginia

First in war, first in peace, and first in the hearts of his countrymen, he was second to none in the humble and endearing scenes of private life.
— "Lighthorse Harry" Lee

George Washington was born into a social class that had always taken an active role in the life of the Virginia Colony. This was the planter aristocracy, people who came to Virginia with attitudes derived from their English country gentry heritage. They believed strongly in participating in the civil and military affairs of the Colony and in performing duties without complaint — even though service might entail sacrifice of individual comfort and welfare.

This philosophy explains much about Washington's willingness to serve the cause of liberty, to participate in the building and structure of government, to become the country's first Chief Executive, and to live on as an inspiration and example for all who followed. As he noted, "The welfare of the country is the great object to which our cares and efforts ought to be directed."

Like so many great men, Washington never forgot his roots. Whenever possible, he returned to Mount Vernon to rejuvenate body, mind, and spirit, far from the incessant pressures of war and government. An overwhelming sense of responsibility, nurtured by his heritage, sustained his efforts and kept him from his oft-spoken desire to be a simple farmer.

> No pursuit is more congenial with my nature and gratifications, than that of agriculture; nor none I so pant after as again to become a tiller of the earth.

When his service to the nation was completed in 1797, Washington returned for good to Mount Vernon, an eight-thousand-acre plantation tended by three hundred slaves. The Father of our Country finally fulfilled his ambition of becoming a full-time farm manager.

> I can truly say that I had rather be at Mount Vernon with a friend or two about me, than to be attended at the Seat of Government by the Officers of the State and the Representatives of every Power in Europe.
>
> —George Washington

George Washington Birthplace
National Monument
Washingtons Birthplace, Virginia

In the early part of the eighteenth century George Washington's father, Augustine Washington, bought property on Popes Creek where it fed into the Potomac River, forty miles east of Fredericksburg, Virginia. The elder Washington planted the land in tobacco and erected a fine home around 1725.

George Washington was born at Popes Creek Plantation in 1732 but spent only a few years there before the family moved upriver to Little Hunting Creek Plantation, later named Mount Vernon. Popes Creek became the property of George's half-brother, Lawrence, and young George visited frequently.

The Main House at Popes Creek was named Wakefield in 1774 by George's nephew, William, then the occupant. Wakefield was destroyed by fire in 1779, and William chose not to rebuild. The property lay fallow for many years and passed from the family in the early nineteenth century.

In the 1920s a group of ladies who were picnicking on the grounds had the idea to form the Wakefield National Memorial Association, their intention being to restore the site to its early eighteenth century condition.

With significant public support, and with additional funding from the Rockefeller family, 394 acres were purchased and dedicated as a National Historic Site in 1932, the two-hundredth anniversary of Washington's birth at Popes Creek.

Archaeological searches during the past seventy years have uncovered many artifacts, as well as the structural remains of the Main House, the smokehouse, the kitchen, and other buildings, some of which have been replicated, although the original Main House in which Washington was born has not been reconstructed. Rather, its original foundation has been outlined with a design of oyster shells.

Nearby is a Memorial House, set in a grove of magnificent red cedars (Figure 6). Constructed in time for the 1932 dedication, it represents a typical upper-class home of the eighteenth century, with four rooms and a central hallway on each floor. The bricks

Figure 6. The Memorial House at George Washington Birthplace National Monument, Washingtons Birthplace, Virginia. Photograph by Richard Frear; use courtesy of National Park Service.

used for the outer walls were handmade from the clay of a nearby field, and the furnishings, although not original, are of the period when the Washington family resided there. The Memorial House dramatically illustrates the setting into which Washington was born and the lifestyle led by his family.

A working farm, established in 1968, recreates scenes and activities reminiscent of Washington's boyhood. The farm features a colonial herb and flower garden and contains livestock, poultry, and crops characteristic of the 1700s. Douglas Southall Freeman wrote:

> As George came into consciousness and learned to walk, there was around him an amazing world of dogs and chickens and pigs and calves, as well as those towering creatures called cows.

The buildings, furnishings, animals, and crops at Popes Creek offer an experience of aesthetic and historic interest. Visitors are able to view a way of life that has disappeared forever — that of a great river plantation active at the time our nation was emerging as a commercial force in the world.

Family plantations were the focus of economic life, and the planter was the patriarch of a plantation community, with slaves forming the base. Even the architecture and design of the plantation reflected social distinction, with outbuildings, gardens, fields, and slave quarters surrounding the Main House in formal symmetry.

The large landowner-planters dominated the Virginia colony, perpetuating their fortunes and lifestyle through intermarriage and inheritance. Thus each planter, a member of what was basically a ruling class, not only bequeathed his sons the land, but ensured that they received a formal education and were taught a sense of honor, dignity, and dedication to public service. Love of glory and pursuit of fame and fortune also were considered to be noble virtues indicative of character. These values, observed at all of the great Virginia plantations, were instilled in George Washington, a man of his time — planter by birth, public servant when chosen.

DIRECTIONS: Washingtons Birthplace is 40 miles east of Fredericksburg, Virginia. From Fredericksburg, take State Route 3E, which connects with State Route 204. Proceed north on 204 to the Birthplace.

PUBLIC USE: Season and hours: Daily, 9 A.M.– 5 P.M. Closed Christmas and New Year's Day. **Fees:** Adults, $1, with discounts for groups, students, and seniors. Allow several hours to enjoy Popes Creek Plantation. Picnic area. **Gift shop. For people with disabilities:** The Visitor Center is fully accessible. Transportation is provided for those unable to walk the 300 yards to the historic area.

EDUCATIONAL FACILITIES: The Visitor Center features exhibits and a 14-minute film, *A Childhood Place,* that represents life at the plantation in the early eighteenth century. It is screened every 30 minutes beginning at 9:30 A.M. Guided tours are offered, and there are periodic craft-making demonstrations.

FOR ADDITIONAL INFORMATION: Contact: George Washington Birthplace National Monument, RR #1, Box 717, Washingtons Birthplace, Virginia 22443, (804) 224–1732. **Read:** Douglas Southall Freeman. 1948–1952. *George Washington,* 6 volumes. New York: Charles Scribner's Sons. (Volume 7 edited posthumously by J. A. Carroll and M. W. Ashworth.)

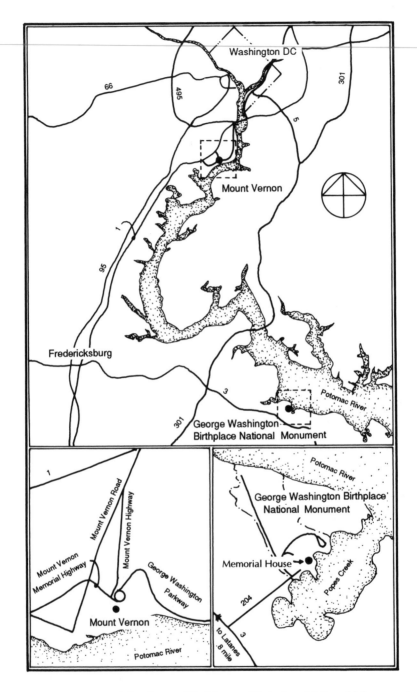

Figure 7. Location of the George Washington Birthplace National Monument and Mount Vernon in northern Virginia.

Mount Vernon

Mount Vernon, Virginia

I have no objection to any sober or orderly person's gratifying their curiosity in viewing the buildings, Gardens &ct about Mount Vernon.
—George Washington, 1794

Little could President Washington have dreamed that two hundred years after he wrote those words, his beloved and treasured estate would be visited each year by over one million people, who experience the splendor and charm of Mount Vernon (Plate 1), America's most popular historic home.

Washington's elegant mansion, overlooking the majestic Potomac River, has been restored meticulously. From the paint colors on the walls to the actual arrangement of the furniture, much of which is original, the appearance of the interior during the last year of his life has been replicated. Bright green and vivid blue walls, handsome wood grains, and dimity and satin window hangings all reflect the ambiance and history of an exciting era.

An outside exhibition area contains more than thirty acres of colorful gardens and forests open for strolling. Close by the mansion are the outbuildings where much of the day-to-day maintenance activity of the plantation took place in Washington's time. Here bread was baked, wool and flax were woven into cloth, laundry was washed and ironed, and meat was cured.

Mount Vernon is currently working on a four-acre exhibition area designed to introduce visitors to George Washington's pioneering work as a farmer. This working-farm exhibit will highlight Washington's experiments with crop rotation and other farming methods that were unusual in the eighteenth century. Visitors will see reproductions of eighteenth-century tools in use and observe brick-making and timber-framing. The main structure of the exhibit will be a reproduction of Washington's unique sixteen-sided barn, which will be built of trees cut from Washington's estate and of bricks made at Mount Vernon. All finishing work on the barn will be done by using eighteenth-century tools and methods. The new area will also include a forest walking trail. The entire exhibit is scheduled to be completed by 1996.

Not far from the mansion is the tomb of George and Martha Washington, and nearby is a slave burial ground, marked by a memorial to the men and women who worked hard to make Mount Vernon profitable. The estate also includes a museum, where a large number of Washington's personal possessions are displayed.

Mount Vernon was not built in a piece; it evolved, beginning as a simple 1 1/2-story dwelling, probably built by Augustine Washington, at Little Hunting Creek Plantation. The house passed through the hands of Augustine's eldest son, Lawrence, who renamed it Mount Vernon in honor of Admiral Edward Vernon, a British naval officer under whom he had served.

When George Washington first acquired the house — by lease from Lawrence's widow in 1752 — he began to enlarge and redecorate it in preparation for his marriage to Martha Custis. These were the first of many improvements he made to the house and farm. Washington inherited the property outright in 1761, and from then on he continued to add outbuildings, improve the gardens and fields, and enlarge the house itself. The work was sporadic, however, interrupted for extended periods as Washington answered the call to serve his country.

Washington's home at Mount Vernon was not completed until 1787. It is considered an excellent example of Colonial architecture, although there are indications of other influences in the Palladian windows and in the originality of the front portico. The home is white, simple, uncluttered, and relaxed. It is one of America's greatest treasures, an evocation of eighteenth-century plantation life: the retreat, haven, and home of our nation's guiding spirit.

Fourteen rooms in the mansion are open for visitation today. Each is filled with original Washington pieces — furniture, paintings, silver, porcelain, bric-a-brac — each room vibrant with rich window hangings, decorated ceilings, carved mantels, and polished woodwork.

Between the doorway to the downstairs bedroom and the doorway of the dining room hangs a gift presented to Washington by General Lafayette in 1790. It is a key to the Bastille. In an accompanying letter, Lafayette wrote:

Give me leave, my dear general, to present you with a picture of the Bastille, just as it looked a few days after I ordered its demolition, with the main key of the fortress of despotism. It is a tribute which I owe as a son to my adoptive father — as an aide-de-camp to my general — as a missionary of liberty to its patriarch.

For 135 years, Mount Vernon has been owned and operated by the Mount Vernon Ladies' Association, which has kept fresh and alive the lifestyle, heritage, and glory of George Washington.

DIRECTIONS: By car: Mount Vernon is located at the end of the Mount Vernon Memorial Highway, 8 miles south of Alexandria, Virginia, and 16 miles from downtown Washington, DC (Figure 7). **By bus:** For schedules, contact Metro Bus and Rail in Washington, (202) 637–2437, or Tourmobile Sightseeing, (202) 554–7950. **By boat:** The motor vessel *Spirit of Mount Vernon* is available mid-March to October. Call (202) 554–8000 for schedules and prices, which include admission to Mount Vernon.

PUBLIC USE: Season and hours: March, September, October, 9 A.M.– 5 P.M. April-August, 8 A.M.– 5 P.M.; November-February, 9 A.M.– 4 P.M. **Fees:** Adults, $8, with discounts for groups, students, and seniors. Allow several hours to enjoy Mount Vernon. **Food service:** Food and drink are not permitted on the grounds, but a full-service snack bar and a restaurant are located just outside the main gate. **Gift shops:** One, located in the museum on the grounds, features regional crafts, foodstuffs and historical reproductions. A second gift shop is located just outside the gate. **For people with disabilities:** A limited number of wheelchairs are available. The first floor of the mansion and many of the outbuildings are accessible.

EDUCATIONAL FACILITIES: Museum: The museum located on the grounds offers an intimate glimpse of the Washingtons' personal possessions, including clothing, military equipment, silver, porcelain, and other artifacts. The Ladies' Association also sponsors a full range of special activities and educational programs throughout the year, including lectures, seminars, holiday fetes, anniversary celebrations, after-hour tours, and student tours.

FOR ADDITIONAL INFORMATION: Contact: Mount Vernon Ladies' Association, Mount Vernon, Virginia 22121, (703) 780–2000. **Read:** (1) Charles Cecil Wall. 1988. "The Architect of Mount Vernon." In *George Washington: Citizen-Soldier*. Mount Vernon: The Mount Vernon Ladies' Association, 92–103. (2) Charles Cecil Wall, et al. 1985. *Mount Vernon: A Handbook*. Mount Vernon: The Mount Vernon Ladies' Association.

John Adams

Second President
1797 – 1801

Born October 30, 1735, Braintree (Quincy), Massachusetts
Died July 4, 1826, Braintree (Quincy), Massachusetts

All of us in America are constantly bemused and astounded by this extraordinary golden age in our history which produced so many men of exceptional talent ... the record of the Adams family, this tremendous devotion to the public interest, this vitality which goes from generation to generation is, really, the most exceptional scarlet thread which runs through the entire tapestry of American political life.

—John F. Kennedy

Few families have so dominated the American political scene as has the family of John Adams. Adams was Vice President under George Washington. He was elected President. He was father of a President, grandfather of an American Minister to Great Britain, and great-grandfather to distinguished politicians, historians, writers, and other men and women of the arts and letters.

John Adams, the son of a farmer, graduated from Harvard with a bachelor's degree and later earned a law degree. He had an unquenchable curiosity about the world, its people, its history, and its political institutions. His writings on the latter subject brought him national attention as the differences between England and her colonies began to widen. Adams was elected a Massachusetts delegate to the Continental Congress and then served as an invaluable American representative to the European states during the War for Independence.

Adams returned to Massachusetts with the intention of becoming a farmer-attorney. He purchased a farm and named it Peacefield, both to emphasize the tranquility he enjoyed there and to memorialize the Paris Peace Treaty, which he had written and helped to negotiate. About Peacefield he once said, "It is but the farm of a patriot," but he proved to be much more than a patriot farmer as the country called him to serve as Vice President and President.

In 1801 Adams finally retired to Peacefield, nicknamed The Old House by his grandchildren, and it became home to many Adams family members, including son John Quincy Adams, well on the way to his own singular and successful diplomatic and political career.

John Adams died in the study of The Old House on July 4, 1826, the fiftieth anniversary of the adoption of the Declaration of Independence. His last spoken words included a reference to his old compatriot Thomas Jefferson, who, coincidentally, had died at Monticello, Virginia, only a few hours earlier.

This confluence of tragic events had an almost mystical effect on the nation. Certainly the deaths of the two great patriots were to be mourned. But the coincidence of the deaths on such a significant anniversary day seemed to signal a divine blessing on the two men and the free nation they had helped to nurture and bring forth in glorious birth.

Adams National Historic Site
Quincy, Massachusetts

John Adams, second President, and his son John Quincy Adams, sixth President, were born in adjacent houses on Franklin Street in Quincy, which at that time was called Braintree.

The John Adams house at 133 Franklin is a New England "saltbox" building with multiple fireplaces around a central chimney. It originally consisted of two upper and two lower rooms, but rooms were later added to both floors. The house dates to around 1680; it is the oldest existing Presidential birthplace.

Upon his father's death, John Adams inherited a similar house next door that became his home and law office, the birthplace of his son John Quincy and, in 1779, the birthplace of the Massachusetts State Constitution. That document, framed by John Adams, his cousin Samuel Adams, and others, became the model used by James Madison in writing the Constitution of the United States.

Both houses are typical of those built in the late seventeenth century by New England carpenters. They were framed with huge beams secured with wooden pegs, floored with wide planks, and covered with clapboard siding over brick-filled walls to ward off the rigors of New England winter weather. The ceilings were low and the windows small, the houses utilitarian and comfortable.

John Adams spent considerable time in Europe as a diplomatic representative of the young United States. During that period John and his wife, Abigail, purchased, sight unseen, a farm and house just 1 1/2-miles from Franklin Street. The house had been built in 1731 by Major Leonard Vassall, a wealthy West India sugar planter.

Peacefield, or The Old House (Plate 2), was not large. It consisted of six rooms and a kitchen wing. Almost before Adams could unpack and settle into his new life at Peacefield, however, he was called to the capital as George Washington's vice president. It would be twelve more years before he would retire to Massachusetts permanently.

During those twelve years, Mrs. Adams was busy overseeing major improvements to the house, including doubling the capacity with the addition of an east wing in 1800. Years later, her great-grandson Henry Adams would recall The Old House:

The old house at Quincy was 18th century. What style it had was its Queen Anne mahogany panels and its Louis XV chairs and sofa. The panels belonged to an old colonial Vassall who built the house; the furniture had been brought back from Paris in 1789 or 1801 or 1817, along with porcelain and books and much else of old diplomatic remnants; and neither of the two 18th century styles . . . was comfortable for a boy, or for anyone else. The dark mahogany had been painted white to suit daily life in winter gloom.

John joined Abigail at last, to enjoy the garden, his books, his children, and his grandchildren. "I long for rural and domestic scenes," he noted, "for the warbling of birds and the prattle of my children."

In 1801 Abigail Adams wrote to a friend, "the beauties which my garden unfolds to my view from the window at which I now write . . . all unite to awaken the most pleasing sensation. . . ." Much has changed at Peacefield in two hundred years, but the present-day garden's fragrance and beauty offer a link to the splendor and serenity of an earlier day. A white York rose brought to Peacefield from England in 1788 still thrives today. A walk on the gravel paths through the orchards and colorful blooms engenders in each of today's visitors a renewed sense of the history, tradition, and quietude of Peacefield.

Son John Quincy Adams loved The Old House as the home of his beloved parents, but he was too engrossed in politics to pay much attention to it. After their deaths he left the supervision and maintenance to his son, Charles Francis. In the middle of the nineteenth century, Charles Francis Adams converted the property from a farm to a country gentleman's home and built a separate building, The Stone Library, to house the extensive Adams collections. He also edited the Adams family papers for the Library.

Generations of Adamses remained in The Old House until 1927, when the Adams Memorial Society was formed and took possession of the home. In 1946 the Society deeded the home to the federal government. The birthplaces of John Adams and John Quincy Adams were owned by the City of Quincy until 1979, when they, too, were presented to the federal government. The two areas, separated by 1 1/2-miles, are considered a single National Historic Site, administered by the National Park Service.

DIRECTIONS: Quincy is 8 miles south of Boston. **By car:** Take I–93 (Southeast Expressway) or Route 128 south to Exit 7 (Massachusetts State Route 3). The first exit from Route 3 is Exit 18 (Quincy Adams T), which flows into Burgin Parkway. Proceed straight on Burgin Parkway through 6 sets of traffic lights. Turn right at the 7th light onto Dimmock Street and drive 1 block to Hancock Street. Turn right on Hancock Street and go for 2 blocks to the Visitor Center on the left. Northbound from Cape Cod on Route 3, take Exit 19 (Quincy Adams T), and follow the above directions. **By MBTA:** Take the Red Line to the Quincy Center Station. Exit on the Hancock Street side. The Visitor Center is across the street (Figure 8).

PUBLIC USE: Season and hours: April 18 to November 10, daily 9 A.M.– 5 P.M. **Fees:** Adults, $2. Under 16, free. Admission includes tours of all three houses with a $2 charge for those who wish to tour the United First Parish Church where the Adamses are interred. **Book store. For people with disabilities:** The lower floors of The Old House are accessible. There is a two-step entry to the Franklin Street houses.

FOR ADDITIONAL INFORMATION: Contact: Adams National Historic Site, Visitor Center, 1250 Hancock Street, Quincy, Massachusetts 02269, (617) 770–1175. Read: (1) Paul Nagel. 1983. *Descent from Glory: Four Generations of the John Adams Family.* New York: Oxford University Press. (2) Wilhelmina S. Harris. 1983. *A Family's Legacy to America.* Washington, DC: US Department of the Interior, National Park Service.

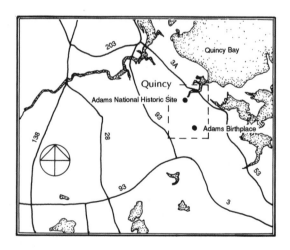

Figure 8. Location of Adams National Historic Site, Quincy, Massachusetts.

Thomas Jefferson

Third President
1801 – 1809

Born April 13, 1743, Goochland County, Virginia
Died July 4, 1826, Monticello, Charlottesville, Virginia

I think this is the most extraordinary collection of talent, human knowledge, that has ever been gathered together at the White House, with the possible exception of when Thomas Jefferson dined alone.

— John F. Kennedy, hosting a dinner for
Nobel Laureates, April, 1962

If Jefferson were living today he would be called a Renaissance man, or perhaps a Universal Genius, for he had an eclectic mind, great curiosity, and high intellect. At different times — sometimes concurrently — he was a planter, lawyer, writer, politician, philosopher, scientist, architect, agronomist, diplomat, educator, statesman and, not incidentally, President of the United States. It's been noted, too, that he was a reasonably accomplished violinist and had a fine singing voice!

Thomas Jefferson was born into a well-to-do plantation family. His father, Peter Jefferson, died when Thomas was fourteen; Thomas inherited land and slaves, for which he became responsible after he attained his majority.

Jefferson attended the College of William and Mary for two years, from 1760 to 1762. After that, he took the path to law and politics. He served in the Virginia legislature and the Continental Congress where he was made a member of the committee drafting a Declaration of Independence. The other members deferred to Jefferson's rare writing skill, and the final document bears the singular marks of his lucid style.

Jefferson's Presidency is noted for numerous achievements, including the Louisiana Purchase, but perhaps the most important day of his administration was the very first one. There were doubters throughout the country who wondered if the new form of government, with its system of checks and balances, would really work. Would peaceful succession prove practical? Vice President John Adams had followed Washington into the Presidency, but Jefferson would be the first opposition candidate to assume the office. Would the system be a blessing or a curse? Would periodic changes of administration solidify citizens' rights to govern themselves, or would they result in chaos — or, even worse, would they mean a return to the political and economic yoke of England?

The campaign between Jefferson and Adams in 1800 had been bitter, with rancor on both sides. Even after the election, the conflict continued, as Adams appointed his infamous "midnight judges" and left town before Jefferson was sworn into office on March 4, 1801. It would be many years before the rivals would reconcile. Nevertheless, the young nation passed its first great constitutional test, as power flowed from the Federalists to the Democratic-Republican party. The system had worked.

Jefferson left the White House in 1809 and lived at Monticello for the next seventeen years as a farmer-philosopher, honored by men and nations for his many contributions to the cause of freedom. Yet he felt that his greatest accomplishment was the founding of the University of Virginia in Charlottesville. He had a hand in every facet of its birth: he served as head of the governing board; he designed the buildings; he approved the curriculum; he hired the staff. The cornerstone was laid October 6, 1817. The university was chartered January 25, 1819, and was opened to students March 7, 1825. A quotation still used in the University's publications is reflective of Jefferson's philosophy and is a stirring and profound creed for free persons everywhere.

> *We are not afraid to follow truth wherever it may lead, nor to tolerate any error so long as reason is left free to combat it.*
> — Thomas Jefferson, December 27, 1820

Tuckahoe Plantation
Richmond, Virginia

Thomas Randolph, a second-generation Virginia settler, built Tuckahoe (Figure 9) in 1712 and bequeathed the estate of over one square mile to his eldest son, William, who managed the property profitably.

William Randolph's will, probated in 1745, requested that Peter Jefferson, who had married William's cousin, Jane Randolph, assume management of the property during the minority of William's son, Thomas Mann Randolph, and that a tutor be hired to direct the boy's education. Thus Peter Jefferson's son, another Thomas, went to live at Tuckahoe and to join Thomas Randolph in lessons from the same educator. The Jefferson family was to remain at Tuckahoe for seven years.

The mansion at Tuckahoe, an H-shaped Georgian, is considered by some historians to be America's finest existing eighteenth-century plantation home. Professor Frederick Nichols of the University of Virginia has written, "Not only is the house priceless

Figure 9. The Mansion of Tuckahoe Plantation, Richmond, Virginia. Photograph courtesy of Tuckahoe Plantation.

because of its completeness, but it contains some of the most important architectural ideas of the early Georgian period."

The Georgian style was English, and it is no surprise that many of the finer homes in colonial America copied it as a reminder of the mother country. The style was simple and balanced, with a planned relationship between the architecture and the landscape. It evolved in no small measure from the Palladian style.

The English adaptation of the Palladian style lay in the development of formal gardens and straightforward architecture that eliminated unnecessary decorations and made maximum use of the buildings. Primary examples at Tuckahoe are the paired outside structures, of which one was the office and the other the schoolhouse where the two Thomases attended class. Both buildings, still standing, are part of a pleasant stroll through the gardens and fields of Tuckahoe.

Tuckahoe is unique in another regard, for little has been done in the way of change since it was built. There have been no additions or other changes made to its exterior, and the interior paneling and embellishments are original. Thus its natural context and personality have been preserved. The interior of the main house, in sparkling mint condition, contains outstanding carved staircases and paneling, built-in cupboards, and beautiful period furniture. All interior rooms face the outside, with a view of either the gardens, the fields, or the river.

A visit to Tuckahoe prompts one to pause in the midst of today's hectic pace to recall its story — a story of European pioneers and Native Americans — of colonial revels and tragic wars — of changing masters and years of suffering. Jessie T. Krusen, in her book, *Tuckahoe Plantation,* has written, "it is a rare old place dowered with many charms. It is restful, and the quiet of the fine old rooms makes one forget the worries of today — for at Tuckahoe all the world seems at peace."

Almost three centuries old, Tuckahoe remains a working farm and home, privately owned by a family partnership and managed by Mr. and Mrs. Addison Thompson, who graciously open the plantation to visitors by appointment.

DIRECTIONS: Tuckahoe is 7 miles west of Richmond, Virginia. From I–64, take the Gaskins Road exit south to River Road. Turn right on River Road, go 2 1/2 miles, and enter a country lane through white pillars. From I–95, exit to Cary Street and follow it west. At the junction with Huguenot Road, Cary Street becomes River Road. Continue on River Road to Tuckahoe (Figure 10).

PUBLIC USE: Season and hours: Year-round, by appointment only. **Fees:** Adults, $7.50, with discounts for groups, students and seniors. Allow 2 hours to enjoy Tuckahoe. **Picnic area. Gift shop. For people with disabilities:** No special facilities.

FOR ADDITIONAL INFORMATION: Contact: Tuckahoe Plantation, 12601 River Road, Richmond, Virginia 23233, (804) 784–5736. **Read:** (1) Jessie T. Krusen. 1976. *Tuckahoe Plantation.* Richmond: Whittet and Shepperson. (2) Richard T. Couture, ed. 1986. *Goochland County Historical Magazine,* volume 18.

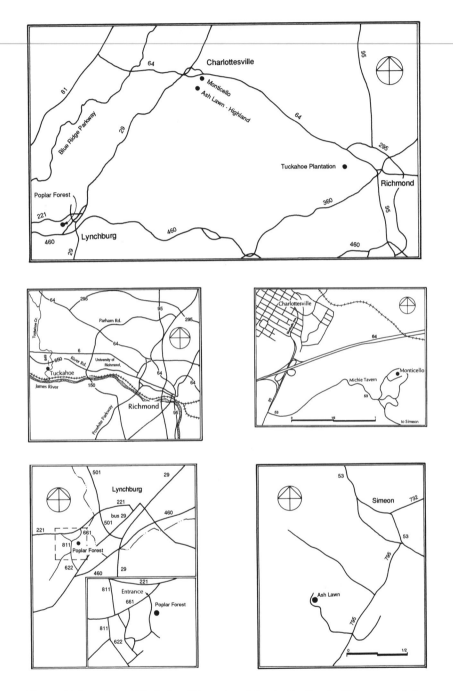

Figure 10. Location of Tuckahoe Plantation, Monticello, Poplar Forest, and Ash Lawn–Highland in central Virginia.

Monticello
Charlottesville, Virginia

Architecture is my delight, and putting up and pulling down, one of my favorite amusements.
— Thomas Jefferson

Monticello, or "Little Mountain," (Plate 3), stands proudly atop an 867-foot peak, with a commanding view of the lush Virginia countryside. Rarely does a home more accurately reflect the personality of its owner than does Monticello, a testimony to Jefferson's ingenuity and breadth of interests. Jefferson began clearing the mountain top in 1768, and for the next forty years Monticello was at the center of his thoughts. He designed and supervised its construction, and he never stopped altering, changing, or improving. Every facet of his home mirrored the pleasure he found in architectural planning and design. Monticello's thirty-three rooms recall Jefferson's quest for perfection in artistic execution, with the key elements existing in perfect balance. Everything in and around the mansion is a reminder of its owner's keen mind and his deep interest in the arts, sciences, agriculture, and architecture. The house has been restored to the splendor of its appearance in 1809 — 1809 being generally accepted as the date when the house was "finished." Recently, the roof was restored to its appearance in 1825, when Jefferson, out of concern about fire hazards and leakage, put on a new roof of tin-plated iron shingles. Altogether, Monticello is one of the country's architectural masterpieces.

Apparently, the house in its initial form was unlike anything ever seen in this country. In 1782 a visitor to Monticello, The Marquis de Chastellux, described the house as "consisting of a large, square pavilion." Even at that early stage of the house's evolution, Chastellux was compelled to remark, "Mr. Jefferson is the first American who has consulted the Fine Arts to know how he should shelter himself from the weather." Early drawings of the "first Monticello" reveal the neoclassic influence of Palladio, whose works Jefferson had read.

Monticello was unfinished at the time Jefferson left for a European diplomatic mission in 1784. He remained in Paris for five years, during which time he absorbed the classic art, literature, music, and architecture of the continent. Upon returning to Monticello, he began to redesign the house.

The upper story was removed and walls were razed in order to add rooms and a new front. The dome was added, its design inspired by an ancient Roman temple illustrated in Palladio's *Four Books of Architecture*. The exterior look of Monticello is deceiving, as it appears to be only one story tall. In fact, Jefferson blended the mezzanine and lower windows into single units and hid the upper floor behind a balustrade.

The interior halls and rooms are filled with Jefferson's gadgetry, such as a double-faced clock designed to be read from both indoors and out, alcove beds, and twin hall doors rigged with a device that opens both doors as one.

Jefferson's interest in architecture was matched only by his interest in garden design and landscape architecture. His plans for Monticello included ornamental and vegetable gardens, orchards, vineyards, and an ornamental forest. The gardens disappeared after Jefferson's death, but researchers found his sketches and meticulous records, which allowed an unusually accurate restoration of the grounds, a project begun by the Garden Club of Virginia.

The ornamental flower gardens were designed to complement and beautify the property, to define the perimeters of the lawns, and to balance the aesthetics of the house, lawns, fields, and view. There are twenty oval-shaped flower beds around the house and a roundabout flower walk on the West Lawn. Jefferson used a large number of species, including some brought from Europe. The beds are filled with varieties that bloom at different times, thus ensuring constant flowering and color.

In addition to being a landscape architect, Jefferson was a horticultural scientist; he tested hundreds of vegetables and herbs. In 1987, the Thomas Jefferson Center for Historic Plants was opened at Monticello as a modern, living tribute to Jefferson's many contributions to plant study. The Center features gardens, exhibits, and a shop where historic varieties of seeds and plants are sold. This continuation of Jefferson's work would have suited the feelings he expressed about gardening:

> *No occupation is so delightful to me as culture of the earth, and no culture comparable to that of the garden. . . . But though an old man, I am but a young gardener.*

Thomas Jefferson died at Monticello on July 4, 1826, more than $100,000 in debt. A dispersal sale held in 1827 included Jefferson's slaves, stock, crops, and household and kitchen furniture. Monticello was deeded to James T. Barclay in 1831 but with the establishment of the Thomas Jefferson Memorial Foundation in 1923, the house — and eventually over 2,000 surrounding acres — became a place for all people to visit. It is a monument to Jefferson's unparalleled gifts and his contributions to the United States and the cause of freedom everywhere.

The graveyard in which Jefferson is buried is located where family tradition says he and his close friend Dabney Carr studied under a favorite oak tree as boys. Carr's was the first burial there, in 1773, in accordance with the two friends' agreement that the survivor would bury the other beneath the oak. Jefferson's grave is marked by an obelisk inscribed with the epitaph that he wrote for himself:

> *Here Was Buried Thomas Jefferson*
> *Author of the Declaration of American Independence*
> *Of the Statute of Virginia for Religious Freedom*
> *And Father of the University of Virginia*

DIRECTIONS: Monticello is 3 miles south of Charlottesville, Virginia (Figure 10). From I–64, exit on State Route 20, proceeding south to State Route 53. Go left on Route 53 and follow the historical markers to Monticello. A Visitor Center serving Monticello and other local attractions is situated on Route 20 at the I–64 exit.

PUBLIC USE: Season and hours: March-October, daily 8 A.M.– 5 P.M. November-February, daily 9 A.M.– 4:30 P.M. Closed Christmas. **Fees:** Adults $9, with discounts for groups, students, and seniors. Visitors park below the mountain and are taken to Monticello by shuttle bus. Guided tours are conducted every 5 minutes in groups of up to 25. Allow several hours to enjoy Monticello. **Food service:** Picnic tables are located in the parking area; a luncheonette is open April to mid-November. **Museum shop. For people with disabilities**: Fully accessible.

EDUCATIONAL FACILITIES: Monticello conducts a regular program of lectures, nature walks, seminars, and special events ranging from wine and apple-tasting to gardening demonstrations. The Monticello Education Department offers special enrichment programs for student groups. Advanc registration is required. **Visitor Center:** The Monticello Visitor Center, located 2.5 miles west of Monticello on SR 20 at I-64, features a Jefferson Museum and award-winning film *Thomas Jefferson: The Pursuit of Liberty*. The Center also provides maps, brochures, and up-to-date information on local services. It sells tickets to Monticello, James Monroe's Ash Lawn-Highland, and Michie Tavern. A combination ticket for all three attractions costs $20 for ages 12–61, less for younger children and seniors.

FOR ADDITIONAL INFORMATION: Contact: Monticello, Box 316, Charlottesville, Virginia 22902, (804) 984-9800; Monticello Visitors Center, Box 161, Charlottesville, Virginia 22902, (804) 977-1783. **Read:** (1) Edwin M. Betts and Hazelhurst Bolton Perkins. 1986. *Thomas Jefferson's Flower Garden at Monticello*, 3rd ed. (2) Jack McLaughlin. 1988. *Jefferson and Monticello: The Biography of a Builder*. New York: Henry Holt Co., Inc. (3) Monticello Monograph Series. Charlottesville: Jefferson Memorial Foundation. April 1993 and following.

Poplar Forest
Lynchburg, Virginia

Often overwhelmed by the intrusion of visitors to Monticello, Jefferson sometimes fled to a secret retreat in the foothills south of Lynchburg, there to enjoy the "solitude of a hermit."

Poplar Forest (Figure 11) was unimproved property inherited by Mrs. Martha Jefferson in 1773. It was rarely used by the family, as there was only a tiny house on the grounds. Poplar Forest proved useful in 1781, however, when the British attacked Monticello in search of Virginia Governor Thomas Jefferson. Forewarned, the family fled to the safety of Poplar Forest.

It was not until 1806, well after his wife's death and near the end of his Presidency, that Jefferson laid the foundation for an unusual octagonal house, considered to be of a particularly cre-

Figure 11. Poplar Forest from the north, showing the front of the house. Photograph courtesy of Thomas Jefferson's Poplar Forest.

ative design. "When finished," Jefferson wrote, "it will be the best dwelling house in the State, except that of Monticello; perhaps preferable to that, as more proportioned to the faculties of a private citizen."

Poplar Forest is owned by the Corporation for Jefferson's Poplar Forest, a non-profit organization dedicated to the restoration of the historic house and property. Extensive archaeological work is being conducted on the grounds in a search for clues to an early age, and in the house for evidence of the ideas and plans of its genius-owner. The house is open to the public, but it is unfurnished.

DIRECTIONS: Poplar Forest is located on Virginia State Route 661, 1 mile from US Route 221, southwest of Lynchburg (Figure 10).

PUBLIC USE: Season and hours: April-November, Wednesday-Sunday, 10 A.M.– 4 P.M. Group tours are conducted year-round by appointment. **Fees:** Adults, $5, with discounts for groups, students, and seniors. Allow 1 1/2 hours to enjoy Poplar Forest. **Museum shop. For people with disabilities:** Due to the restoration and archaeological work in progress, the site is not accessible. Some assistance may be provided with advance notice.

EDUCATIONAL FACILITIES: Poplar Forest is an archaeological work-in-progress with no timetable for completion. The staff conduct a series of public programs about their work. During the summer they also conduct archaeological and architectural field schools that are open both to students and to professionals.

FOR ADDITIONAL INFORMATION: Contact: The Corporation for Jefferson's Poplar Forest, Box 419, Forest, Virginia 24551–0419, (804) 525–1806. **Read:** (1) Allen S. Chambers, Jr. 1993. *Poplar Forest and Thomas Jefferson.* Lynchburg: The Corporation for Jefferson's Poplar Forest. (2) Jane Brown Gillette. "Mr. Jefferson's Retreat," *Historic Preservation.* July/August 1992, 42+.

James Madison

Fourth President
1809 – 1817

Born March 16, 1751, Port Conway, King George County,
Virginia
Died June 28, 1836, Montpelier, Orange County, Virginia

*I believe there are more instances of the abridgment of free-
dom of the people by gradual and silent encroachment of
those in power than by violent and sudden usurpation.*
— James Madison

Madison, like two of his predecessors, was a member of the planter aristocracy; his family had prospered in the Virginia Colony since 1653. He was provided with the best possible education that included private tutoring and eventual matriculation at the College of New Jersey, now Princeton University. After graduation, Madison struggled within himself over the question of whether he should pursue a religious vocation, but he ultimately chose a career in law and became involved in the affairs of Virginia as a member of the House of Delegates.

In 1787, the War for Independence was over, and freedom had become a reality. Madison became a member of the Constitutional Convention, where his intelligence and clarity of thought were instrumental in developing and writing the Constitution.

A year later Madison, Alexander Hamilton, and John Jay wrote a series of essays known collectively as The Federalist Papers. They were distributed to citizens of the new nation as explanatory material on the Constitution. and are still studied as brilliant examples of cogent constitutional thought.

In 1794 Aaron Burr introduced the forty-three-year-old Madison, a bachelor, to Dolley Payne Todd, a twenty-six-year-old mother and widow. Soon after, they married and began a life of fine living, entertaining, political service, and deep devotion to the nation and to each other.

Madison served as a United States congressman and as Secretary of State in Jefferson's cabinet before being elected President of the United States.

> *I can say conscientiously that I do not know in the world a man of purer integrity, more dispassionate, disinterested and devoted to genuine republicanism; nor could I in the whole scope of America and Europe point out an abler head.*
> — Jefferson on Madison, 1790

Montpelier

Montpelier Station, Virginia

I wish you had just such a country home as this. It is the happiest and most independent life.

— Dolley Madison

The tract of land that was to become Montpelier was settled by the Madison family in 1723. The nucleus of the present main house was built around 1760 by James Madison, Sr., who bequeathed the estate to his son James in 1801. Montpelier (Plate 4) became a retreat to which Madison returned again and again throughout a long, productive, and distinguished public life.

James and Dolley Madison moved permanently to Montpelier upon Madison's retirement from the Presidency; however, they did not retire from public life and scrutiny. They remained involved in national and world affairs, and James' voluminous correspondence and Dolley's lavish entertaining kept them in the public eye.

The original main house at Montpelier seems to have combined some principles of Georgian architecture with a vernacular style. Its simple lines included a colonnade designed by Dr. William Thornton; the broad porch offered a sweeping view of the lawn and the distant Blue Ridge Mountains.

The derivation of the name Montpelier is unclear. Montpellier, a medieval French term for "Mount of the Pilgrim," was the name of a well-known resort and university town in France. Since the Madisons had no ties to the town, it is likely that the name is associated with the beauty, clean air, and healthy climate of the Montpellier area in France.

President Madison died in 1836; in 1844 Dolley sold the property and returned to Washington. Montpelier changed hands and appearance many times before it was acquired in 1901 by Mr. William duPont who made extensive alterations, including enlargement of the main house, addition of outbuildings, and planting of a formal garden. The estate remained in the duPont family until 1984, when Mr. duPont's daughter bequeathed it to the National Trust for Historic Preservation.

Today the fifty-five rooms of the main house are "preservation in progress;" guided tours of the house are oriented toward architecture and construction with access limited to portions of the first floor. Several rooms that were furnished in a modern style by the duPonts are open but little remains of the Madison occupancy, as Dolley and her son sold much of the Madison furniture upon their departure.

Considerable archaeological work has been undertaken at Montpelier, the most interesting find being evidence that Montpelier's largest source of income in the late eighteenth century was iron working. Documents have shown that Thomas Jefferson was a customer for Montpelier's finely-tooled iron equipment.

Madison's four-acre garden was designed by a full-time French gardener, and slaves were trained to care for it. In the early 1900s Mrs. duPont undertook a transformation of the garden and initiated a formal twentieth-century horticultural masterpiece. Following Montpelier's acquisition by the National Trust, further changes began under the direction of the Garden Club of Virginia.

Visitors are encouraged to explore Montpelier's vast acreage and to enjoy the garden and the lush woods, which form an arboretum of mature native and non-native trees. Madison corresponded with horticulturists in America and Europe and imported a number of exotic plants. A large cedar-of-Lebanon is one specimen that may have been introduced by Madison.

The graves of James and Dolley Madison are in a wooded copse on the grounds, a considerable distance from the main house.

DIRECTIONS: Montpelier Station is 4 miles south of Orange, Virginia (Figure 12). From Charlottesville, take State Route 20 north to Orange and follow the historical markers. From Washington, DC, take I-66 west to Gainesville, then US Route 15 south to Orange, picking up State Route 20 south to Montpelier.

PUBLIC USE: Season and hours: Daily, 10 A.M.– 4 P.M. Open for tours on weekends only during January and February. Closed Thanksgiving, Christmas, and New Year's Day. The main house is also closed on Montpelier Race Day, the first Saturday in November. **Fees:** Adults, $6, with discounts for groups, students, and seniors. The ticket office is located in the Montpelier Supply Company Gift Shop, the starting place for tours. A short orientation film is shown before visitors board shuttle buses for a 1 1/2– mile ride to the main house. Allow 3 hours to enjoy Montpelier. **Picnic area. Gift shop. For people with disabilities:** Fully accessible.

EDUCATIONAL FACILITIES: Special events are conducted by the Garden Club of Virginia on Madison's birthday and during April's Historic Garden Week. The Montpelier Educational Department provides an array of services and programs, including tours of Montpelier as well as seminars and workshops devoted to such topics as "James Madison and the Principles of Democratic Government."

FOR ADDITIONAL INFORMATION: Contact: Montpelier, 11407 Constitution Highway, Montpelier Station, Virginia 22957, (703) 672–2728. **Read:** (1) Ann L. Miller. 1990. *Historic Structure Report - Montpelier, Orange County, Virginia: Phase II: Documentary Evidence Regarding the Montpelier House 1723–1983.* (Prepared for Montpelier, a museum property of the National Trust for Historic Preservation.) (2) Irving Brant. 1942–1962. *James Madison,* 6 volumes. Indianapolis: The Bobbs-Merrill Company, Inc. (3) Larry Dermody. 1992. "Fire and Ice: Col. James Madison's Ironworks, 1762 to 1801." The Society for Historical Archaeology 1992 meetings, January 1992, Kingston, Jamaica. (On file in the Research Center, Montpelier.) (4) Lynne G. Lewis. "Archaeology on Ice: The Tempietto/Ice House at Montpelier." (Report on excavations conducted during the summer of 1989, on file at the Office of Technical Services, National Trust for Historic Preservation, Washington, DC.)

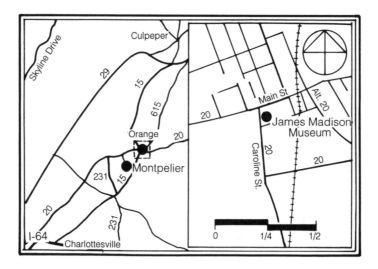

Figure 12. Location of Montpelier and the James Madison Museum in central Virginia.

James Madison Museum
Orange, Virginia

James Madison's home at Montpelier is an architectural work-in-progress that contains very few artifacts from the Madison occupancy. However, the James Madison Museum (Figure 13) is only a few miles away and provides an interesting complement to Montpelier with permanent exhibits tracing the life and times of Madison and detailing his enormous contribution to our political system. The museum contains a number of Madison artifacts — furnishings from Montpelier, the Madisons' correspondence and books, fashions associated with Dolley — and features a slide presentation about the estate at Montpelier.

A lower floor is devoted to a display of farm implements used in the early eighteenth century and features a complete one-room farmhouse of the period.

DIRECTIONS: Orange is 35 miles north of Charlottesville, Virginia (Figure 12). From Charlottesville and I–64, take State Route 20 north to Orange and follow historical markers to the museum. From Washington, DC, take I–66 west to Gainesville, then US Route 15 south to Orange.

Figure 13. The entrance to The James Madison Museum, Orange, Virginia. Photograph courtesy of The James Madison Museum.

PUBLIC USE: Season and hours: March-November, daily 9 A.M.– 4 P.M.; weekends 1 P.M.– 4 P.M. Closed Thanksgiving, Christmas, New Year's Day, Memorial Day, July 4, Labor Day. Closed weekends in December, January, and February. **Fees:** Adults, $3, with discounts for groups, students, and seniors. Allow 1 hour to enjoy the James Madison Museum. **For people with disabilities:** Partially accessible. Call museum for details.

FOR ADDITIONAL INFORMATION: Contact: James Madison Museum, 129 Caroline Street, Orange, Virginia 22960, (703) 672–1776. **Read:** Irving Brant. 1970. *The Fourth President.* Indianapolis and New York: The Bobbs-Merrill Company, Inc.

Octagon House
Washington, DC

During the War of 1812, the White House was partially destroyed by British invaders. When President Madison was finally able to return to the capital, the house was uninhabitable, with only the outer walls standing. The French ambassador to the United States was living nearby in the Octagon House (Figure 14),

Figure 14. The Octagon House, Washington, DC. Photograph courtesy of The Octagon Museum of The American Architectural Foundation, Washington, DC.

probably spared the torch out of diplomatic courtesy. In any event, the house was offered to Madison as temporary headquarters until the President's House could be repaired.

"Octagon House" is a misnomer, as the structure is only six-sided, not eight, but its design is unique and graceful. The first owner was Colonel John Tayloe, III, a wealthy plantation owner who wished to build a fine townhouse so that his wife could be near her friend, Nelly Custis of Mount Vernon. The house hosted many distinguished personages of our early history. Its historical significance was cemented in 1815 when President Madison, in residence, signed the Treaty of Ghent, which established peace with Great Britain.

The Octagon House deteriorated gradually, until it was rescued by the American Institute of Architects (AIA) at the turn of the century. They used it as their national headquarters, but in 1968 ownership was transferred to the non-profit AIA Foundation, which was mandated to maintain and operate the house as an historic landmark. AIA moved its headquarters to a modern building, leaving The Octagon House, which the AIA describes as follows:

> an excellent example of American Federal period architecture, designed by one of the renowned architects of the capital city. With its great originality of design, the mansion was undoubtedly one of the finest residences of its time, and it offers today's visitors an insight into the urban lifestyle of the period. Second, in terms of events in our nation's history, the Octagon is significant because of the part it played in establishing peace with Great Britain and for its role in the early life of the capital as a meeting place for the people who helped shape our country's future.

DIRECTIONS: Octagon House is two blocks from the White House, where New York Avenue intersects 18th Street (Figure 15).

PUBLIC USE: Season and hours: Tuesday-Sunday, 10 A.M.– 4 P.M.; Closed on major holidays. **Fees:** None. Donation is requested. Allow 45 minutes to enjoy Octagon House. **Book shop. For people with disabilities:** The first floor is accessible, with a videotaped presentation of the upper floors.

FOR ADDITIONAL INFORMATION: **Contact:** The Octagon, 1799 New York Avenue, NW, Washington, DC 20006, (202) 638–3105. **Read:** (1) Barbara G. Carson. 1990. *Ambitious Appetites.* Washington, DC: AIA Press. (2) Kenneth R. Bowling. 1988. *Creating the Federal City, 1774–1800: Potomac Fever.* Washington, DC: AIA Press. (3) Orlando V. Rideout. 1989. *Building the Octagon.* Washington, DC: AIA Press.

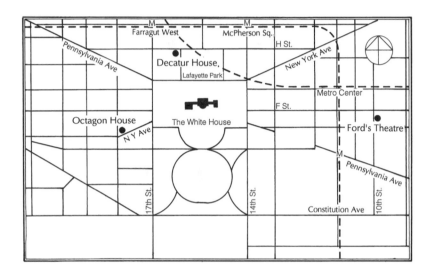

Figure 15. Location of the Octagon House, Decatur House, Ford's Theatre, and Woodrow Wilson House, Washington, DC.

James Monroe

Fifth President
1817 – 1825

Born April 28, 1758, Westmoreland County, Virginia
Died July 4, 1831, New York City, New York

The American continents are henceforth not to be considered
as subjects for future colonization by any European powers.
— The Monroe Doctrine

James Monroe was one of the four Virginians who, as a group, presided over the United States for 32 of the republic's first 36 years. He came from a more middle-class background than the others, but received an excellent education at the College of William and Mary in Williamsburg. The War for Independence interrupted his education, and he joined the revolutionary army as an eighteen-year-old lieutenant, serving with distinction; he was wounded at Trenton and wintered with Washington at Valley Forge.

He returned to Virginia to finish his education, then applied himself to law and politics. His political resume has rarely been equaled: delegate to the Virginia Assembly; member of the Virginia Convention to ratify the US Constitution; United States Senator; Governor of Virginia; Minister to France, Spain and England (he signed the treaty for the Louisiana Purchase); Secretary of State under Madison; and Secretary of War during the War of 1812.

Monroe's term as President became known as the "Era of Good Feelings," and he was so popular that he ran for a second term unopposed, an honor shared only with Washington. One member of the Electoral College disregarded public opinion, however, and cast a vote for John Quincy Adams, which gave Monroe a plurality of 231–1, thus assuring George Washington the singular honor of being the only President to be elected unanimously.

Ash Lawn – Highland
Charlottesville, Virginia

Ash Lawn-Highland (Plate 5) is an historic house museum, a 535-acre working farm, and a center for the performing arts in central Virginia. It was named Highland by the Monroes, but the estate's name was changed to Ash Lawn by a subsequent owner and both are used today.

Highland was the home of James and Elizabeth Monroe from 1799 to 1823. They had moved to Albemarle County at the urging of Thomas Jefferson, who admired Monroe and had the idea of creating a social and intellectual community close by Monticello.

Jefferson selected the site for Highland, located only two miles from Monticello, and assisted in its planning.

Unimposing compared to Jefferson's mansion, Highland reflected Monroe's less prosperous background and his belief in the simple life of a farmer — although from our modern perspective Highland was hardly "simple." The house was a modest frame structure that, with additions made through the years, now encompasses almost forty-four-hundred square feet. Like other farms of the era, it was a community unto itself, employing the services of resident craftsmen and a number of slaves. There were many outbuildings, and the property included woods, orchards, vineyards, and cleared fields that grew to an imposing thirty-five-hundred acres.

Monroe sold the Highland plantation in 1826, and it remained a working farm for more than a century. In 1931 philanthropists Jay and Helen Johns purchased Ash Lawn-Highland and opened it to visitors. In 1974, Mr. Johns bequeathed the property to Monroe's alma mater, the College of William and Mary, stipulating that it be operated "as a historic shrine for the education of the general public."

Thus the house became a museum, its period rooms filled with Monroe possessions and mementos of his achievements. The entrance hall, for example, showcases the Monroe Doctrine in pictures and documents. The Doctrine was a warning against European intervention into the Western Hemisphere, a warning gratefully received by our neighbors. One of the displays is a gift of appreciation to Monroe from the people of Santo Domingo — now the Dominican Republic — a magnificent drop-leaf table carved from a single section of Honduras mahogany.

Furniture in the Hepplewhite and Sheraton styles, a Thomas Gibson pianoforte, and James Madison's writing desk are but a few of the objets d'art filling the rooms. French wallpapers and period paintings provide a fitting background for the Monroe treasures. The Monroes spent considerable time in France on diplomatic service, and they returned not only with exquisite furniture, but with the ideas, tastes, and manners of the continent.

Outside the house, visitors enjoy exploring the still-active working farm, which features periodic crafts demonstrations. Particularly popular is a stroll through a distinctive boxwood garden and out onto the spacious lawn that is enlivened by colorful, strutting peacocks.

A non-profit subsidiary of the College of William and Mary, Ash Lawn-Highland seeks to fulfill the educational agenda of Jay Johns' will in many ways. An example of the varied activities is a summer arts festival dedicated to interpreting the cultural milieu of the Monroe era.

Ash Lawn-Highland generates income from a variety of sources — admission fees, donations, and grants — used to support the maintenance and restoration activities of the facility. But Ash Lawn-Highland, true to the spirit and strong convictions of James Monroe, also provides $50,000 annually to the College of William and Mary for James Monroe Scholarships.

Monroe would surely be touched by this living memorial, for in 1818 he wrote:

> *The principal support of free government is to be derived from the sound morals and intelligence of the people; and the more extensive means of education, the more confidently we may rely upon the preservation of our public liberties.*

DIRECTIONS: Ash Lawn-Highland is 2 1/2 miles south of Monticello on Virginia State Route 795 (Figure 10). From I-64 in Charlottesville, exit to State Route 20 and proceed south to State Route 53. Turn left on Route 53 to State Route 795 and turn right to Ash Lawn-Highland. See previous directions to Monticello for information about the Visitor Center that serves both homes.

PUBLIC USE: Season and hours: March-October, daily 9 A.M.– 6 P.M. November-February, daily 10 A.M.– 5 P.M. Closed Thanksgiving, Christmas, and New Year's Day. **Fees:** Adults, $6, with discounts for groups, students, and seniors. Allow 1 1/2 hours to enjoy Ash Lawn-Highland. **Food service: Picnic area.** Catered lunches are available by advance reservation. **Museum shop. For people with disabilities:** Fully accessible, including Braille material for the sightless, and special facilities for the hearing-impaired.

EDUCATIONAL FACILITIES: In addition to lectures and seminars throughout the year, a Summer Arts Festival features dramatic and musical entertainment, lectures, crafts demonstrations, and children's activities.

FOR ADDITIONAL INFORMATION: Contact: Ash Lawn-Highland, James Monroe Parkway, Route 6, Box 37, Charlottesville, Virginia 22902–8722,

(804) 293–9539. **Read:** (1) *Ash Lawn-Highland: A Guide.* 1991. Williamsburg: The College of William and Mary. (2) Harry Ammon. 1991. *James Monroe: The Quest for National Identity.* Charlottesville: University Press of Virginia. (3) James E. Wootton 1987. *Elizabeth Kortright Monroe.* Charlottesville: Ash Lawn-Highland Publishing.

James Monroe Museum
Fredericksburg, Virginia

James Monroe practiced law in Fredericksburg from 1786 to 1789 before progressing to a brilliant career in political and diplomatic service. The museum that honors him (Figure 16) is on land that he owned while he lived in Fredericksburg and is possibly the site of his former office.

Monroe served as American Minister to France from 1794 to 1797 and again from 1803 to 1807. While in Paris in the 1790s, Monroe purchased several suites of exquisite Louis XVI furniture crafted by masters, and subsequently used by the Monroes in the

Figure 16. The James Monroe Museum, Fredericksburg, Virginia. Photograph courtesy of James Monroe Museum.

White House. This handsome furniture is displayed in the James Monroe Museum, a favorite piece being the Louis XVI desk, upon which President Monroe signed his annual message to the Congress in 1823, a portion of which became known as the "Monroe Doctrine." Mrs. Monroe's impressive gem collection, costumes worn by the Monroes at the Court of Napoleon, other personal and historic items, changing exhibitions, and special events all serve to make a trip to Fredericksburg and this museum an interesting and rewarding experience.

The James Monroe Museum is owned by the Commonwealth of Virginia and administered by Mary Washington College through the Center for Historic Preservation.

DIRECTIONS: Fredericksburg is a 1-hour drive from Washington, DC (Figure 17). Take I–95 south and exit east on State Route 3, which leads into Fredericksburg. Turn right on Charles Street and proceed 1/2 block to the Museum, on the right. Street parking is available.

PUBLIC USE: Season and hours: March 1-November 31, daily 9 A.M.– 5 P.M. December 1-February 28, daily 10 A.M.– 4 P.M. Closed Thanksgiving, December 24, 25, 31, and January 1. **Fees:** Adults, $3, with discounts for groups, children 6–18, and seniors. Allow several hours to enjoy Fredericksburg and the James Monroe Museum. **Museum shop. For people with disabilities:** Fully accessible.

EDUCATIONAL FACILITIES: The James Monroe Museum is located in the center of the forty-square-block Historic District, which includes period

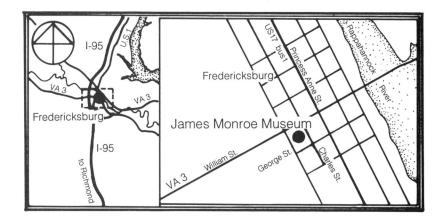

Figure 17. Location of James Monroe Museum in Fredericksburg, Virginia.

homes, shops, museums, and other buildings dating from the Colonial and Federal times. One is the Mary Washington House — the fine home that George Washington purchased for his mother. This and many other attractions in the picturesque town are open to the public year-round.

FOR ADDITIONAL INFORMATION: Contact: James Monroe Museum and Memorial Library, 908 Charles Street, Fredericksburg, Virginia 22401, (703) 899–4559; Fredericksburg Visitor Center, 706 Caroline Street, Fredericksburg, Virginia 22401, (703) 373–1776. **Read:** (1) James Monroe. 1959. *The Autobiography of James Monroe.* Syracuse: Syracuse University Press. (2) Lee Langston-Harrison, senior ed. 1992. *Images of a President: Portraits of James Monroe.* Fredericksburg: The James Monroe Museum.

John Quincy Adams

Sixth President
1825 – 1829

Born July 11, 1767, Braintree (Quincy), Massachusetts
Died February 23, 1848, Washington, DC.

I want a garden and a park
My dwelling to surround
A thousand acres (bless the mark!)
With walls encompassed round,
Where flocks may range and herds may low,
And kids and lambkins play
And flowers and fruits comming led grow,
All Eden to display.

— John Quincy Adams

John Quincy Adams was the only President's son to have attained the same high office once held by his father. The younger Adams was an ascetic man, sometimes aloof in dealing with others, but possessing a love of country and deep devotion to public service.

As a boy he accompanied his father on diplomatic assignments to Europe, so it was not surprising that his own political career began with similar diplomatic postings. He spent considerable time overseas before returning to serve as Secretary of State in the cabinet of James Monroe, wherein he was influential in framing the Monroe Doctrine.

John Quincy Adams was elected President by a vote in the House of Representatives, as none of the several candidates in 1824 received a majority of either the electoral or the popular vote. In the first house tabulation, Adams was second to Andrew Jackson, but Henry Clay swung his considerable support to Adams. Adams later named Clay Secretary of State, a highly suspect political appointment, looked upon unkindly by the electorate, who swept Jackson into the Presidency four years later.

Adams' Massachusetts constituents were loath to lose his brilliance and political influence, however, and elected him to Congress in 1830, the first ex-President to serve so. He remained a congressman for almost eight terms, until he suffered a stroke on the House floor. To his last breath he was a passionate political fighter for his personal beliefs, for the good of Massachusetts, and for the glory of the nation.

Where could death have found him, but at the post of duty?
— Senator Thomas Hart Benton

The Adams National Historic Site is a memorial to a remarkable legacy in our political heritage. It is a tribute to one of the Founding Fathers, John Adams, who made a rich contribution to the American way of life, and to his son, John Quincy Adams, who continued the valuable family tradition of public service.

[See page 32 for **DIRECTIONS** to Quincy and The Adams National Historic Site, and other relevant information.]

Andrew Jackson

Seventh President
1829 – 1837

Born March 15, 1767, The Waxhaws, South Carolina
Died June 8, 1845, The Hermitage, Nashville, Tennessee

*[Jackson is] incompetent both by his ignorance and by the
fury of his passions. He will be surrounded and governed by
incompetent men, whose ascendancy over him will be secured by their servility and who will bring to the Government of the nation nothing but their talent for intrigue.*

— John Quincy Adams, describing his opponent
during the 1824 Presidential election

Faults he had, undoubtedly; such faults as often belong to an
ardent, generous, sincere nature — the weeds that grow in
rich soil. Notwithstanding this, he was precisely the man for
the period in which he fell and nobly discharged the duties
demanded of him by the times.

— William Cullen Bryant, 1836

Today Andrew Jackson might be considered a "troubled youth." His father died before he was born, his family was poor, and the boy was a hellion — undisciplined and a constant mischief-maker. Jackson often told the story of having participated in the Revolutionary War at age thirteen as a messenger. He was captured by the British and held prisoner with one of his brothers; when he refused to polish a pair of boots, he received a blow on the head from a British officer's sword. He carried the scar proudly through life.

Jackson had an innate sense of his own ability and a compelling determination to overcome his impoverished background. He moved to Salisbury, North Carolina, where he read for the law and qualified for the bar in 1787. He settled in the western district of North Carolina — the district that was to become Tennessee. Serving as Attorney General for the district, he became known for his excellent record in that office; he established a successful private practice as well. He went on to serve in the Tennessee Constitutional Convention and in the United States Congress before returning to Nashville to sit on the Tennessee Supreme Court.

In 1802, Jackson was elected major general of the Tennessee militia. During the war of 1812 he received a commission as a major general in the US Army after defeating the Creek Indians in the pivotal Battle of Horseshoe Bend. As a commander of US forces, Jackson then achieved a dramatic victory over the British at the Battle of New Orleans. The result was national attention and a political boom that would lead to the Presidency. Although he lost his first bid for the office in a disputed contest in the House of Representatives in 1824, he was elected handily by popular and electoral vote in 1828, and again in 1832. He proved to be an active Chief Executive, greatly expanding the power and prestige of the office.

The Hermitage
Nashville, Tennessee

The 425-acre Hermitage Plantation that Andrew and Rachel Jackson bought in 1804 was a far cry from The Hermitage that visitors enjoy today. It was merely a clump of log cabins — storerooms, slave quarters, and a two-story house (Figure 4) — where the Jacksons lived until 1821. At that time they moved into a more modern home, built in the Federal style popular in America at that time. The house was plain, its symmetrical facade embellished only with a fanlighted entry. In 1831 Jackson began the addition of two wings and a colonnade, completed in 1833.

Three years after the addition, The Hermitage was partially destroyed by fire. The upper floor was lost, and the ground floor sustained severe damage. Jackson, who was serving as President at the time, had the house rebuilt within the original walls and foundation. The roof lines were changed, and columns were added to the portico in the Greek Revival style then becoming popular. The interior underwent a total renovation, with enlarged rooms and new wallpaper, carpets, and furniture. To unify the elements of the home and complete the Greek Revival look, the front brick walls were painted white, although three sides remained red brick (Plate 6).

Jackson entertained simply but constantly, and The Hermitage, with its large rooms and handsome furniture, reflected a gracious lifestyle. After Jackson's death in 1845, however, The Hermitage fell into decline. By 1856, Andrew Jackson, Jr., Jackson's adopted son, had come into financial difficulty and was forced to sell the mansion and five hundred acres of property to the State of Tennessee. The state intended to propose The Hermitage as a branch of the United States Military Academy, but that scheme died, and in 1860 the Jackson family was invited back to manage the state-owned property.

During the Civil War, The Hermitage was protected from physical damage, but the loss of agricultural production was ruinous. The future of the property remained in doubt for many years, and in 1889 the state considered converting the estate into a home for indigent Confederate soldiers. At the same time, Amy Jackson, wife of Andrew Jackson, III, inspired by the success of the Mount Vernon Ladies' Association, formed a similar organization of Nashville women to reclaim The Hermitage. On February 19, 1889, The Ladies' Hermitage Association was officially recognized under charter of the State of Tennessee and, a century later, is still custodian of The Hermitage.

Today's visitors to The Hermitage enter a sprawling Visitor Center that houses a museum shop, a restaurant, and a small but impressive museum. The museum contains original Jackson artifacts, memorabilia, and graphic displays tracing Jackson's career and the history of The Hermitage.

Tours of the property begin with the screening of a sixteen-minute orientation film. As guests leave the theater, they receive audio cassette players and tapes that accompany a self-guided tour of the estate and mansion. Trained docents are stationed in the buildings to answer questions, the most frequent being about the panoramic wallpaper covering the entire front hall of the mansion. Scenic paper was popular in fine homes of the period; in this case the paper depicts the epic legend of Telemachus, on the island of Calypso, in search of his father, Odysseus.

Another popular item is the portrait of Rachel Jackson that hangs over the mantel in the President's bedroom. Mrs. Jackson died only weeks after her husband's election in 1828, and the portrait was shipped to Washington, where it was placed, as at The Hermitage, opposite Jackson's bed. He told a friend that it was placed so that "it might be the first object to meet his eyes when his lids opened in the morning and the last for his gaze to leave when they closed in sleep at night."

The grounds at The Hermitage are colorful, lush, and manicured. The walk from the Visitor Center to the mansion passes a guitar-shaped driveway bordered by cedar trees planted in 1838. To the east is "Rachel's Garden," an excellent example of a southern plantation garden. Over an acre in size, it is maintained with the same species of flowers that were available when Rachel Jackson gathered bouquets for departing guests or made floral arrangements for the house. There are over fifty varieties of flowers, shrubs, herbs, and trees; the central beds are arranged in a formal geometric design, with brick borders. At the southeast corner of the garden is the Jackson tomb, a stone monument built along classic Greek lines, with a copper dome supported by fluted columns.

To the rear of the mansion are a number of outbuildings: the smokehouse, two original log cabins, and a springhouse. Just down Rachel's Lane stands Tulip Grove, the residence of Andrew Jackson Donelson, Jackson's secretary and Rachel's nephew. Nearby is the Old Hermitage Church, built on land donated by Andrew Jackson in 1823. He attended services there regularly and became a member in 1838. Both the Tulip Grove Mansion and the church are part of a visit to The Hermitage.

At The Hermitage, Andrew Jackson was the opposite of his public persona — the tough old general or the stern, squabbling politician. Childless, the Jacksons had adopted one of Rachel's nephews; eventually the mansion was filled with friends, children, and grandchildren, all of whom delighted Jackson, "The Old Spoiler."

The Hermitage was a friendly house, filled with children, joy, and security. It is easy to understand why Jackson, frequently absent in the service of the nation, always returned home to The Hermitage.

DIRECTIONS: The Hermitage may be reached by taking the Old Hickory Boulevard exit from I-40 East, I-65 North, or I-24 North from Nashville, Tennessee (Figure 18). The entrance off Old Hickory Boulevard is prominently marked.

PUBLIC USE: Season and hours: Daily, 9 A.M.– 5 P.M. Closed Thanksgiving, Christmas, and the third week in January. **Fees:** Adults, $7, with discounts for groups, students, and seniors. **Food service:** There is a 120-seat cafeteria in the Visitor Center, plus an outdoor picnic area. **Museum shop. For people with disabilities:** Accessible, with the exceptions of the second floor of the mansion and Tulip Grove mansion. Allow several hours to enjoy The Hermitage.

EDUCATIONAL FACILITIES: The Hermitage conducts an extensive research and educational program including archaeological work-in-progress, summer garden tours, and a "hands-on" history series for students.

FOR ADDITIONAL INFORMATION: Contact: The Hermitage, 4580 Rachel's Lane, Hermitage, Tennessee 37076–1331, (615) 889–2941. **Read:** (1) Arthur M. Schlesinger. 1953. *The Age of Jackson.* Boston: Little, Brown and Company. (2) Larry McKee. 1992. "Reinterpreting the Construction History of the Service Area of the Hermitage Mansion." In Text-Aided Archaeology, ed. Barbara J. Little. Boca Raton, Ann Arbor, London: CRC Press, Inc. (3) Patricia L. Hudson. 1990. "Old Hickory's House." Americana. February. (4) Stanley Horn. 1976. *The Hermitage.* Nashville: Ladies' Hermitage Association. (Reprint. Originally published 1941.)

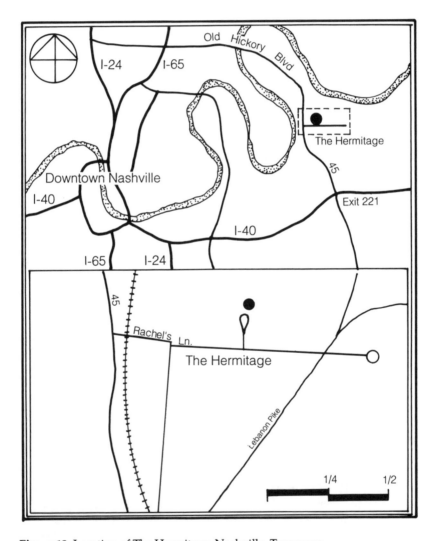

Figure 18. Location of The Hermitage, Nashville, Tennessee.

Martin Van Buren

Eighth President
1837 – 1841

Born December 5, 1782, Kinderhook, New York
Died July 24, 1862, Kinderhook, New York

*I, Martin Van Buren . . . heretofore Governor of the State and
more recently President of the United States, but for the last
and happiest years of my life, a Farmer in my native town.*
— Martin Van Buren, beginning his will

Martin Van Buren was the first President to have been born as a citizen of the United States and the first Governor of New York to seek the Presidency. He was born in the tiny hamlet of Kinderhook, New York, the son of a tavern keeper. He attended local schools, studied law, gravitated to politics, and served as a United States Senator, as New York's Governor, and as Secretary of State and Vice President under Andrew Jackson.

Van Buren was elected to the Presidency in 1836, but his term was clouded by the Panic of 1837, which began immediately upon his inauguration and contributed to the defeat of his reelection attempt in 1840. The 1840 campaign highlighted Van Buren's dismal economic record — inherited from the Jackson Presidency — and was notable for a masterpiece of political prowess displayed by his opponents.

Van Buren's opposition nominated William Henry Harrison, a Virginia aristocrat with a distinguished frontier military record. Harrison was craftily portrayed by the Whigs as "a man of the people" and "the candidate of hard cider and a log cabin." On the other hand, Van Buren, who was of humble beginnings and had been born in his parents' tavern, was depicted as a champagne-swilling dilettante who used silver spoons and dainty tea cups in the White House. The tactic was successful, and Harrison carried the day.

Van Buren's term in office has been described by scholars as "undistinguished," but a linguistic legacy of his final nomination and campaign lives on: the everyday expression "O.K." There are conflicting theories as to its derivation, but one of the more interesting ones is that it stands for one of Van Buren's nicknames, "Old Kinderhook." The first recorded use of the expression to signify approval took place in 1839, when a newspaper referred to a Democratic party meeting of the "roarers, the butt-enders, ring-tails, and O.K.s," the allusion apparently being to those who marked ballots "O.K.," for Martin Van Buren.

Van Buren's political nickname was "The Little Magician." He was a master of cool, competent persuasion — perhaps the first great political manipulator in our history. So, defeated by Harrison, but unbowed, he sought the Democratic nomination once again, in 1844, only to be defeated by James K. Polk. In 1848, never-say-die Van Buren switched political affiliation and ran for the Presidency as candidate of the Free-Soil party, a group opposing the extension of slavery. His subsequent defeat finally brought a remarkable political career to an end.

Martin Van Buren National Historic Site
Kinderhook, New York

Martin Van Buren returned to Kinderhook (Plate 7) in 1841. Two years earlier he had paid $14,000 for a two-story red brick house situated on a fine piece of prime farm land once owned by his ancestors. He named the place "Lindenwald," Dutch for "Grove of Linden Trees," for the lovely trees that surrounded the property.

Belying his humble background, Van Buren, by now a wealthy and fastidious man with expensive tastes, lavished money and attention on renovations, both outside and in. On the outside he decided on a "Venetian Villa look" that involved a third story and the addition of a library wing, a porch, a 4 1/2-story tower, and additional rooms. The red brick exterior was painted yellow. The interior was refurbished with fresh hangings, new furniture, and spectacular wallpaper. The front hall was handsomely decorated with fifty-one panels of rich French wallpaper that provided a mural-like depiction of a European hunting scene. Like Andrew Jackson's scenic paper, Van Buren's was typical of the homes of the wealthy at that time.

Van Buren's daughter-in-law once described her young son's "little shrieks of delight [that] can be heard all over the house when he is shown the dogs and cows of the hall paper." Modern visitors share that delight when visiting Lindenwald. The paper, the White House china, fine paintings, and expensive furnishings recall a time when gentleman farmer Martin Van Buren "drank the pure pleasure of a rural life" at Lindenwald.

After a number of ownerships and political disinterest, Lindenwald was purchased by the National Park Service in 1976 and restored to the charm it possessed when owned by "The Red Fox of Kinderhook," Martin Van Buren.

DIRECTIONS: Kinderhook is 125 miles north of New York City, 18 miles south of Albany. From New York City, take the Taconic Parkway north to State Route 23. Travel west on Route 23 for 6 miles to US Route 9H and turn north for 10 1/2 miles to Lindenwald. From Albany, take 90E to Exit 12; then go 5 miles on 9 to 9H. Go 5 miles south on 9H to Lindenwald (Figure 19).

PUBLIC USE: Season and hours: May-October, daily 9 A.M.– 4:30 P.M. November-December 5 (Van Buren's birthday), closed Mondays and Tuesdays. Closed December 6-April 30. Closed Thanksgiving. Schedule is subject to change; call site for information. **Fees:** Adults, $2; under 17, free; 62 and over, free. Allow 1 hour to enjoy Lindenwald. **For people with disabilities:** No special facilities.

FOR ADDITIONAL INFORMATION: Contact: Martin Van Buren National Historic Site, Box 545, Kinderhook, New York 12106,(518) 758–9689. **Read:** John Nivin. 1983. *Martin Van Buren, the Romantic Age of American Politics.* New York: Oxford University Press.

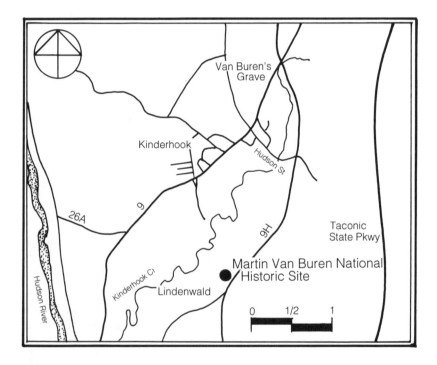

Figure 19. Location of Martin Van Buren National Historic Site, Kinderhook, New York.

Decatur House
Washington, DC

While serving as Secretary of State in the cabinet of Andrew Jackson, Martin Van Buren lived in Decatur House (Figure 20), an elegant Federal-style red brick townhouse designed by Benjamin H. Latrobe. Decatur House is on the northwest corner of Lafayette Square, facing historic St. John's Church across the park. The White House is a block south, just across Pennsylvania Avenue.

Decatur House was built in 1818 for Commodore Stephen Decatur, hero of the War of 1812 and of conflicts with the Barbary Pirates. It has also served as home to cabinet officers, congressmen, secretaries of state, foreign ministers, and other important figures in our history. As a gathering place for politicians and statesmen, Decatur House has played an important part in our nation's progress.

Figure 20. The Decatur House, Washington, DC. Photograph courtesy of Decatur House, a museum property of the National Trust for Historic Preservation.

Following the Civil War, when it served as a clothing depot, Decatur House was purchased by Mr. Edward Beale. The Beale family was socially prominent and the house was host to hundreds of distinguished visitors. In 1956 its last owner, Mrs. Marie Oge Beale, bequeathed it to the National Trust for Historic Preservation, under whose attention the mansion is now maintained as a museum representing 175 years of residential living in Washington. The ground floor rooms reflect the Federal style of the Decatur Era, and the formal parlors on the second floor remain decorated in the Victorian style of the Beale family.

DIRECTIONS: Decatur House is on Lafayette Square, the center of Washington's most famous historic district (Figure 15). It is within walking distance of both the Farragut West and Farragut North Metro subway stations.

PUBLIC USE: Season and hours: Tuesday-Friday, 10 A.M.– 3 P.M. Saturday and Sunday, Noon – 4 P.M. **Fees:** Adults, $3, with 50% discount for students and seniors. Allow 1 hour to enjoy Decatur House. **Museum shop:** Open Monday-Friday, 10 A.M.– 5 P.M. Saturday and Sunday, Noon – 4 P.M. Shop is closed on weekends after Father's Day and until after Labor Day. **For people with disabilities:** Accessible.

FOR ADDITIONAL INFORMATION: Contact: Decatur House, 748 Jackson Place, NW, Washington, DC 20006, (202) 842–0920. **Read:** (1) Helen Duprey Bullock, et al., eds. n. d. Decatur House. First published as numbers 3–4 in Volume 19 (1967) of *Historic Preservation*. (2) *Initial Investigations of the Decatur House, Volume II: Phase One of an Historic Structure Report.* 1990. Washington, DC: National Trust for Historic Preservation. (3) Marie Beale. 1954. *Decatur House and Its Inhabitants.* Washington, DC: National Trust for Historic Preservation.

William Henry Harrison

Ninth President
March, 1841 – April, 1841

Born February 9, 1773, Charles City, Virginia
Died April 4, 1841, Washington, DC

What has caused this great commotion
All the country through?
It is the ball-a-rolling on
For Tippecanoe and Tyler too.

— Campaign song, 1840

Campaign songs and rhetoric to the contrary, William Henry Harrison was anything but a common man. His father, Benjamin, was a signer of the Declaration of Independence and three-time governor of Virginia. William Henry was born at Berkeley, the great James River plantation that had been in the family for a century.

William was eighteen and a medical student when his father died. Attracted by the West and by the idea of fighting against the British, who still occupied some areas of the western territories, he visited his father's friend George Washington, who obtained William a commission as ensign in the young American army. He was assigned to the western frontier, where he remained for many years.

In 1801, only twenty-seven years of age, he was appointed Governor of the Northwest Territory, which later became Indiana, and took up military and residential headquarters in Vincennes. He wrote:

> I am much pleased with this country. Nothing can exceed its beauty and fertility.

Although engaged in periodic Indian wars — in the most famous, he defeated the Shawnees at the Tippecanoe River, earning his familiar nickname, "Old Tippecanoe" — he began to build a family home called Grouseland, in a design reminiscent of his boyhood home in Virginia. Harrison and his family resided at Grouseland until his retirement from the army in 1814.

The family moved to Ohio, where Harrison began a career in local and regional politics. To his surprise, and to the surprise of many others, he was nominated for the Presidency by the newly-formed Whig party in 1836. He was defeated in that election but ran a strong enough race to be nominated again in 1840. With the nation's economy in disarray, he easily defeated the incumbent, Martin Van Buren.

His term in office was shockingly brief. He died of pneumonia only one month after taking office, the first President to die while living in the White House.

Berkeley Plantation
Charles City, Virginia

Berkeley Plantation (Plate 8) is famous as the ancestral home of the Harrisons; it is the birthplace of one president, two governors of Virginia, and one signer of the Declaration of Independence, Its historic legacy began in 1619 when thirty-eight Englishmen put ashore and established a colony under a grant from the London Company. The colonists called themselves the Berkeley Company, a name they transferred to the new adventure. On December 4, 1619, the tiny group fell to their knees in thankful prayer — the first official Thanksgiving in America. The Berkeley settlement was short-lived, however, as it fell victim to a bloody Indian massacre in 1622.

In 1691, Berkeley Plantation was acquired by the Harrisons, a family of English descent who had been in this country for two generations. They expanded Berkeley to include a shipyard and tobacco warehouse, but it was not until 1726 that Benjamin Harrison IV built a Georgian mansion that was to become the base for a commercial and agricultural empire.

The manor house, the oldest three-story brick house in Virginia, is situated atop a landscaped hilltop within a fourteen-hundred-acre estate. The grounds include a formal boxwood garden and textured lawns sloping from the front door of the mansion to the bank of the James River.

Handsome Adam woodwork and double arches in the "Great Rooms" were installed in 1790 at the direction of Thomas Jefferson. All of the interior rooms are furnished with authentic furniture and fine antiques. Visitors are particularly interested in the bedroom in which William Henry Harrison was born. After his election to the Presidency, Harrison returned to the room to write his inaugural address at the simple desk which remains in place.

By the mid-nineteenth century, financial setbacks had caused the Harrison family to lose Berkeley. During the Civil War it was appropriated as headquarters for General George McClellan and the Army of the Potomac. During that bivouac McClellan's aide, General Daniel Butterfield, composed the plaintive "Taps," played for the first time by company bugler O. W. Norton. A commemorative plaque on the grounds marks the historic event. Abraham Lincoln visited Berkeley twice during the war to confer with McClellan and to review the troops.

Following the war, the estate steadily declined until 1907 when it was purchased by Scottish-born John Jamieson, a man who had served as a drummer boy in McClellan's army. John Jamieson's son, Malcolm, and his wife, Grace, inherited Berkeley in 1927, and are responsible for its restoration; the property is much the same now as it was in its days of glory under the Harrisons.

As Parke Rouse, Jr., and Susan Burtch remark in their booklet, *Berkeley Plantation and Hundred*, "Berkeley Hundred Plantation stands today as a reminder of those men of vision, Americans of long ago who worked and fought to make this country free and prosperous. It is at once a birthplace and an inheritance: not only a plantation home, but in a very real sense, an ancestral home common to Americans nationwide."

DIRECTIONS: Berkeley Plantation is on Virginia State Route 5, equidistant between Richmond and Williamsburg (Figure 21). Historical markers direct visitors to Berkeley.

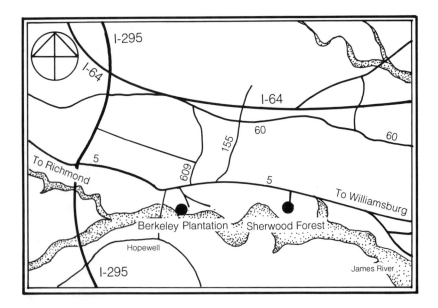

Figure 21. Location of Berkeley Plantation and Sherwood Forest, The Peninsula, eastern Virginia.

PUBLIC USE: **Season and hours:** Mansion and grounds, daily 8 A.M.– 6 P.M. Closed Christmas. **Fees:** Adults, $8.50; Children 6–12, $4; Discounts for groups, seniors, military, and AAA members. Allow 2 hours to enjoy Berkeley. **Food service:** The Coach House Restaurant, on the grounds, is open for lunch and traditional colonial dining. Reservations are required. (804) 829–6603. **Gift shop. For people with disabilities:** Accessibility is limited. Some assistance is available with advance notice.

FOR ADDITIONAL INFORMATION: **Contact:** Berkeley Plantation, 12602 Harrison Landing Road, Charles City, Virginia 23030, (804) 829–6018. **Read:** (1) Bruce Roberts. 1990. *Plantation Homes of the James River.* Chapel Hill: University of North Carolina Press, pages 28–39. (2) Clifford Dowdey. 1957. *The Great Plantation.* Charles City: Berkeley Plantation. (Reprinted 1988.) (3) Parke Rouse, Jr., and Susan T. Burtch. 1980. *Berkeley Plantation and Hundred.* Williamsburg: Williamsburg Publishing Company.

Grouseland

Vincennes, Indiana

I wish that my husband's friends had left him where he is, happy and contented in retirement.
— Anne Harrison, leaving for Washington
to become First Lady

In 1800, William Henry Harrison was serving as governor of Indiana Territory, which was the western frontier at that time. Accustomed to quality eastern living, he commenced, between 1803 and 1804, construction of a house similar in appearance to his boyhood home, Berkeley Plantation. There are significant structural differences, however. The threat of Indian raids in Indiana was real; hence the outer walls of Grouseland are 18 inches thick. In addition, the walls and ceilings were reinforced against the stress caused the structure by Harrison's many guests.

Grouseland (Figure 22) contains seventeen rooms, including six in the basement, and ten fireplaces. The rooms were full in the Harrisons' time, as the family had eight children; they entertained frequently and offered an open "Y'all come" invitation to their neighbors in the event of an Indian attack.

Figure 22. Grouseland, Vincennes, Indiana. Photograph courtesy Francis Vigo Chapter, Daughters of the American Revolution.

After the Harrisons moved from Indiana in 1812, Grouseland underwent many changes of occupancy. A period of ignominy included its use as a grain storage facility and as a less-than-four-star hotel at the time that the railroad was built. Shortly after the Civil War, Grouseland was reclaimed as a private residence, but by 1909 it was decaying and was scheduled for demolition to make room for a water company settling tank.

It was saved from the wrecker's ball by the intervention of the one-year-old Francis Vigo Chapter, Daughters of the American Revolution. The ladies were granted custody and, in 1911, they opened the house both outside and in, filling the rooms with some genuine Harrison possessions and other period pieces. Almost a century later, the active Chapter maintains Grouseland with enthusiasm and great attention to detail.

One of the rooms has been converted into a small museum, with historical displays, war material, uniforms, maps, and other artifacts delineating the life and career of the outstanding military figure who served our young nation with distinction, but led it as President for only thirty-one days.

DIRECTIONS: Vincennes is in the southwestern corner of Indiana on US Route 41. From Route 41 take the Hart Street exit. Proceed west on Hart to North 2nd Street. Go right on North 2nd and continue 3 blocks to Harrison Street. Turn left on Harrison and go to North 1st Street. Turn left and go 1 block to Scott Street, then right on Scott for 1 1/2 blocks to Grouseland, which is on the right (Figure 23).

PUBLIC USE: Season and hours: Daily, 9 A.M.– 5 P.M. January and February, daily 11 A.M.– 4 P.M. Closed Thanksgiving, Christmas, and New Year's Day. **Fees:** Adults, $3, with discounts for groups, students, and seniors. Allow 1 hour to enjoy Grouseland. **Museum shop. For people with disabilities:** No special facilities.

FOR ADDITIONAL INFORMATION: Contact: Grouseland, 3 West Scott Street, Vincennes, Indiana 47591,(812) 882–2096. **Read:** (1) Freeman Cleaves. 1990. *Old Tippecanoe: William Henry Harrison and His Time.* American Political Biography Press. (2) Lorethea Hamke, et al. 1985. *All About William Henry Harrison,* 2nd edition. (Photocopied and bound by author. Available from the site museum shop.)

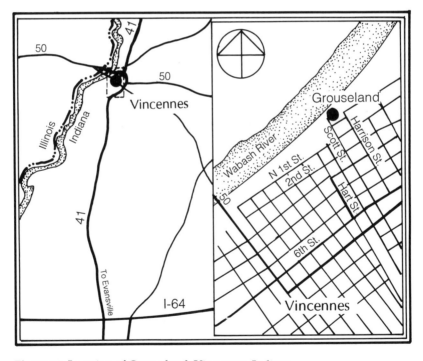

Figure 23. Location of Grouseland, Vincennes, Indiana.

John Tyler

Tenth President
1841 – 1845

Born March 29, 1790, Charles City, Virginia
Died January 18, 1862, Richmond, Virginia

*My daughters, you are now occupying a position of great
importance. I desire you to bear in mind three things; show
no favoritism, accept no gifts, receive no seekers after office.*
— John Tyler's admonition to his family
at his inauguration

John Tyler was the first vice president to succeed a President who died in office. Fletcher Webster, son of Daniel Webster, was dispatched to Williamsburg to tell Tyler of the death of President Harrison, who was only one month into his term. Tyler was asleep when Webster arrived on horseback at one o'clock in the morning.

Tyler's ascendancy was a shock to the entire nation, particularly to some political leaders who found the country led by a new President not under their control and influence. Some even suggested that Tyler resign and not assume office, but Tyler stood tall on strong constitutional grounds and refused to be swayed by such sentiments. He wrote:

> *I can never consent to being dictated to. I, as President, shall be answerable for my administration. My resignation would amount to a declaration to the world that our system of government has failed.*

Thus Tyler set the legal and moral example for the vice presidents who have followed. Another constitutional crisis passed; the trial and error process of the new democracy — and the strength of John Tyler — had resulted in victory for the people. "His Accidency," as he was called by his enemies, proved to be a man of vigor and honesty — with solid beliefs in the Constitution and our developing democracy.

Tyler's first wife, Letitia, died in 1842, early in his term, and in 1844 the President remarried, taking twenty-four-year-old Julia Gardiner as his bride in a New York ceremony; he became the first President to marry while in office. The couple enjoyed eight months in the White House. They campaigned together for the annexation of Texas, which Tyler signed into effect two days before his term ended in 1845. Tyler presented the bill-signing pen to his wife, who hung it around her neck as a necklace and wore it to Polk's inauguration. Upon their departure from the White House the Tylers moved to Sherwood Forest, their retirement estate on the James River.

Sherwood Forest
Charles City, Virginia

While serving as President, John Tyler, anticipating retirement, purchased a James River plantation not far from where he had grown up. He christened the house "Sherwood Forest," (Plate 9) as he considered himself a political "Robin Hood." It was a Georgian clapboard structure that Tyler renovated in the Greek Revival style and increased in size by connecting the kitchen and laundry to the east wing by a colonnade and by connecting the law offices to the main house with a sixty-eight-foot long ballroom. Three stories tall and only one room deep, the completed house ended up with a three hundred-foot facade, the longest frame house in America.

The large house was necessary to accommodate Tyler's second family of seven children. (His prolificacy remains a Presidential record; he had fathered eight children in his first marriage.) Its spacious rooms include a family sitting room occupied by a two hundred-year-old ghost, the Gray Lady. Legend has it that she descends a hidden staircase each night and rocks till dawn in a non-existent rocking chair. Presumably she is the only ghost to haunt a Presidential home.

The Gray Lady notwithstanding, Sherwood Forest has been owned and occupied continuously by direct Tyler descendants; it is still a working sixteen hundred-acre plantation, and it remains the repository of family heirlooms of the eighteenth and nineteenth centuries.

A complete set of original outbuildings is on the grounds. The colorful gardens and lush woods also attract visitors. There are over eighty varieties of century-old trees, including a large Ginkgo from Japan. Captain Matthew C. Perry, who opened the Trade Route to Japan in 1853, presented the tree to Tyler to commemorate Tyler's 1844 opening of the Trade Route to China.

DIRECTIONS: Sherwood Forest is on Virginia Route 5, 35 miles east of Richmond and 18 miles west of Williamsburg (Figure 21, page 78). Historical markers direct visitors to Sherwood Forest.

PUBLIC USE: Season and hours: Daily 9 A.M.– 5 P.M. Tours of the mansion are guided, with self-guided access to the grounds. Closed Thanksgiving, Christmas Day, New Year's Day. **Fees:** Adults, $7.50; Students $4.40; discounts available for groups, military, AAA, and senior citizens. Allow 1 1/2 hours to enjoy Sherwood Forest. **Food service:** Picnic area. Refreshments available. **Gift shop. For people with disabilities:** Assistance may be provided with advance notice.

FOR ADDITIONAL INFORMATION: Contact: Sherwood Forest Plantation, Box 8, Charles City, Virginia 23030, (804) 829–5377. **Read:** (1) Bruce Roberts. 1990. *Plantation Homes of the James River.* Chapel Hill: University of North Carolina Press. 46–51. (2) Jane Gillette. "Family Affair," *Historic Preservation.* September 1993. (3) Mary Ann Hemphill. "Restoring a President's House," *Washington Post* 20 May 1993: Home Section 8.

James Knox Polk

Eleventh President
1845 – 1849

Born November 2, 1795, Pineville, North Carolina
Died June 15, 1849, Nashville, Tennessee

I would relieve the burdens of the whole community as far as possible, by reducing the taxes. I would keep as much money in the treasury as the safety of the Government required, and no more. I would keep no surplus revenue there to scramble for, either for internal improvements, or for anything else. I would bring the Government back to what it was intended to be . . . a plain economical Government.

— James K. Polk

James K. Polk is recognized today as a strong and forceful President. He was a compromise candidate for his party's nomination, but he won the general election and went on to accomplish every goal of his administration — acquisition of California, settlement of the Oregon question, reduction of the tariff, and establishment of an independent treasury. These remarkable achievements are a credit to Polk's singular dedication, sincerity, and business-like conduct of government affairs.

Polk was born on a North Carolina farm, first child of a strict, God-fearing Presbyterian family. When Polk was eleven, his family moved to Tennessee; their determination and hard work led to financial success on the frontier. Polk graduated from college with honors, practiced law, and entered politics as a protégé of Andrew Jackson. Polk represented Tennessee in Congress for seven terms and returned to Nashville to run successfully for the governorship of the state. He served one term before resuming his law practice. When the Democratic convention of 1844 deadlocked, his name was brought forward as "Jackson's choice," and "Young Hickory" was nominated as the darkest dark horse.

As he promised, he served a single term, but, worn physically by the pressures of the Presidency, he passed away a few months after returning to Tennessee in 1849. At the news of his death, James Buchanan said of him:

> *He was the most laborious man I have ever known; and in a brief period of four years had assumed the appearance of an old man.*

James K. Polk Memorial
Pineville, North Carolina

James K. Polk, like other early Presidents, was a son of the soil; he was born on a farm of approximately four hundred acres worked by his parents.

The Polk Memorial (Figure 24) is located on twenty one acres of the original farm. Visitors to the Memorial can imagine young James performing his daily chores: feeding the animals, planting,

Figure 24. James K. Polk Memorial, Pineville, North Carolina. Photograph by Larry Misenheimer; use courtesy of North Carolina Department of Archives and History.

hoeing, and reaping. The work was hard, the only rewards being the development of industry, family responsibility, frugality, and devotion — ingrained qualities that served Polk and the nation well throughout his time of public service. Reconstructed homestead buildings — log house, kitchen house, and barn — have been furnished with period items to approximate their appearance at the time of the Polk residency.

The Polk Memorial is owned by the State of North Carolina and administered by the State Division of Archives and History. There is a Visitor Center on the grounds that features a twenty-five-minute film on Polk, plus colorful exhibits and displays illustrating the most significant events in his Presidential term: the war with Mexico, the annexation of California, and the establishment of an independent Treasury.

DIRECTIONS: Pineville is south of Charlotte, North Carolina, on US Route 521. The Memorial is 1 mile south of the junction with North Carolina State Route 51 (Figure 25).

PUBLIC USE: Season and hours: April 1-October 31, Monday-Saturday 9 A.M.– 5 P.M., Sunday 1 P.M.– 5 P.M.; November 1-March 31, Tuesday-Saturday 10 A.M.– 4 P.M., Sunday 1 P.M.– 4 P.M. **Fees:** None. Allow 1 hour to enjoy the Polk Memorial. **Picnic area. Gift shop. For people with disabilities:** No special facilities.

FOR ADDITIONAL INFORMATION: Contact: James K. Polk Memorial, Box 475, Pineville, North Carolina 28134, (704) 889–7145.

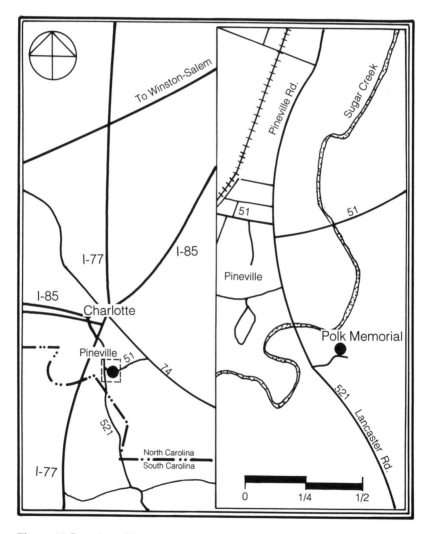

Figure 25. Location of James K. Polk Memorial, Pineville, North Carolina.

Polk Ancestral Home
Columbia, Tennessee

Searching for a more secure future, the Samuel Polk family moved west from North Carolina when James was eleven, settling at last in Columbia, Tennessee. By 1816, Samuel Polk had begun to prosper as a farmer and land surveyor and was able to build a comfortable home for his family, which included the future President, James. James was to live with his parents until his own marriage in 1824.

The house (Plate 10) is a two-story Federal of handmade bricks. The interior is typical of the home of a well-to-do Tennessee farmer: there is a double parlor off the entrance hall, with three bedrooms above. Outside there were gardens and a kitchen building. The house next door was home to Polk's sisters; the building was similar in design to the main house and was appropriately called "Sisters." Today it serves as a Visitor Center.

Tours of the Polk property begin at the Visitor Center with screening of an orientation film, then move to a museum area featuring memorabilia and exhibits that highlight Polk's life and career. Visitors are always intrigued by the "National Fan," a gift from the President to the First Lady, which Mrs. Polk carried to the Inaugural Ball. On one side of the fan are miniature portraits of the ten previous Presidents, with "President-elect" written above the picture of Polk. On the reverse side is a rendering of the signing of the Declaration of Independence. Other popular items are Sarah Polk's satin ball gown and the Bible upon which James Polk swore his oath of office as President.

Guests are then taken to the Polk home, filled with original furniture, silver, crystal, and Polk's set of White House china, decorated with Tennessee wildflowers and bordered by the shield of the United States.

In anticipation of his retirement from the Presidency, Polk had purchased a colonnaded mansion in Nashville that, together with its formal gardens, occupied a full city block. It was called "Polk's Place" and was the home in which he died in 1849. Mrs. Polk died in 1891 and, contrary to Polk's explicit instructions, "Polk's Place" was razed, a tragedy for all Americans who love, appreciate, and learn from the places where great men lived.

DIRECTIONS: Columbia is 50 miles south of Nashville, Tennessee, near I–65. From I–65, take Exit 46 (US Route 412) into Columbia and turn left on US Route 31 to West 7th Street; turn west and go 1 block to the Polk house. An alternate exit from I–65 is Saturn Parkway, which becomes Route 31 (Figure 26). Parking is on the street.

PUBLIC USE: Season and hours: April-October, Monday-Saturday 9 A.M.– 5 P.M., Sunday 1 P.M.– 5 P.M.; November-March, Monday-Saturday 9 A.M.– 4 P.M., Sunday 1 P.M.– 5 P.M. **Fees:** Adults, $2.50; discounts for groups, students, and seniors. Staff-conducted tours. Allow 1 hour to enjoy the Polk House. **Gift shop. For people with disabilities:** Partially accessible.

FOR ADDITIONAL INFORMATION: Contact: Polk Ancestral Home, Box 741, 301 West 7th Street, Columbia, Tennessee 38402, (615) 388–2354. Read: Betty D. Elder. 1980. *A Special House.* Columbia: James K. Polk Memorial Association.

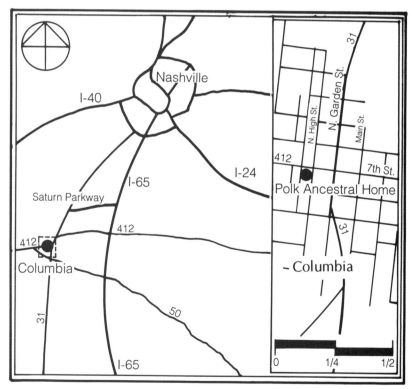

Figure 26. Location of Polk Ancestral Home, Columbia, Tennessee.

Zachary Taylor

Twelfth President
1849 – 1850

Born November 24, 1784, Orange County, Virginia
Died July 9, 1850, Washington, DC

It would be much more congenial to my feelings to be sitting with you under your own vine and fig-tree discussing the best mode of raising cotton.
   — Zachary Taylor to his son-in-law, Jefferson Davis

"Old Rough and Ready" Zachary Taylor was the first career army officer to achieve the Presidency. Taylor's father had also been in the army, assigned to the frontier near Louisville, Kentucky. The Taylor family's circumstances were modest, but their home was filled with warmth and affection, which Taylor recalled fondly through frequent moves to the rugged and sometimes primitive frontier posts of his own career.

Taylor rode into history during the War with Mexico by virtue of a brilliant victory at Buena Vista against overwhelming odds. Although he had no formal political party affiliation — he had never even voted — his fame propelled him to the Presidency. Only sixteen months into his term he died of pneumonia, brought on by fatigue, fever, and the effects of arduous military campaigning.

The only Taylor home still in existence is a boyhood home, called Springfield, in Louisville. It is privately owned and not open to the public.

Millard Fillmore

Thirteenth President
1850 – 1853

Born January 7, 1800, Locke, New York
Died March 8, 1874, Buffalo, New York

God knows I detest slavery . . . but we must endure it and give it such protection as is guaranteed by the Constitution, till we can get rid of it without destroying the last hope of free government in the world.

— Millard Fillmore

Millard Fillmore, as much as any man, epitomized the Horatio Alger story: "rags to riches, log cabin to the White House, and poverty to worldly success." He was born on a frontier farm in upstate New York, in a home where everyone had to work, and with precious little food or attention to go around. Under such mean circumstances, his parents apprenticed Millard to a cloth maker when he was fourteen years of age. Historical lore has told us that the ambitious lad used whatever spare time he could find to study and that by eighteen he had purchased his freedom and was studying law, paying his way as an itinerant teacher.

Just out of his teens, he fell in love with a pretty schoolteacher who recognized the talent in the raw, unlettered youth. With her encouragement, he continued to work hard and at twenty-three passed the New York bar, obtained employment in an East Aurora law firm, and felt secure enough to marry the schoolteacher, Miss Abigail Powers.

After a few years, the Fillmores moved on to Buffalo, where the young attorney caught the eye of political impresario Thurlow Weed. Fillmore spent the next fifteen years in a succession of elected and appointed political capacities. In 1848 he was nominated as vice president in order to "balance the ticket" with westerner Zachary Taylor. Fillmore assumed the Oval Office upon Taylor's death in 1850.

As President, Fillmore proved to be more than a political hack, and his short administration was one of stable competence. His party nevertheless refused to nominate him for a full term in 1852. He was persuaded to run four years later, however, as the candidate of the "Know-Nothings," a fringe party that sought to unite the country against foreigners and aliens in hopes of diverting attention from the divisive issue of slavery.

Fillmore was badly defeated and retired to Buffalo, New York, where he lived in baronial splendor, a far cry from the log cabin home and impoverished boyhood on the farm. Fillmore was respected but not loved by his neighbors, as he opposed President Lincoln's policies throughout the Civil War. The home in Buffalo has not survived.

Millard Fillmore Log Cabin
Moravia, New York

Deep dark woods, log cabin below,
Everywhere the drifting snow.
Raw wind whistling through the trees,
Never a place to take one's ease.
Ever on watch for wolf or bear,
Wildcat catching one unaware
Who in that wilderness could foresee
A youth destined for history.

— Ruby Morse

In 1921 the citizens of Moravia dedicated a local park to the honor of Millard Fillmore, and in 1925 the state of New York opened it to the general public as Fillmore Glen State Park. It encompasses 938 acres of woodlands, with playgrounds, campsites, fishing facilities, and other family attractions. Fillmore Glen lies in the middle of one of New York's beautiful vacation areas, at the southern end of Owasco Lake, one of the famous Finger Lakes.

The log cabin in which Fillmore was born a few miles away has been lost to progress and the elements, but in the 1960s a campaign was begun to replicate the cabin on a site within the park. Construction of the cabin (Figure 27) was completed in 1965. With the exception of a new hidden cement foundation, the materials used are from the period: logs, nails, glass, and bricks were reclaimed from other cabins that still remained in the area. Building techniques were authenticated and supervised by scholars on the nineteenth century. One newspaper noted:

> *with the pluck of pioneers . . . and no state aid . . . the citizens*
> *of Moravia have held a cabin raising to honor a log cabin*
> *President and the area's most distinguished native, Millard*
> *Fillmore.*

As Robert Scarry, a Fillmore biographer, noted, "It is hoped that this cabin will serve as an inspiration to the young people of America in years to come in that it exemplifies the American

Figure 27. The Millard Fillmore Log Cabin, Moravia, New York. Photograph by Robert J. Scarry.

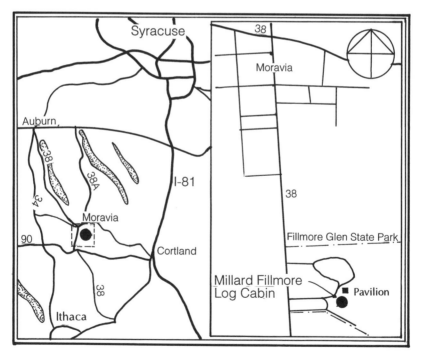

Figure 28. Location of the Millard Fillmore Log Cabin, Moravia, New York.

dream, that a person from humble surroundings can rise to hold the highest office in the land."

DIRECTIONS: Fillmore Glen State Park is 40 miles south of Syracuse, New York, just off I–81. Get off I–81 at Exit 12 (Homer) and turn north on State Route 11, proceeding 1/2 mile to State Route 90 and turning west to Locke. At Locke, turn north on State Route 38 and proceed to the park (Figure 28).

PUBLIC USE: Season and hours: Mid-May to mid-October, Dawn - dusk. **Fees:** $4 per vehicle for those entering the park between the hours of 9 A.M. and 6 P.M. Allow 30 minutes to enjoy the Fillmore Cabin. **Picnic area. For people with disabilities:** Accessible.

FOR ADDITIONAL INFORMATION: Contact: Fillmore Glen State Park, Moravia, New York 13118, (315) 497–0130. **Read:** Robert Scarry. 1993. *Millard Fillmore: Thirteenth President of the United States.* Published privately by Robert Scarry, Moravia, New York.

Fillmore House Museum
East Aurora, New York

Millard and Abigail Fillmore's life in East Aurora, from the time of their marriage, in 1826, until 1830, was an important period in Fillmore's odyssey from log cabin to the White House. He practiced law and became involved in politics in East Aurora, and his first child was born in a modest frame house on Main Street (Plate 11).

Eventually the house was abandoned, and it stood in disrepair until 1930, when it was purchased by a local artist and converted to a studio. In 1975 the Aurora Historical Society bought the house, hoping to restore it to the style of 1826 and the Fillmore occupancy. Extensive research uncovered the original floor plans, paint colors, and interior details. These were combined with period furniture and other nineteenth-century artifacts to recreate the sense of a typical small dwelling of the Federal period.

DIRECTIONS: East Aurora is 20 miles southeast of Buffalo, New York, on State Route 20A. From the New York State Thruway, take State Route 77 south to East Aurora and follow the historical markers. From I–90 (Buffalo to

Erie), take Expressway 400 east 15 miles to East Aurora. Exit at Maple Street and proceed to Main Street. Turn right on Main; go 1 block to Shearer. Turn right on Shearer; the Fillmore house is the first house on the right (Figure 29).

PUBLIC USE: Season and hours: June to mid-October, Wednesday, Saturday, and Sunday 2 P.M.– 4 P.M. **Fees:** Adults, $1; Children free. Allow 30 minutes to enjoy the Fillmore House. **For people with disabilities:** No special facilities.

FOR ADDITIONAL INFORMATION: Contact: Millard Fillmore House, Aurora Historical Society, Box 472, East Aurora, New York 14052, (716) 652–8875 or 652–0167. **Read:** Robert J. Rayback. 1959. *Millard Fillmore.* Buffalo: Buffalo Historical Society.

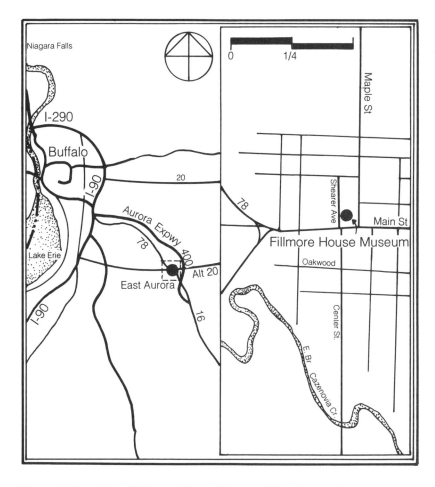

Figure 29. Location of Fillmore House Museum, East Aurora, New York.

Franklin Pierce

Fourteenth President
1853 – 1857

Born November 23, 1804, Hillsborough, New Hampshire
Died October 8, 1869, Concord, New Hampshire

Some men are so constituted that they do not incline to bend before a storm.

— Franklin Pierce

Franklin Pierce, like Millard Fillmore, has been called a "Forgotten President." His single term was considered unsuccessful — although it is doubtful that any President could have halted the runaway train of disharmony, distrust, anger, and folly that was America in 1852.

Pierce was the son of a veteran of the Revolutionary War, a man who had overcome a poor background to attain prosperity, reputation, success in business, and two terms as governor of New Hampshire. Franklin inherited his father's political instincts as well as his principles of hard work and his belief in public responsibility. He served New Hampshire as legislator, speaker of the house, United States Congressman, and United States Senator.

In 1852, Pierce became a compromise candidate for President, nominated by his party on the forty-ninth ballot, then was elected by a deeply divided electorate. Exacerbating an already volatile and hopeless situation, Pierce entered the White House bearing the scars of a personal tragedy so horrifying that Presidential scholars are convinced that it affected his ability to govern.

Only two months before Pierce's inauguration, he and his wife, Jane, along with their only surviving son — two others had died in infancy — were involved in a railway accident. Pierce and his wife were uninjured, but young Bennie was killed before their eyes. Jane never recovered from her deep trauma, and Franklin's gloom and sense of guilt haunted him for the rest of his life.

As President, Pierce proved to be a strict constitutional constructionist. Every attempt he made toward appeasement and understanding between the political forces of the North and the South failed. He pleased no one. When elected, he had been the most popular figure in the state of New Hampshire. When he returned from the White House four years later, the city of Concord refused him an official welcome home.

Nevertheless, Pierce and his wife seem to have had several good years together after Pierce left the Presidency. Mrs. Pierce's health, which had been frail, improved when they made a trip to the Bahamas, after which they also traveled to Europe. She had never liked politics; in addition, the distance from the death of their son helped her spirits. Mrs. Pierce died a few years before her husband, and he lived alone, suspected of harboring a drinking problem, until his own death in 1869.

Franklin Pierce Homestead
Hillsborough, New Hampshire

Benjamin Pierce was a bluff, determined veteran of the War for Independence. Able and ambitious, he migrated to New Hampshire after the war as a land surveyor, but he became a successful farmer, entrepreneur, tavern keeper, and politician. In 1804 Pierce completed a fine Colonial house (Figure 30) in Hillsborough just in time for the birth of his fourth son, Franklin, destined to become President of the United States.

The pioneer era was passing in New Hampshire in the early part of the nineteenth century as settlers moved west, and the Pierce home reflected a new age of comfort and luxury. Spacious rooms, hand stenciling on the walls, imported wallpaper, and fine paintings were indications of prosperity, good taste, and gracious living. The Pierce house even featured a second-floor ballroom that became the center of important political gatherings and grand social affairs. The rooms echoed with the inspirational, sometimes conspiratorial, sounds of the discussion of public affairs during this period of development and maturation in America's democratic history.

Figure 30. Franklin Pierce Homestead, Hillsborough, New Hampshire. Photograph by William G. Clotworthy.

Thus Franklin Pierce was exposed early to the excitement of politics and the thrill of debate. His father, although a self-made man, was poorly educated, dominating, and iron-willed in his determination that his son reap the benefits denied himself. He set a patriarchal example to his children of ambition, discipline, strong religious belief, and absolute determination. These were qualities that Franklin desperately needed when faced with the rigors of the Presidency many years later.

DIRECTIONS: Hillsborough is near the junction of New Hampshire routes 9 and 31, 30 miles northwest of Manchester. The Pierce Homestead is on Route 31, 100 yards north of Route 9 (Figure 31).

PUBLIC USE: Season and hours: Memorial Day weekend, June, and September through Columbus Day, Saturday 10 A.M.– 4 P.M.; Sunday 1 P.M.– 4 P.M.; July and August, daily 10 A.M.– 4 P.M.; Sunday 1 P.M.– 4 P.M. **Fees:** Adults, $2; children under 18, free. Allow 1 hour to enjoy the Pierce Homestead. **For people with disabilities:** No special facilities.

FOR ADDITIONAL INFORMATION: Contact: The Pierce Homestead, PO Box 896, Hillsborough, New Hampshire 03244, (603) 478–3165 or 478–3913. **Read:** Norman S. Boas. 1983. *The Pierce-Aiken Papers.* Stonington: Seaport Autographs.

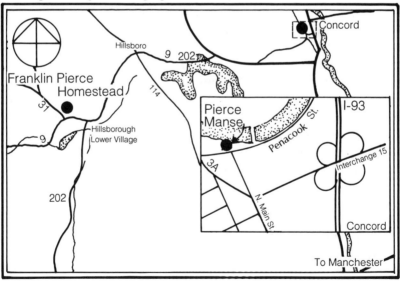

Figure 31. Location of The Pierce Homestead, Hillsborough, New Hampshire, and The Pierce Manse, Concord, New Hampshire.

The Pierce Manse
Concord, New Hampshire

While Franklin Pierce was serving a second term in Congress, his wife, unhappy in Hillsborough and devastated by the death of an infant son, persuaded him to move their permanent home to Concord (Plate 12). The new surroundings were to bring no happiness, however, as a second son died of typhus at the age of four.

Mrs. Pierce came to consider Washington as a place of exile and dread, so Pierce interrupted his political career and returned to Concord to practice law. He remained in Concord for many years, leaving only for service in the War with Mexico, enlisting as a private and rising to the rank of brigadier general. After returning home, he was plucked from political obscurity to be named Democratic candidate for President in 1852.

The Concord house is similar to dozens that one sees throughout New England. It is a two-story white Greek Revival with multiple chimneys. The kitchen, parlor, and dining room are on the first floor; the bedrooms are above. The house was saved from destruction in 1966 by a group of citizens interested in preserving the heritage of Pierce. They called themselves The Pierce Brigade, in honor of his rank during the Mexican War. To keep the house from being lost in the process of urban renewal, they had it moved from downtown Concord to a park-like setting, where it was refurbished to represent the time during which it was occupied by the Pierce family. Many of the furnishings are original, or were brought from the White House. In 1993 the carriage house was rebuilt, board by board, from one in Belmont, New Hampshire, that fit the dimensions and age of the original Pierce carriage house, which was built in the 1840s.

The word "manse" is applied to this house simply to differentiate it from the other home connected to Pierce.

DIRECTIONS: Concord, New Hampshire's capital, is located on I-93, 100 miles northwest of Boston, Massachusetts. Take Exit 15W in Concord, turn right on Main Street, then follow the historical markers 2 blocks to the Pierce Manse (Figure 31).

PUBLIC USE: Season and hours: Mid-June to Labor Day, Monday through Friday 11 A.M.– 3 P.M. Closed holidays. **Fees:** Adults, $2.00; students, .50; discounts for groups. Allow 45 minutes to enjoy the Pierce Manse. **For people with disabilities:** A wheelchair ramp provides entry to the house through the carriage house.

FOR ADDITIONAL INFORMATION: Contact: The Pierce Manse, 14 Penacook Street, Box 425, Concord, New Hampshire 00301, (603) 224–7668 or 224–0094. **Read:** Larry Gara. 1991. *The Presidency of Franklin Pierce.* Lawrence: University Press of Kansas.

James Buchanan

Fifteenth President
1857 – 1861

Born April 23, 1791, Cove Gap, Pennsylvania
Died June 1, 1868, Lancaster, Pennsylvania

If you are as happy, dear sir, on entering this house as I am on leaving it and returning home, you are the happiest man in the country.
—James Buchanan at Lincoln's inauguration

James Buchanan was born in a log cabin trading post in Cove Gap,Pennsylvania. In 1791 the area was the western edge of civilization, the surrounding Allegheny mountains forming a formidable barrier to the west.

The trading post did well and enabled the Buchanans to move into Mercersburg to open a small dry goods store. James performed well in school and graduated from nearby Dickinson College. He then moved east and settled in Lancaster, which he came to consider home. As a young attorney, he gravitated to politics, starting a distinguished career that included service in the Pennsylvania Legislature and the United States Congress, and appointments as ambassador to Russia and England and Secretary of State.

Buchanan's fate, of course, was to be elected President at a time when the national crisis over slavery and states' rights was all but impossible to solve. Buchanan's attempts to appease the South only alienated important factions in the North and did nothing to reduce southern militancy.

He left office strongly supporting the Union and Lincoln's policies, but happy to return to Lancaster, far from the daily pressures and cares of the White House.

Buchanan Historic Site
Mercersburg, Pennsylvania

Mercersburg is a picturesque small town nestled in the beautiful Cumberland Valley of southern Pennsylvania, unspoiled by the hustle and bustle of modern life — a town proud of its roots. In 1975, as part of its 225th anniversary celebration, Mercersburg created an historic district to preserve many of the town's fine structures — some of which date back to the early eighteenth century — and, of more significance, to perpetuate and maintain a lifestyle that was in danger of being lost forever. Included in the redevelopment were several buildings associated with President James Buchanan, Mercersburg's most famous son. These include:

Stoney Batter: An early trading post operated by the Buchanan family in Cove Gap. Buchanan's father gave it the name Stoney

Batter, after the Buchanan home in Northern Ireland. It is but a few miles from downtown Mercersburg. The birth site of James Buchanan is marked by a stone monument located within an eighteen-acre state park.

Log Cabin: Buchanan's actual birth cabin (Figure 32) has been relocated to a woody copse on the campus of Mercersburg Academy. Consisting of but one room, it is unfurnished; the interior may be viewed through a window.

Lane House: Harriet Lane, Buchanan's niece and ward, served the bachelor President as White House hostess and became the belle of Washington. Her girlhood home, a Federal-style house dating to 1825, is part of a self-conducted walking tour of Mercersburg's historic district. The house is privately owned and the interior is not open to the public.

Buchanan Hotel: When James was five years of age, the Buchanan family moved from Cove Gap to Mercersburg and opened a small store. The family's living quarters were on the second floor. Years later the store was converted to a hotel, and the owner honored Buchanan by naming the hostelry for him. It remains open as a pub and a residential hotel.

Mansion House: In 1856 Buchanan gave the speech that launched his campaign for the Presidency from the balcony of Mansion House, once a dormitory for Marshall College. Now in use for stores and offices, the balcony is not open for visitation.

Figure 32. Log Cabin, The Buchanan Historic Site, Mercersburg, Pennsylvania. Photograph by William G. Clotworthy.

DIRECTIONS: Mercersburg is on Pennsylvania Route 16, 10 miles west of I–81. From the North use Exit 6 (Greencastle); follow US Route 30 west to State Route 416 and proceed 8 miles south to Mercersburg. From the South, take Exit 2 or 3 (Greencastle); proceed 10 miles west from Greencastle on Route 16, which becomes Main Street. From the Pennsylvania Turnpike, take Exit 13 (Fort Littleton), then US Route 522 south to McConnellsburg, then Route 16 east to Mercersburg (Figure 33).

PUBLIC USE: Season and hours: Mercersburg is a thriving community, active the year-round. Allow 2 hours to enjoy Mercersburg. **Fees:** None. **For people with disabilities:** No special facilities.

FOR ADDITIONAL INFORMATION: Contact: Mercersburg Borough Hall, 113 South Main Street, Mercersburg, Pennsylvania 17236, (717) 328–3116. **Read:** Philip Shriver Klein. 1962. *President James Buchanan.* Lancaster: The James Buchanan Foundation.

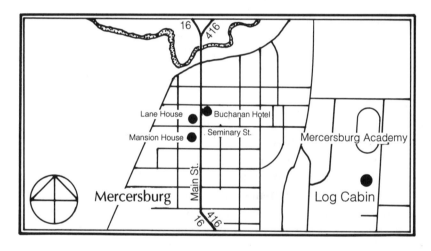

Figure 33. Location of Buchanan Historic Site, Mercersburg, Pennsylvania.

Wheatland

Lancaster, Pennsylvania

I am now residing at this place, which is an agreeable
country residence about a mile and a half from Lancaster . . .
I hope you may not fail to come this way . . . I should be
delighted with a visit.
— James Buchanan, in a letter to a friend

Wheatland (Plate 13) was built in 1828 by a wealthy Lancaster banker and named for its view of the rich wheat fields surrounding it. In 1848 it was purchased by Secretary of State James Buchanan as a country estate. Buchanan loved his time at Wheatland and praised "the comforts and tranquility of home as contrasted with the trouble, perplexities and difficulties of public life."

Wheatland was destined, however, to become a much more public arena; its library was the center of political activity during Buchanan's Presidential campaigns in 1852 and 1856. It was not until his retirement from the White House that tranquility returned and Wheatland became, once again, "the beau ideal of a statesman's abode." The house, with four acres of woodlands, was purchased and restored in 1936 by the James Buchanan Foundation for the Preservation of Wheatland, an educational, non-profit organization. The Foundation has succeeded brilliantly in preserving not only the residence but also the lifestyle of a wealthy country gentleman — a lifestyle that included liveried servants, leisurely dinner for twenty-five people, and entertainment comprising piano music and lively conversation.

Tours of Wheatland begin with the screening of an orientation film in the converted carriage house and continue in the residence with guides in period costumes. The rooms are spacious, as would have been a necessity for Buchanan's social and political activities. Original furnishings include a Chickering grand piano, which was played by Harriet Lane, Buchanan's hostess and niece.

In his description of Wheatland, A. Cranston Jones said:

The great charm in visiting Wheatland is that so much of the
tang and aroma of this pastoral existence can still be sensed.
So magnificently are the rooms maintained, with their

Lancaster hostesses in period crinolines, that one almost expects to catch sight of Miss Hetty tidying up the parlor, Harriet Lane once again adjusting her skirts before her fingers ripple the first chords on the Chickering grand, or find elegant and reserved President Buchanan himself standing at the head of the table, ceremoniously greeting each guest in turn."

DIRECTIONS: Wheatland is 1 1/2 miles west of Lancaster on Pennsylvania State Route 23 (Marietta Avenue). From US Route 30 East, take Route 23 east and follow the historical markers. From Route 30 West, take Route 23 west through downtown Lancaster (Figure 34). There is ample parking in the rear.

PUBLIC USE: Season and hours: April 1-November 30, daily 10 A.M.– 4:15 P.M. Closed Thanksgiving. During one week in December the mansion is open for special Victorian candlelight tours. Exact dates available on request. **Fees:** Adults, $5, with discounts for groups, students, and seniors. Allow 1 hour to enjoy Wheatland. **Food service:** Beverages and snacks are sold at the Carriage House and there is a picnic area. **Gift shop. For people with disabilities:** There are two steps to the porch, and the main floor is accessible. The second floor is not accessible.

FOR ADDITIONAL INFORMATION: Contact: Wheatland, 1120 Marietta Avenue, Lancaster, Pennsylvania 17603, (717) 392–8721. **Read:** Sally Smith Cahalan. 1988. *James Buchanan's Wheatland.* Lancaster: The James Buchanan Foundation.

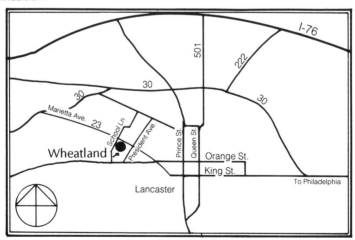

Figure 34. Location of Wheatland, Lancaster, Pennsylvania.

Abraham Lincoln

Sixteenth President
1861 – 1865

Born February 12, 1809, Hardin County (now Larue
County), Kentucky
Died April 15, 1865, Washington, DC

*We can see the past, though we may not claim to have
directed it; and by seeing it . . . we feel more hopeful and
confident for the future.*

— Abraham Lincoln

Heritage, environment, and human associations all combine to shape our thoughts into beliefs, prejudices, and attitudes. Abraham Lincoln's work ethic and ambition were molded by hard farm life. His compassion was learned from his beloved mother. His attitude toward slavery may have been defined by his first teacher, a determined emancipationist, or perhaps by the sight of slaves being driven down the road past the Lincoln cabin.

When Abraham was seven the Lincoln family, along with other neighbors, was evicted from a Kentucky farm called Knob Creek because of land title problems. They moved farther west to Indiana, where, during the next fourteen years, young Abe helped carve a farm from the wilderness and experienced the emotional wrench of his mother's death and his father's remarriage. His education was sporadic; he was, to a great extent, self-taught. All these factors were critical to the development of his future.

Lincoln eventually struck out on his own and moved to New Salem, Illinois, where he achieved a reputation as "Honest Abe," working as clerk in a general store. A voracious reader with a thirst for knowledge and an insatiable curiosity about society and his fellow man, he continued his scattered education until he was admitted to the Illinois bar at the age of twenty-eight.

Lincoln's New Salem experiences were a crucible for the skills and dogged determination that propelled him to the successes that lay ahead, the first of which occurred just twenty miles down the road in the state capital, Springfield.

Abraham Lincoln Birthplace National Historic Site
Hodgenville, Kentucky

I was born and have ever remained in the humble walks of life.

— Abraham Lincoln

In 1911, almost one hundred years after Thomas Lincoln and his family resided at Sinking Spring Farm, President William Howard Taft dedicated a memorial on the site (Figure 35). It is an imposing neoclassical building of marble and granite that may

Figure 35. Abraham Lincoln Birthplace National Historic Site, Hodgenville, Kentucky. Photograph courtesy of National Park Service.

seem too grandiose to memorialize such a simple man as Thomas' son Abraham, but the tiny rough cabin that is preserved inside its stone walls dramatizes the basic values that sustained Abraham Lincoln throughout his life, especially as he led his nation through its darkest hours.

The building sits atop a hill and is approached by a flight of fifty-six steps, each representing one year of Lincoln's life. Above the six granite columns at the entrance are inscribed his most famous words, "with malice toward none, with charity for all."

The Memorial Building is at the center of a 110-acre park that encompasses most of the original Lincoln farm. Extensive research suggests that the cabin within the Memorial Building is not Lincoln's actual birth cabin, although it is undoubtedly of the same construction, size, and historical period. However, it is within the same farmland, surrounded by the same forest and fields. Standing on the hill one is moved, hearing the same sounds, smelling the same natural odors, and experiencing the same atmosphere that Lincoln did almost two hundred years ago.

DIRECTIONS: The Abraham Lincoln Birthplace National Historic Site is 55 miles south of Louisville, Kentucky, on US Route 31E, a few miles from I–65. From I–65 northbound, take Exit 81 and follow State Route 84 east to Hodgenville, where historical markers lead visitors to the Site. From I–65 southbound, take Exit 91 and follow State Route 61 to Hodgenville (Figure 36).

PUBLIC USE: Season and hours: June, July, and August, daily 8 A.M.– 6:45 P.M.; all other months, daily 8 A.M.– 4:45 P.M. Closed Thanksgiving and Christmas. Contact park for seasonal changes in hours of operation and for holiday closings. **Fees:** None. Allow 2 hours to enjoy the birthplace site. **Picnic area: Gift shop:** Cards and books are available at the Visitor Center. **For people with disabilities:** Main features are accessible.

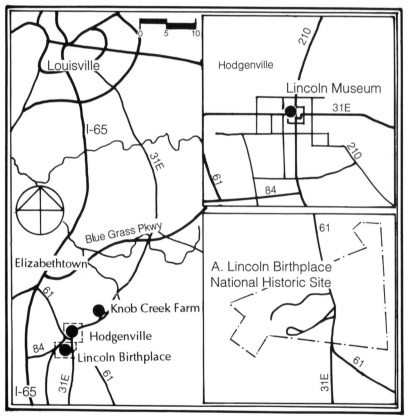

Figure 36. Location of Abraham Lincoln Birthplace National Historic Site, The Lincoln Museum, and Knob Creek Farm, Hodgenville, Kentucky.

115

EDUCATIONAL FACILITIES: The National Park Service has developed a self-guided historic walking tour through the site of the Lincoln farm that demonstrates the resourcefulness of the early settlers. Explanatory material provided by the park rangers helps guide visitors as they observe the forest and realize its importance as a source of food, building material, kitchen utensils — even of thread and buttons used in making clothing. On the far side of the Site is an environmental study area reserved for the use of school groups.

FOR ADDITIONAL INFORMATION: Contact: Abraham Lincoln Birthplace National Historic Site, 2995 Lincoln Farm Road, Hodgenville, Kentucky 42748, (502) 358–3137. **Read:** Louis A. Warren. 1929. *Lincoln's Parentage and Childhood.* New York: The Century Company.

The Lincoln Museum
Hodgenville, Kentucky

Fellow citizens, we cannot escape history. We will be remembered in spite of ourselves.

— Abraham Lincoln

The Lincoln Museum in Hodgenville is the most recent addition to the facilities dedicated to America's greatest President. The museum opened in 1989 and is located on the Hodgenville Square, the square dominated by A. A. Weinmann's bronze statue of "The Great Emancipator."

Hodgenville had never acted on periodic attempts to honor its most famous son, but in 1986 a retired museum curator came to town looking to sell some used wax figures. What she sold was Hodgenville's most valuable tourist attraction, as the community rallied around to use the wax figures in building a tribute to Lincoln.

The figures are used to represent twelve significant episodes in Lincoln's life. "The Railsplitter," "Gettysburg Address," and "Ford's Theatre" are three examples of the scenes that are depicted in vivid, life-like detail. The upper floor of the museum is devoted to a small display area, a collection of original artwork related to Lincoln, and an auditorium where visitors are treated to a film, *Lincoln's Kentucky.*

Each year Hodgenville Square is the site of "Lincoln Days," a festival held during the second weekend of October. The festival features local crafts, a pioneer exhibit, and an art contest. The winning work in the Lincoln category of the art contest is purchased and added to the Lincoln Museum's collection.

DIRECTIONS: Hodgenville is on US Route 31E, a few miles east of the Birthplace National Historic Site. See page 115 (Figure 36) for directions for reaching Hodgenville.

PUBLIC USE: Season and hours: Monday-Saturday, 8:30 A.M.– 5 P.M., Sunday 1 P.M.– 5 P.M. Closed Christmas, New Year's Day. **Fees:** Adults, $3; seniors and military, $2.50; ages 5–12, $1.50; under five, free. **Group rates:** students, $1.00; adults, $2.00. Allow 1 hour to enjoy the museum. **Gift shop. For people with disabilities:** The first floor, which displays the scenic representations, is accessible. The second floor is not.

FOR ADDITIONAL INFORMATION: Contact: The Lincoln Museum, 66 Lincoln Square, Hodgenville, Kentucky 42748, (502) 358–3163.

Abraham Lincoln's Boyhood Home, Knob Creek Farm
Hodgenville, Kentucky

My earliest recollection is of the Knob Creek place.
— Abraham Lincoln

When Lincoln was two years of age, his family moved from Sinking Spring to Knob Creek Farm (Plate 14), ten miles to the east, where they lived until moving to Indiana in 1816.

The six years during which the Lincolns farmed Knob Creek were important ones in the maturation of Abraham Lincoln. Years later he recalled incidents from these years: listening to his mother read from the Bible, observing dealers driving slaves past the cabin, attending school for the first time, and experiencing the sheer joy of boyhood on the farm.

The original Lincoln cabin has been lost to time, but it was replicated in 1931 with logs from a neighboring cabin, and the construction took place under the direction of Robert Thompson, who had helped his father, a childhood playmate of Lincoln's, tear down the original cabin in 1870.

DIRECTIONS: Knob Creek Farm is 10 miles east of Hodgenville, Kentucky, on US Route 31E. Many visitors begin their visit at the Birthplace National Historic Site, travel east on Route 31E to the Lincoln Museum, and continue eastward to Knob Creek Farm (Figure 36).

PUBLIC USE: Season and hours: Memorial Day-Labor Day, 9 A.M.– 7 P.M.; April, May, September, October, 9 A.M.– 5 P.M. Closed November, December, January, February, March. **Fees:** Adults, $1; ages 6–12, .50. Allow 30 minutes to enjoy Knob Creek. **Picnic area. Gift shop. For people with disabilities:** Accessible.

FOR ADDITIONAL INFORMATION: Contact: Lincoln's Boyhood Home, Knob Creek Farm, US 31E, Route 4, Hodgenville, Kentucky 42748, (502) 549–3741.

Lincoln Boyhood National Memorial
Lincoln City, Indiana

The things I want to know are in books. My best friend is the man who'll get me a book I ain't read.
— Abraham Lincoln

In 1816 the slavery issue, in addition to the lawsuits over their Kentucky farm, induced the Thomas Lincoln family to move west to Indiana. There they carved out a farm from the wilderness and remained for fourteen years. On that farm young Abraham Lincoln shared family life, learned to work, and earned his first money. He experienced joy and tragedy and grew from boy to man.

Lincoln Boyhood National Memorial (Figure 37) is the ideal place to learn about young Lincoln, his times, and the circumstances that molded him. An integral part of the area is a living historical farm. The buildings are not original, but were built in an attempt to depict a typical farm of Lincoln's period in Indiana. The theme of the farm is self-sufficiency and use of the natural environ-

Figure 37. Lincoln Boyhood National Memorial, Lincoln City, Indiana. Photograph by Richard Frear; use courtesy of National Park Service.

ment. The farm workers dress in period clothing to demonstrate daily activities of Lincoln's time, including domestic arts and crafts, animal husbandry, farming, and gardening.

A memorial Visitor Center contains two halls, with a connecting cloister, a small auditorium, and five nine-ton sculptured panels marking important periods in Lincoln's life. The Nancy Hanks Lincoln Hall is a retreat; its design and furnishings, reminiscent of early Indiana, create a sense of the simplicity and warmth of a pioneer home.

The Abraham Lincoln Hall, across the cloister, is used for meetings, church services, weddings, and other special events. The stone and wood used in its construction are meant to reflect the grandeur, yet the simplicity, of Lincoln himself. Its church-like ambiance engenders a feeling of reverence and respect. Visitors are urged to pause and "think about the meaning — to America and you — of this great American's life."

The grave of Lincoln's beloved mother, Nancy Hanks Lincoln, is located on a pleasant knoll overlooking the farm.

DIRECTIONS: The Memorial is south of I–64 near Dale, Indiana, 35 miles east of Evansville. From I-64, take Exit 57 south on US Route 231 to Gentryville, then east on Indiana State Route 162 to the Memorial (Figure 38).

PUBLIC USE: Season and hours: Visitor Center: daily 8 A.M.– 5 P.M. Closed Thanksgiving, Christmas, and New Years Day. Farm: mid-April through late September, daily 8 A.M.–5 P.M. During the rest of the year the farm is an exhibit in place, and the farm buildings and demonstrations are closed. **Fees:** $2.00 per person, with maximum charge of $4.00 per family group. Ages 16 and under, free; ages 62 and over, free; qualified educational groups free. Allow 2 hours to enjoy the Boyhood Memorial. **Small picnic area. Gift shop. For people with disabilities:** Braille exhibit text; most facilities accessible.

FOR ADDITIONAL INFORMATION: Contact: Lincoln Boyhood National Memorial, Box 1816, Lincoln City, Indiana 47552, (812) 937–4541. **Read:** (1) Don Davenport. 1991. *In Lincoln's Footsteps: A Historic Guide to the Lincoln Sites in Illinois, Indiana and Kentucky.* Madison: Prairie Oak Press. (2) *Lincoln Lived Here.* 1992. Williamsburg: Miller Bicast Publishing Company.

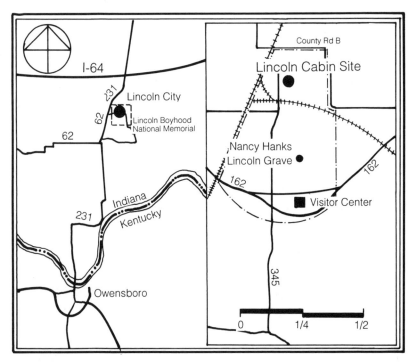

Figure 38. Location of Lincoln Boyhood National Memorial, Lincoln City, Indiana.

The Lincoln Museum
Fort Wayne, Indiana

An honest man is the noblest work of God.
— Abraham Lincoln

In 1905, the Lincoln National Life Insurance Company was founded, the name most likely chosen to symbolize integrity at a time when the insurance industry was temporarily identified with corruption. Abraham Lincoln's son, Robert, granted the company permission to use the name and provided a portrait of his father for use on the company letterhead. His letter and the portrait survive as prominent exhibits in The Lincoln Museum, located in one of the headquarters building of what is now known as the Lincoln National Corporation (Figure 39).

Figure 39. Statue of Abraham Lincoln at the Lincoln National Corporation, Fort Wayne, Indiana. Photograph courtesy of The Lincoln Museum, Fort Wayne, Indiana, a part of the Lincoln National Corporation.

121

The Museum was founded in 1928 and is the repository for the world's largest private collection devoted to the life of Abraham Lincoln. Sixty chronological exhibits, 5000 original photographs, 5000 art prints, 20,000 books, 200,000 newspaper and magazine articles, along with statues, busts, plaques, masks, medals, and more are on display or are available for study by research scholars and historians. Eleven galleries, four theaters, and eighteen computerized hands-on exhibits describe in dramatic detail how Lincoln preserved the Union and American ideals.

An original cast-bronze statue, "Abraham Lincoln: The Hoosier Youth," commissioned by the company and executed by Paul Manship in 1932, stands outside another building of the corporate headquarters a few blocks away on Harrison Street. The statue and its granite base are twenty-two feet tall and weigh 79 1/2 tons. With the exceptions of the Lincoln Memorial and Mount Rushmore, the statue is the largest representation of Lincoln yet made.

DIRECTIONS: From either I–69 or US Route 30, proceed south on US Route 27, which becomes Clinton Street (one-way) in Fort Wayne. The Museum is on the left after about 1 mile, at the corner of Clinton and Berry streets (Figure 40).

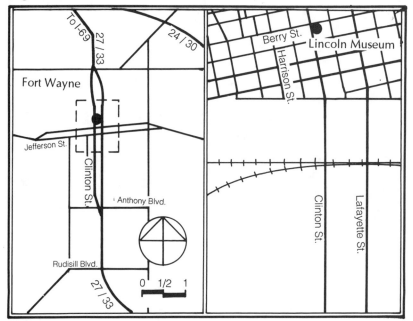

Figure 40. Location of The Lincoln Museum, Fort Wayne, Indiana.

PUBLIC USE: **Season and hours:** Monday-Saturday 10 A.M.– 5 P.M., Sunday 1 P.M.– 5 P.M. Closed Thanksgiving, Christmas, New Year's Day. **Fees:** Adults, $2.99; Children and seniors $1.99. Allow 1 hour to enjoy the Museum. **Museum shop. For people with disabilities:** Fully accessible.

FOR ADDITIONAL INFORMATION: **Contact:** The Lincoln Museum, 200 East Berry Street, Fort Wayne, Indiana 46802, (219) 455–3864. **Read:** Harold Holzer and Mark E. Neely, Jr. 1990. *The Lincoln Family Album.* New York: Doubleday.

Lincoln's New Salem
Petersburg, Illinois

All my successes were because of that opinion of me which the people express when they call me "Honest Abe."
— Abraham Lincoln

Young Abraham Lincoln stopped in the village of New Salem while piloting a flatboat down the Illinois waterways. The ambitious Lincoln saw a great potential in the future of the growing community and settled there in 1831. He spent six years of his early adulthood in New Salem, growing from a gangling youngster with no objectives, a self-admitted "aimless piece of driftwood," into a man of purpose. He clerked in a store, chopped wood, served as postmaster and surveyor, enlisted in the Black Hawk War, and was elected to his first public office. Most important to his future and that of the nation was that it was in New Salem that Lincoln, by flickering firelight, began to study law.

In 1839, two years after Lincoln had left New Salem for Springfield, the Menard County seat was established in nearby Petersburg, and the fortunes of New Salem declined. Interest in the history of the first part of the twentieth century resurrected New Salem, however, with reconstruction of the village (Figure 41) undertaken at times by the State of Illinois, the Chautauqua Association, and even the Civilian Conservation Corps in the 1930s.

Visits to today's New Salem begin at a modern Visitor Center with the screening of an orientation film and a "Time Walk" exhibit tracing Lincoln's life in pictures and documents. Then one

Figure 41. A log cabin and outbuilding in winter at Lincoln's New Salem State Historic Site, Petersburg, Illinois. Photograph courtesy of Lincoln's New Salem State Historic Site.

steps into a 160-year-old town and strolls through a nineteenth-century village that includes stores, mills, taverns, twenty-three residences, a schoolhouse, and a church. Over nine hundred authentic period articles have been discovered and donated for furnishing the houses and equipping the farms and industrial shops. Interpreters wearing period dress go about the daily work of the town: farming, carding wool, blacksmithing, and cooking.

A walk through the winding paths of New Salem brings history to life. The town affords witness to an era and a village that influenced the personality, principles and career of Abraham Lincoln.

DIRECTIONS: Lincoln's New Salem is 20 miles northwest of Springfield, Illinois, on State Route 97 (Figure 42).

PUBLIC USE: Season and hours: March-October, daily 9 A.M.– 5 P.M.; November-February, daily 8 A.M.– 4 P.M. Closed Thanksgiving, Christmas, New Year's Day, Martin Luther King's birthday, Washington's birthday, Veteran's Day, Election Day. **Fees:** None. Allow several hours to enjoy New Salem. **Food service:** A full-service restaurant, River Ridge, is across Route

97 from the entrance to New Salem. **Gift shops:** One, adjacent to the Visitor Center, and another, in the Pioneer Shop, located in the Historic Village, feature craft items appropriate to the 1830s. **For people with disabilities:** The Visitor Center is accessible; the village is not.

EDUCATIONAL FACILITIES: Lincoln's New Salem is part of an Illinois State Historic Site operated by the Illinois Historic Preservation Agency. The site features picnicking, camping, riverboat rides, and many special events. Theater in the park, a cornucopia of family entertainment, is held in the amphitheater of the park from mid-June through late August.

FOR ADDITIONAL INFORMATION: Contact: Lincoln's New Salem, RR #1, Box 244A, Petersburg, Illinois 62675, (217) 632–2277.

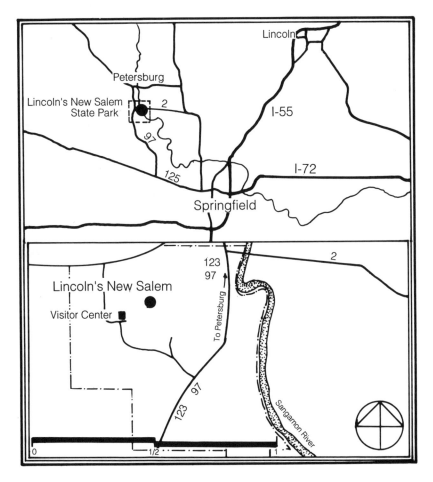

Figure 42. Location of Lincoln's New Salem, Petersburg, Illinois.

The Abraham Lincoln Museum

Harrogate, Tennessee

*On the subject of education, I can only say that I view it as
the most important subject in which we as people can be
engaged.*

— Abraham Lincoln

General O. O. Howard, founder of Lincoln Memorial University, met Lincoln only a few times, but one of those meetings was for Howard a memorable one. In September 1863, Howard and his corps were to be transferred from the eastern theater to the western. According to Howard's journal, when he met with Lincoln about the transfer, the President pulled down a map and pointed to the Cumberland Gap, where many eastern Tennesseeans had remained pro-Union in spite of the fact that Tennessee was a Confederate state. President Lincoln suggested that, after the war, maybe they could "do something for these people." Howard returned to the Cumberland Gap area thirty years later; having remembered Lincoln's words, he founded Lincoln Memorial University in the hope of establishing a better way of life for the people of southern Appalachia. The Abraham Lincoln Museum, located on the University's beautiful campus, was conceived by its administration through a desire to provide the University with a philosophical direction and, as they have stated:

> to provide the public with a moving and creative portrayal of
> Abraham Lincoln's dramatic commitment to the American
> way of life and confront each of us with the need to reaffirm
> that commitment.

The Museum houses an outstanding collection of books, manuscripts, relics, and pictures related to Lincoln and the Civil War period. As a research center it provides an opportunity for students and scholars to research and write from original materials. A heroic sculpture of the martyred President, by Gutzon Borglum, and the cane Lincoln carried on the night of his assassination are two of the many exhibits.

DIRECTIONS: Lincoln Memorial University is in Harrogate, Tennessee, just south of Middlesboro, Kentucky, on US Route 25E, 55 miles northeast of Knoxville (Figure 43).

PUBLIC USE: Season and hours: Monday-Friday 9 A.M.– 4 P.M., Saturday 11 A.M.– 4 P.M., Sunday 1 P.M.– 4 P.M. Closed major holidays. **Fees:** $2, with discounts for groups, students, and seniors. Allow 1 hour to enjoy the museum. **Gift shop. For people with disabilities:** First floor accessible, but there is no access to the second floor gallery.

EDUCATIONAL FACILITIES: The Museum is an educational institution devoted to learning. Teaching kits for student visitors at all levels are available. Adjacent to the campus is the Cumberland Gap National Park, established to commemorate the pioneer passage to the western frontier. The park contains 20,000 acres, with 50 miles of scenic trails.

FOR ADDITIONAL INFORMATION: Contact: The Abraham Lincoln Museum, Cumberland Gap Parkway, Harrogate, Tennessee 37752, (615) 869–6235. **Read:** (1) Joseph Suppiger. 1977. *Phoenix of the Mountains*. Harrogate: Lincoln Memorial University Press. (2) Stephen Hague, ed. *The Lincoln Herald*. Harrogate: Lincoln Memorial University Press. Quarterly, February 1938 and following. (3) Weldon Petz. 1973. *In the Presence of Lincoln*. Harrogate: Lincoln Memorial University Press.

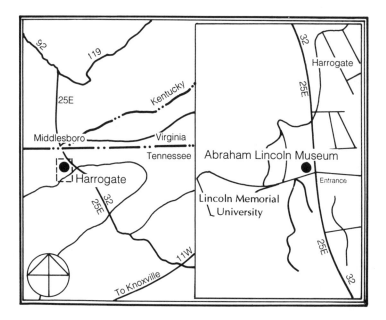

Figure 43. Location of The Abraham Lincoln Museum, Harrogate, Tennessee.

127

Lincoln Home National Historic Site
Springfield, Illinois

No one not in my situation can appreciate my feeling of sadness at this parting. To this place, and the kindness of these people, I owe everything . . . .
— Lincoln's farewell, Springfield, 1861

The Lincoln Home (Figure 44) at 8th and Jackson Streets is the centerpiece of a four-square-block restoration project of the National Park Service — a project intended to create an historic district that will preserve the nineteenth-century neighborhood where Abraham and Mary Todd Lincoln lived for seventeen years. It was in the Lincoln home, within this neighborhood, as part of Springfield, that Abraham Lincoln fully matured. His farewell remarks make clear his sense of connection to the town: "here I have lived a quarter of a century, and have passed from a young to an old man. Here my children have been born, and one is buried . . . ." Here he practiced law, served in the state legislature, gained national recognition as an orator and political thinker, learned of becoming a candidate, and heard, finally, of his election as President of the United States.

In 1844, shortly after the birth of his first son, Lincoln purchased the house on 8th Street for $1500 cash. The Greek Revival house was 1 1/2-stories, built of wood, with a cistern, well, privy, barn, and carriage house. An exterior retaining wall was built in 1850, and major changes were effected in 1856 to make room for the Lincoln's growing boys; the house was expanded to two full stories with the addition of bedrooms and a storage room. Approximately fifty Lincoln-associated artifacts are on exhibit in the Home.

The city of Springfield is justly proud of Abraham Lincoln, and the city features many other attractions associated with him. The Lincoln-Herndon law office, the family pew at the First Presbyterian Church, the Old State Capitol Building where Lincoln served — all have been preserved and are open to the public. The Illinois State Historical Society, housed in the Old State Capitol, maintains the Lincoln Collection, one of the largest and most valuable single collections of papers, documents, letters, and memorabilia devoted to the life and times of Abraham Lincoln.

All attractions are within walking distance of the Lincoln Home, including the Great Western Depot where Lincoln made his farewell address to Springfield's citizens before boarding the train for his inauguration journey to Washington and into history. Five years later the train would again stop at Springfield, bringing back the body of America's martyred President, to be placed in the vault at Oak Ridge Cemetery on the outskirts of Springfield. Today it rests in an impressive monument building at Oak Ridge, together with Mary and three of their children.

Figure 44. Lincoln Home National Historic Site, Springfield, Illinois. Photograph courtesy of Lincoln Home National Historic Site.

After Lincoln's death, Mrs. Lincoln never returned to Spring-field. The house was rented until Robert Todd Lincoln deeded it to the State of Illinois in 1887. It was declared a National Historic Site in 1972 and is currently administered by the National Park Service.

DIRECTIONS: Springfield is southwest of Chicago at the junction of I–55 and I–72, I-72 becomes Clearlake Avenue in Springfield, merging into Jefferson Street (one-way west). Turn left on 7th Street to get to the Visitor Center, between Capitol and Jackson Streets. From St. Louis and I-55 northbound, follow I–55 Business Loop into Springfield where it becomes 6th Street (one-way north). Turn right on Capitol Street; go 1 block to 7th Street and turn right; go 1/2 block to the Visitor Center (Figure 45).

PUBLIC USE: Season and hours: Memorial Day-Labor Day, daily 8 A.M.–8 P.M.; September, October, April, May, daily 8:30 A.M.– 6 P.M. November-March, daily 8:30 A.M.– 5 P.M. Closed Thanksgiving, Christmas, New Year's Day. **Fees:** None, but free tickets, available at the Visitor Center on a first-come, first-served basis, are required. Tours of the Home are led by Park Rangers. Allow 1 1/2 hours to enjoy the Site. The Visitor Center features two films on Lincoln, *At Home with Mr. Lincoln* and *Mr. Lincoln's*

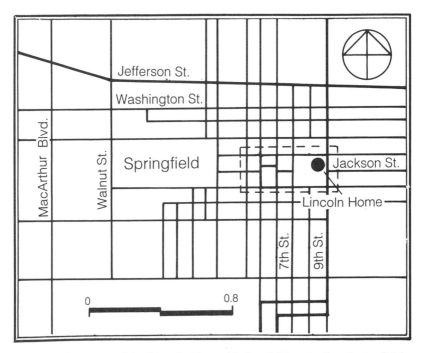

Figure 45. Location of the Lincoln Home National Historic Site, Springfield, Illinois.

130

Springfield. **Book shop:** Located in the Visitor Center. **For people with disabilities:** There is a lift to the first floor of the Home, but the second floor is not accessible. The Visitor Center is fully accessible and offers an open-captioned film for the hearing impaired.

FOR ADDITIONAL INFORMATION: Contact: Lincoln Home Visitor Center, 426 South 7th Street, Springfield, Illinois 62701, (217) 492–4150; Superintendent, Lincoln Home National Historic Site, 413 South 8th Street, Springfield, Illinois 62701, (217) 492–4241. Read: Wayne C. Temple. 1984. *By Squares and Compasses: The Building of Lincoln's Home and Its Saga.* Bloomington: Ashlar Press.

Lincoln Memorial Shrine
Redlands, California

Those who deny freedom to others deserve it not for themselves.

— Abraham Lincoln

Robert Watchorn emigrated from England to the United States in 1880, impoverished and without education. Like Horatio Alger, he studied and worked hard and became a highly successful and respected labor leader, government official, corporation president, and philanthropist.

Watchorn was fascinated with Abraham Lincoln and the Civil War period and believed that people throughout the world could benefit from a more complete knowledge of Lincoln's principles, character, and life of service. Thus Watchorn began to formulate plans for a memorial to Lincoln that would also serve as repository for his own extensive personal collection of Lincolniana. His dream came true when Lincoln Memorial Shrine (Figure 46) was built and dedicated in 1932, presented by Mr. Watchorn to the City of Redlands as a tribute to Lincoln and as a memorial to Watchorn's late son.

The Shrine is an imposing building of reinforced concrete, with Indiana limestone plates upon which are inscribed excerpts from Lincoln's speeches and writings. Bookcases and polished black walnut furniture line the interior. A magnificent bust of "The Great

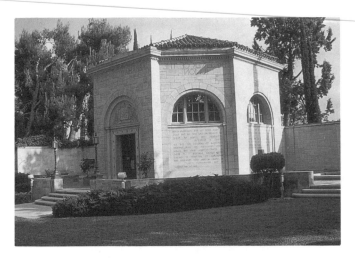

Figure 46. Lincoln Memorial Shrine, Redlands, California. Photograph courtesy of the Collection of The Lincoln Shrine, Redlands, California.

Emancipator" by sculptor George Grey Bernard is the focal point of the interior and is the major art work that inspired the building's design.

The Lincoln Memorial Shrine is the only tribute in the form of a museum to Abraham Lincoln west of the Mississippi. At the dedication ceremony in 1932 Mr. Watchorn said:

> *I have no speech, my speech is over there ... [the Shrine] will stand for other generations to be inspired by the example of the great American who turned the current of freedom into the souls of millions of fellow men."*

DIRECTIONS: From Los Angeles, California, take I-10 east to the Orange Downtown exit and turn right on Eureka Street. Just past the second traffic light is the A. K. Smiley Library. The Shrine is behind the Library (Figure 47).

PUBLIC USE: Season and hours: Tuesday-Saturday 1 P.M.– 5 P.M. Closed holidays except Lincoln's Birthday. **Fees:** None. Allow 1 hour to enjoy the Shrine. **For people with disabilities:** Call ahead for portable wheelchair ramp.

FOR ADDITIONAL INFORMATION: Contact: Lincoln Memorial Shrine, 125 West Vine Street, Redlands, California 92373 (909) 798–7632. **Read:** (1) Larry Burgess. 1981. *The Lincoln Memorial Shrine Genesis: Prelude to the Golden*

132

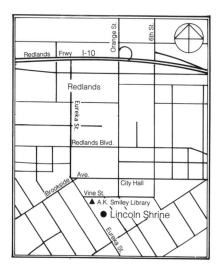

Figure 47. Location of the Lincoln Memorial Shrine, Redlands, California.

Jubilee. Redlands: Lincoln Memorial Shrine. (2) Larry Burgess. 1982. *The Lincoln Memorial Shrine Golden Jubilee: History Looking to the Future.* Redlands: Lincoln Memorial Shrine. (3) "The Lincoln Shrine at Redlands, California." *Pencil Points Magazine.* 1938. Reprinted by Lincoln Memorial Shrine, Redlands.

Lincoln College Museum
Lincoln, Illinois

In 1853, the first lots were sold in a new real estate development north of Springfield, Illinois. Attorney Abraham Lincoln had prepared the papers of incorporation. It was decided that the town should be named for him, and he was asked to christen it. Lincoln took a watermelon, split it open, and duly baptized the little town with watermelon juice!

One cannot develop a complete picture of Abraham Lincoln without visiting Lincoln and surrounding Logan County, for it was in that area that he rode the circuit as a young attorney, invested in property, and spoke as a political candidate. The town of Lincoln was immensely proud when Lincoln became President.

On his last birthday, February 12, 1865, the town dedicated Lincoln College, chartered as Lincoln University, the first school of higher education to be named in Lincoln's honor.

The McKinstry Memorial Library on the campus houses two small historical museums, one dedicated solely to Lincoln. It has catalogued and displays over two thousand volumes, pamphlets, pictures, and other significant items, including the original plat delineating the town of Lincoln as approved by attorney Lincoln in 1853. The other museum is called the Museum of Presidents, designed as a shrine to honor all of the men who have served as Chief Executive. Its main display case contains documents signed by every President and every first lady. Both museums dramatize American history, inspire its study, and remind us, as Lincoln said, that "freedom is the most valuable property of an individual."

The exterior of the McKinstry Library is honored with Merrell Gage's bronze statue, "Lincoln, the Student."

DIRECTIONS: Lincoln is 20 miles northeast of Springfield, Illinois, just off I-55. From either north or south, take the Woodlawn exit, following Woodlawn east until it becomes Keokuk Street. The McKinstry Memorial Library is a few blocks farther, on the left (Figure 48).

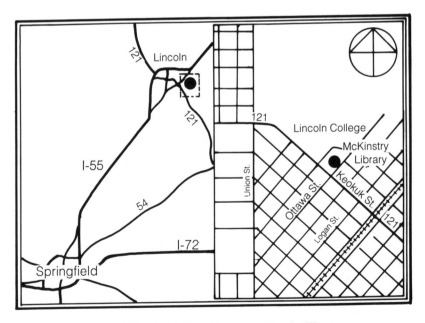

Figure 48. Location of Lincoln College Museum, Lincoln, Illinois.

134

PUBLIC USE: **Season and hours:** Monday-Friday 10 A.M.–4 P.M., Saturday and Sunday 1 P.M.–4 P.M. **Fees:** None. Allow 1 hour to enjoy the museum. **Museum shop. For people with disabilities:** Fully accessible.

FOR ADDITIONAL INFORMATION: Contact: Lincoln College Museum, 300 Keokuk Street, Lincoln, Illinois 62656, (217) 732–3155 (Extension 295). **Read:** Barbara Hughett, ed. 1981-present. *The Lincoln Newsletter.* Lincoln, Illinois: Lincoln College Museum. Quarterly.

Ford's Theatre National Historic Site
Washington, DC

On the evening of April 14, 1865, President Abraham Lincoln arrived at Ford's Theatre in downtown Washington. On this visit he planned to enjoy a performance of the comedy *Our American Cousin.* During the third act, scene III, the President was shot by John Wilkes Booth, a southern political activist who supported the Confederacy. Dr. Charles Leale, a young doctor from New York, went to Lincoln's theatre box. He examined him there and declared, "His wound is mortal. He cannot recover." The President, shot in the brain, was removed to a back room of the Petersen Boarding House, directly across the street from the theatre. Doctors attempted to make him as comfortable as possible as he was dying; his heart stopped the next morning at 7:22 A.M.

The nation was plunged into deep mourning as Lincoln, who had struggled to preserve the Union through a long and bloody civil war, became himself the victim of senseless violence.

Ford's Theatre was gutted within a few months of the assassination and converted into a three-story government office building. This structure collapsed in 1893, killing twenty-two workers and severely injuring sixty-eight others. The building reopened in 1894 as a warehouse.

Restoration of Ford's Theatre was begun in 1964; the building was again gutted, and a basement was added. The interior was made to appear similar to, although not exactly like, its 1865 appearance; the facade, however, remains the same as on that fateful day of Lincoln's last visit (Figure 49). Actress Helen Hayes reopened the stage in January of 1968.

Figure 49. Ford's Theatre National Historic Site, Washington, DC. Photograph courtesy of National Park Service.

The Petersen house has also been restored, and the two structures make up The Ford's Theatre National Historic Site — a site that reminds us of the troubling events of yesterday and perpetuates the spirit, hopes, and ideals that Abraham Lincoln upheld for all Americans.

DIRECTIONS: Travel in Washington is easiest by Metro subway. Take the Red, Orange or Blue lines to Metro Center, which is at 13th Street and "F." Ford's Theatre is a 4-block walk from there, on 10th Street and "E" (Figure 15).

PUBLIC USE: Season and hours: Daily 9 A.M.– 5 P.M. Closed Christmas. Talks by rangers are scheduled periodically. The theatre is closed for tours when rehearsals or matinees are in progress, so calling ahead is recommended. The museum and the Petersen Boarding House are always open during the hours above. **Fees:** None. Allow 2 hours for a tour of the theatre and a visit to the Petersen Boarding House. **For people with disabilities:** Limited access at the theatre, none at the house.

FOR ADDITIONAL INFORMATION: Contact: Ford's Theatre National Historic Site, 511 10th Street, NW (Theatre), 516 10th Street, NW (Petersen Boarding House), Washington, DC 20004, (202) 426–6924. **Read:** (1) Dorothy Meserve Kunhardt and Philip Kunhardt, Jr. 1985. *Twenty Days.* New Hollywood: Newcastle Publishing Co.(2) *Ford's Theatre and the House Where Lincoln Died* (brochure). 1991. Washington, DC: National Park Service, Department of the Interior.

Andrew Johnson

Seventeenth President
1865 – 1869

Born December 29, 1808, Raleigh, North Carolina
Died July 31, 1875, Carter Station, Tennessee

When I die, I desire no better winding sheet than the Stars and Stripes, and no softer pillow than the Constitution of my country.

— Andrew Johnson

Andrew Johnson was a quintessential self-made man who represented the most desirable traits in the American character. He was born into poor circumstances that were made even more difficult by the death of his father when Andrew was only three. Without education or opportunity — unable to read or write — Andrew was indentured at the age of thirteen and became highly skilled as a tailor.

At eighteen he moved to Greeneville, Tennessee, where he opened his own tailor shop and became successful enough to afford marriage and the purchase of a small house. Success as a tailor was not enough, however, for Johnson had an overwhelming desire to advance. He knew that advancement in life hinged on obtaining an education, so he had his wife read to him for hour after hour while he worked with needle and thread. When her time became limited by child-rearing, local men were hired to carry on the lessons. After work he practiced public speaking and entered local debates. Within a few years Johnson had become so respected by his neighbors for his industry, intelligence, and ability that they elected him alderman, then mayor of Greeneville.

Johnson's ambition, energy, dedication, and remarkable solicitude for his fellow citizens carried him far beyond Greeneville: to the Tennessee Statehouse, to the United States Congress, to the vice presidency, and on to the White House.

Assuming the Presidency upon the assassination of Lincoln, Johnson was plunged into a tumultuous political period. A strict constructionist — he was the only southern senator to vote for the Union — he attempted to implement Lincoln's reconstruction plans, to "bind the nation's wounds" with lenient policies toward the defeated South, but he faced a hostile and radical Congress that viewed the South as a conquered nation.

In 1868, following many bruising battles, Presidential vetoes, and congressional overrides, the House of Representatives drew up articles of impeachment against President Johnson after his veto of the Tenure of Office Act. A Senate trial resulted in his acquittal by a one-vote margin.

Johnson finished his term of office and returned to Tennessee in 1869. He went back to Washington as United States Senator in 1875, the only ex-President ever to return to Congress in that capacity. He died later that year, and his body was returned to

Greeneville for burial. In honor of his wishes, he was buried wrapped in Old Glory and with a copy of the Constitution placed beneath his head.

> *I intend to stand by the Constitution as it is, insisting upon a compliance with all its guarantees . . . it is the last hope of human freedom.*
>
> — Andrew Johnson

Andrew Johnson Birthplace
Raleigh, North Carolina

In 1808, Raleigh, capital of North Carolina, was a town of less than a thousand people. Many visitors to early Raleigh lodged at Casso's Inn. Jacob Johnson, inn hostler, cared for horses while his wife, Mary, known as "Polly the weaver," did weaving for the inn. They lived in a small kitchen-dwelling (Plate 15) behind Casso's Inn, where their son Andrew was born.

The Johnsons were poor and uneducated, but possessed qualities of character that earned them the respect and friendship of the townspeople. Andrew learned their positive traits and earned fame and fortune far beyond the borders of Raleigh.

In 1904, the house was purchased by the Wake County Committee of the Colonial Dames of America, who presented it to the city of Raleigh. In 1975, it was moved to Mordecai Historic Park and restored. Mordecai Park is managed by Capital Area Preservation in cooperation with the City of Raleigh. The park contains several buildings of local historical interest in addition to the Johnson house, including the Mordecai plantation house, dating to 1785.

DIRECTIONS: From I–440 north of Raleigh, exit to Capital Boulevard and proceed south. Exit at Blount Street and make a left. This street becomes Wake Forest Road. The park is up the hill on the right. From the south of Raleigh on I–40, exit at Person Street and follow it north through the city to the park, on the left (Figure 50).

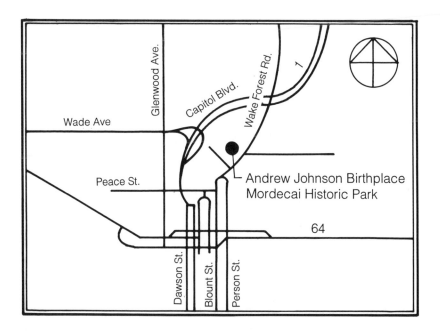

Figure 50. Location of Andrew Johnson Birthplace, Raleigh, North Carolina.

PUBLIC USE: Season and hours: Monday-Friday 10 A.M.– 3 P.M., Saturday and Sunday 1:30 – 3:30 P.M. Closed major holidays. **Fees:** Adults, $3; children 7–17, $1; 6 and under, free. Discount for groups. Allow 1 hour to enjoy the Johnson Birthplace. **Gift shop. For people with disabilities:** Restrooms are accessible.

FOR ADDITIONAL INFORMATION: Contact: Mordecai Historic Park, 1 Mimosa Street, Raleigh, North Carolina 27601, (919) 834–4844. **Read:** (1) Hans L. Trefousse. 1989. *Andrew Johnson.* New York: W. W. Norton and Company.

141

Andrew Johnson National Historic Site
Greeneville, Tennessee

The charming town of Greeneville, proud of its Johnson heritage, hosts a number of attractions associated with the former President. The National Historic Site encompasses several, the most moving being Johnson's tiny tailor shop where he worked at his trade and listened to his readers. The shop is protected from the elements, housed within the walls of a Visitor Center that also contains exhibits, letters, and displays tracing the career of one of America's most unusual Presidents.

Just across the street from the Visitor Center is a small two-story brick house, unfurnished, in which the Johnsons lived during their early days in Greeneville. A few blocks away is a larger brick house, the Johnson Homestead (Figure 51), which Johnson purchased in 1851 and in which he lived until his death. Inside are many mementos of his Presidential years, including a handsome tilt-top table inlaid with five hundred pieces of wood, a gift from the people of Ireland. A guided tour of the three stories includes every room and highlights the relation between the Johnsons and their home.

Figure 51. Andrew Johnson National Historic Site, Greeneville, Tennessee. Photograph courtesy of National Park Service.

The Andrew Johnson National Cemetery is a mile farther up Main Street. Johnson's resting place is marked by a tall marble shaft topped by an American eagle. On one side is a scroll depicting the United States Constitution, which Johnson valiantly defended. His epitaph reads:

His faith in the people never wavered.

DIRECTIONS: Greeneville is 70 miles east of Knoxville, Tennessee, at the junction of US Routes 11E and 321. Historical markers are prominently displayed throughout Greeneville (Figure 52).

PUBLIC USE: Season and hours: Daily 9 A.M.– 5 P.M. Closed Christmas, Thanksgiving, New Year's Day. **Fees:** Adults 18–61, $2 for Homestead only, other attractions are free. Allow 2 hours to enjoy the Andrew Johnson National Historic Site. **For people with disabilities:** The Visitor Center is accessible.

FOR ADDITIONAL INFORMATION: Contact: Andrew Johnson National Historic Site, PO Box 1088, Greeneville, Tennessee 37744, (423) 638–3551. **Read:** (1) Hugh Lawing. "Andrew Johnson National Historic Site." (Reprint from *Tennessee Historical Quarterly;* available from Visitor Center.)

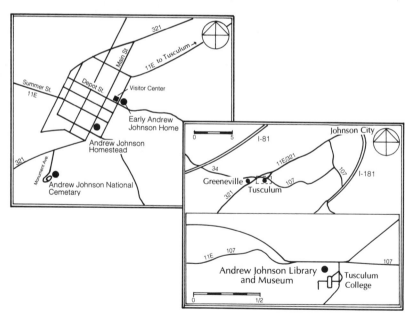

Figure 52. Location of Andrew Johnson National Historic Site and Andrew Johnson Presidential Library and Museum, Greeneville, Tennessee.

143

Andrew Johnson Presidential Library and Museum
Greeneville, Tennessee

Johnson developed and honed his rhetorical and oratorical skills at debates held on the campus of Tusculum College, although he did not matriculate there. He remained grateful to Tusculum and was interested in its affairs throughout his life; he served as a college trustee after his political career had ended.

A library and museum (Figure 53) devoted to Johnson is located on the campus of Tusculum, and a replica of his birth house is on the grounds. The house was presented to the college in 1980 by Johnson's great-granddaughter, Mrs. Margaret Johnson Patterson Bartlett.

DIRECTIONS: Tusculum College is 5 miles northeast of downtown Greeneville on Tennessee State Route 107 (Figure 52).

Figure 53. The Andrew Johnson Presidential Library and Museum on the campus of Tusculum College, Greeneville, Tennessee. Photograph by William G. Clotworthy.

PUBLIC USE: Season and Hours: By appointment only. **Fees:** None. Allow 1 hour to enjoy the museum. **For people with disabilities:** No special facilities at present.

FOR ADDITIONAL INFORMATION: Contact: Museum Director, Andrew Johnson Presidential Library and Museum, Tusculum College, Box 5026, Greeneville, Tennessee 37743, (423) 636–7348.

Ulysses Simpson Grant

Eighteenth President
1869 – 1877

Born April 27, 1822, Point Pleasant, Ohio
Died July 23, 1885, Saratoga Springs, New York

*Whoever hears of me in ten years, will hear of a well-to-do old
Missouri farmer!*

— U. S. Grant, 1853

Jesse Grant owned a tannery and a small farm in rural Ohio, so his son Ulysses was familiar with hard times and harder work. He was ambitious, though, and often thought of college, but mean circumstances seemed to preclude higher education. Jesse, too, dreamt of a college education for his son; his thoughts were on West Point, as the education there was free. When a neighbor's son failed his examinations at the Military Academy, Jesse asked United States Senator Thomas Morris for the opening for Ulysses. Morris replied that he had filled his quota, but he suggested that Congressman Thomas Hamer might have an opening left. Jesse Grant and Congressman Hamer had once had political differences, but Jesse swallowed his pride and made the request. His letter arrived at Hamer's office on the last day of the Congressman's term, just in time for the appointment to be made, thus changing the life of young Ulysses and influencing the course of the nation.

Grant was dogged and determined as a cadet and young officer, but he was forced from the army due to his excessive drinking, which was brought on by prolonged absences from his family. Subsequent careers in farming, real estate, and storekeeping were similarly unsuccessful, and Grant lived in quiet obscurity — a military genius in need of a war to fulfill his destiny.

The right man met the right war at the right time as the Civil War brought Grant back to the military, where his tactics, determination, and leadership skills brought victory — making Grant a popular hero and the inevitable choice to lead the nation in peace.

Success in battle was no guarantee of success in political office, however; Grant's administration was rife with fraud, dishonesty, and scandal. After leaving the Presidency, he and Mrs. Grant toured the world; they were received everywhere with honor and respect, and Grant returned home with some of his popularity restored. He made a feeble attempt to regain the White House but was soundly defeated at the party convention.

A financial swindle wiped out Grant's fortune, so at the urging of Mark Twain and others, he began writing his memoirs, hoping to replenish his fortune and keep his family financially stable. Stricken with cancer of the throat and in constant pain, he struggled with characteristic courage to complete the task. He died only a few days after its completion, unable to enjoy the critical acclaim and the monetary success the memoirs brought.

Grant's Birthplace
Point Pleasant, Ohio

Ulysses Grant was born in the bedroom of a tiny frame house (Plate 16) of white Allegheny pine set high on the banks of the Ohio River. The house, which consisted only of a kitchen, living room, and bedroom, is now owned by the Ohio Historical Society and has been restored and furnished with historic memorabilia and authentic furniture, including the cradle in which infant Ulysses slept.

DIRECTIONS: Point Pleasant is 25 miles south of Cincinnati, on US Route 52E. The house is at the intersection of 52E and Ohio State Route 232 (Figure 54).

PUBLIC USE: Season and hours: April 1–October 31, Wednesday through Saturday 9:30 A.M.– Noon and 1 P.M.– 5 P.M. Sunday, Noon – 5 P.M. **Fees:** $1.00. Allow 30 minutes to enjoy Grant's Birthplace. **For people with disabilities:** Accessible.

FOR ADDITIONAL INFORMATION: Contact: New Richmond Historical Society, 1591 State Route 232, Point Pleasant, Ohio 45153, (513) 553–4911. **Read:** U. S. Grant. 1885. *Personal Memoirs of U. S. Grant*, 2 volumes. New York: Charles L. Webster and Company.

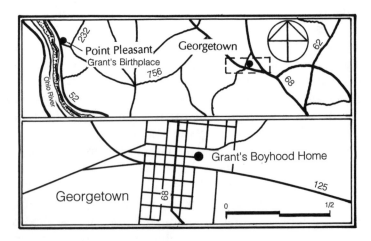

Figure 54. Location of Grant's Birthplace, Point Pleasant, Ohio, and U. S. Grant Boyhood Home, Georgetown, Ohio..

U. S. Grant Boyhood Home
Georgetown, Ohio

When Ulysses Grant was an infant, his family moved thirty miles southeast of Point Pleasant to Georgetown, where his father founded a tannery and built a two-story brick house with one room upstairs and one down (Figure 55). As family fortunes improved he added a kitchen, a parlor, and two more bedrooms.

The Grant home is owned by Mr. and Mrs. John Ruthven, who completed a restoration in 1982, their stated intention "for preservation of its future as a house museum furnished in the period." Mr. Ruthven, a noted wildlife artist, is the proprietor of the Thompson House Art Gallery just north of the Grant House. Visitors should stop at the gallery, where the curator will present a short orientation lecture before conducting a tour of the Grant home.

Visitors are also urged to enjoy a walking tour of Georgetown that encompasses Jesse Grant's tannery, two schoolhouses that young Ulysses attended, the Brown County Courthouse, and other buildings of historic interest.

Figure 55. U. S. Grant Boyhood Home, Georgetown, Ohio. Photograph by Mr. and Mrs. John A. Ruthven.

DIRECTIONS: Georgetown is 50 miles southeast of Cincinnati on Ohio State Route 125. From Route 52E, turn east on State Route 221 to Georgetown (Figure 54).

PUBLIC USE: Season and hours: Tuesday-Saturday 9:30 A.M.–5 P.M. **Fees:** None. Allow 1 1/2 hours to enjoy Georgetown and the Grant home. **For people with disabilities:** No special facilities.

FOR ADDITIONAL INFORMATION: Contact: U. S. Grant Boyhood Home, 217 East Grant Street, Georgetown, Ohio 45121, (513) 378–4222.

Ulysses S. Grant National Historic Site and Grant's Farm

Saint Louis, Missouri

In 1821, Frederick Dent, a Saint Louis businessman, purchased a two-story frame house and farm in the country as an escape from the summer heat of the city, naming the place White Haven. Dent's son, Fred, had roomed with Ulysses Grant at West Point, and Grant, stationed in Saint Louis, visited White Haven often. It soon became clear, however, that Grant called at White Haven not to see Fred Dent, but to see Fred's sister, Julia. Friendship developed into romance, and when Grant's army company was transferred from Saint Louis in 1844, he asked Mr. Dent for Julia's hand in marriage.

White Haven (Figure 56) remained a focal point in the lives of the Grants for over forty years. They lived there briefly following their marriage; their first child was born there in 1850; and when Grant was assigned to California, Julia waited for him at White Haven. Grant returned to St. Louis after his resignation from the army in 1854 to farm one hundred acres of the White Haven property given to Julia by her father. He hand-built a log cabin facetiously named Hardscrabble, not only for the land itself but for the difficulty of the times.

Within six years the farming venture had failed and the Grants moved to Galena, Illinois, where they experienced further disappointment and financial hardship before the Civil War brought opportunity, military success, fame, and fortune.

150

Figure 56. White Haven, Ulysses S. Grant National Historic Site, Saint Louis, Missouri. Photograph courtesy of National Park Service.

Hardscrabble Cabin is now part of Grant's Farm, a 281-acre entertainment and educational complex conceived, owned, and operated by the Anheuser-Busch Company. Trackless trains transport visitors through manicured grounds, with stops for elephant and bird shows and passage through Deer Park, home to thirty exotic species including bison, elk, and antelope living in a natural habitat.

The train passes the original Grant cabin, a carefully preserved symbol of an important part of our national heritage. Fronting the cabin is a dramatic reminder of the Civil War — a fence built from 2563 rifle barrels dating from the great conflict. The tours terminate at the stables of the world-famous Budweiser Clydesdale horses.

The rest of the White Haven property lies directly across Grant Road from Grant's Farm and was recently authorized by an act of Congress as the Ulysses S. Grant National Historic Site. The property houses the original Dent home, a barn, a shed, a springhouse and a stone building. The National Park Service assumed management in 1990 and is currently conducting research on the history of the property, its structures, and its connection with the Dent and

Grant families. When the research is completed the buildings will be restored and the site open to the public. The restoration project is on-going and access to the White Haven house is limited by the status of the reconstruction work.

DIRECTIONS: From Saint Louis, take I–55 south to Reavis Barracks and turn north to Gravois Road. Proceed west on Gravois Road to Grant Road. Turn right on Grant and proceed to the sites, which are across the road from one another (Figure 57).

PUBLIC USE: White Haven: Season and hours: Daily 9 A.M.– 5 P.M., closed Thanksgiving, Christmas, New Year's Day. **Fees:** None. **Gift shop. For people with disabilities:** No special facilities. **Grant's Farm: Season and hours:** Closed October to April. April-May, open Thursday-Sunday; June-August, open Tuesday-Sunday; September-October, open Thursday-Sunday. Tours by tram conducted several times daily with advance reservation only. **Fees:** None. **Food service:** The Bauernhof Restaurant is on the grounds. Gift shop. **For people with disabilities:** Fully accessible.

FOR ADDITIONAL INFORMATION: Contact: Grant's Farm, 10501 Gravois Road, Saint Louis, Missouri 63123,(314) 843–1700; Ulysses S. Grant National Historic Site, 7400 Grant Road, Saint Louis, Missouri 63123, (314) 842–1867. **Read:** (1) Julia Dent Grant. 1975. *The Personal Memoirs of Julia Dent Grant.* New York: Putnam. (2) William S. McFeely. 1981. *Grant: a Biography.* New York: Norton.

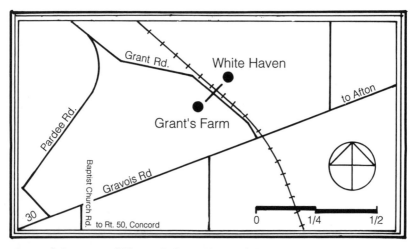

Figure 57. Location of Ulysses S. Grant National Historic Site and Grant's Farm, Saint Louis, Missouri.

Ulysses S. Grant Home State Historic Site
Galena, Illinois

In 1860, Grant and his family moved to Galena, where he hoped to reverse his financial misfortunes by working in a store owned by his father and managed by his brothers. Only a year later, however, he left to rejoin the US Army as colonel of the Twenty-first Illinois Volunteer Infantry Regiment. The rest of the Grant story is, of course, history.

On August 18, 1865, Grant returned to Galena as a conquering hero. After a jubilant parade and patriotic speeches, the citizens of Galena presented General and Mrs. Grant with a handsome, fully-furnished house (Figure 58) as a symbol of their pride, respect, and gratitude. Julia Grant recalled, "after a glorious triumphal ride around the hills and valleys, so brilliant with smiles and flowers, we were conducted to a lovely villa exquisitely furnished with everything good taste could desire."

General Grant was not destined to enjoy Galena for long, as he was called to further service as President. Following his second term, he once again returned, but he soon embarked on an exten-

Figure 58. Ulysses S. Grant Home State Historic Site, Galena, Illinois. Photograph by Jim Quick; use courtesy of Illinois Historic Preservation Agency, Galena State Historic Sites.

sive world tour. When he returned to the United States in 1879 he enjoyed another welcome-home celebration in Galena before settling in residency in New York City.

The Galena house remained in the Grant family until 1904, when Grant's children presented it to the city of Galena "with the understanding that the property is to be kept as a memorial to the late General Ulysses S. Grant, and for no other purpose." In 1931 Galena deeded the property to the State of Illinois, which maintains it under the management of the Illinois Historic Preservation Agency.

Restoration and modernization activities have continued without destroying the charm and ambiance of the period. Ninety percent of the furnishings are original Grant pieces, which make the house an excellent example of mid-nineteenth century taste in exterior design and interior decor.

DIRECTIONS: Galena is in the northwestern corner of Illinois on US Route 20 and Illinois State Route 84. There are historical site markers leading visitors to the Grant house (Figure 59).

PUBLIC USE: Season and hours: Daily 9 A.M.–5 P.M. In January, February, and March, closed Tuesdays and Wednesdays. Closed Thanksgiving and

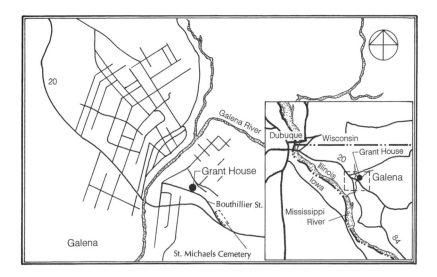

Figure 59. Location of Ulysses S. Grant Home State Historic Site, Galena, Illinois.

the day after, Christmas, New Year's Day, Lincoln's birthday, President's Day, Election Day, and Veteran's Day. **Fees:** None, although a donation is suggested. Allow 1 hour to enjoy the Grant home. Tours are self-guided, with descriptive material posted in each room. **For people with disabilities:** Accessibility is limited to the first floor; photographs of the second floor are displayed for those unable to reach the upstairs.

FOR ADDITIONAL INFORMATION: Contact: Grant Home State Historic Site, 500 Bouthillier Street, PO Box 333, Galena, Illinois 61036, (815) 777–0248 or 777–3310. **Read:** (1) Kenneth N. Owens. 1963. *Galena, Grant, and the Fortunes of War.* DeKalb, Illinois. (2) Thomas A. Campbell, Jr. 1979. "The U. S. Grant Home State Historic Site." *Historic Illinois.* February, 14. (Special reprint available from site.) (3) Thomas A. Campbell, Jr. 1975. "Plans and Specifications for the Ulysses S. Grant Home, Galena, Illinois." *APT.* Volume VII, No. 1, 1225.

Grant Cottage State Historic Site
Mount McGregor, New York

Man proposes, God disposes.

— Ulysses S. Grant

In June 1885, General Ulysses S. Grant and his family journeyed from New York City to a simple vacation cottage, owned by Joseph W. Drexel, on the slope of Mount McGregor near Saratoga Springs, New York (Figure 60). Grant was afflicted with painful throat cancer, and it was hoped that fresh air, the healthy climate, and the beautiful scenery would ease his suffering.

Occasionally he was carried a few hundred yards to a scenic overlook above the Hudson Valley, but he dared not spend much time enjoying the view or his surroundings. He spent most of his day racing desperately to complete his memoirs, which he hoped would sell well enough to replenish a fortune lost in a financial swindle.

He completed the memoirs only a few short days before the struggle with disease ended. At the moment of death the clock in the living room was stopped. It was a spontaneous and symbolic act that prompted arrangements to freeze the moment in time: to preserve the cottage, its furnishings, decorations, and other effects

Figure 60. Grant Cottage State Historic Site, Mount McGregor, New York. Photograph courtesy of The Friends of the Ulysses S. Grant Cottage.

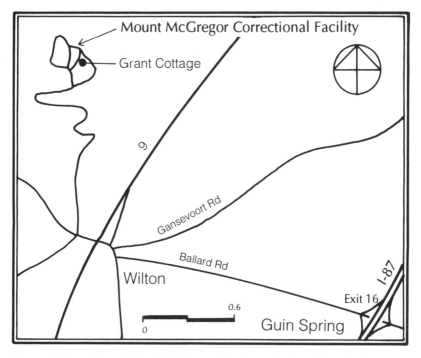

Mount McGregor Correctional Facility

Grant Cottage

9

Gansevoort Rd

Ballard Rd

Wilton

Exit 16

I-87

0.6

0

Guin Spring

Figure 61. Location of Mount McGregor, Saratoga Springs, New York.

just as they were — a dramatic tribute to one of the nation's great military heroes.

DIRECTIONS: Mount McGregor is 40 miles north of Albany, New York. From Albany, take I–87 north to Exit 16, and proceed west on Ballard Road. At the Intersection with US Route 9 there are historical markers directing visitors to the cottage, which is on the grounds of the Mount McGregor Correctional Facility (Figure 61). Visitors will be stopped briefly for identification before driving to the cottage.

PUBLIC USE: Season and hours: Memorial Day-Labor Day, Wednesday-Sunday 10 A.M.– 4 P.M. Each weekend in September and the first two weekends in October, 10 A.M.– 4 P.M. **Fees:** Adults, $2; children, $1; senior citizens $1.50; $1 for groups of 10 or more. (Groups accepted by advance reservation). Allow 1 hour to enjoy Mount McGregor. Picnics allowed at Grant's Overlook. **For people with disabilities:** Fully accessible.

FOR ADDITIONAL INFORMATION: Contact: The Friends of the Ulysses S. Grant Cottage State Historic Site, Box 990, Saratoga Springs, New York 12866, (518) 587–8277. **Read:** (1) Leonard Poggiali. 1993. "Conditional Surrender: The Death of U. S. Grant, and the Cottage on Mount McGregor," *Blue & Gray Magazine.* February, 60–65. (2) Thomas M. Pitkin. 1973. *The Captain Departs: Ulysses S. Grant's Last Campaign.* Carbondale: Southern Illinois University Press. (3) Thomas S. W. Lewis. 1985. *To Be, To Do, To Suffer: The Memoirs of Ulysses S. Grant.* The Edwin M. Moseley Faculty Research Lecture, Skidmore College. Published by The Friends of the Ulysses S. Grant Cottage State Historic Site.

Rutherford Birchard Hayes

Nineteenth President
1877 – 1881

Born October 4, 1822, Delaware, Ohio
Died January 17, 1893, Fremont, Ohio

He serves his party best who serves his country best.
— Rutherford B. Hayes

Just as Abraham Lincoln was known as "Honest Abe," our nineteenth President could have been called "Honest Rud," for it was his reproachless reputation that made him a candidate for President in 1876. After the Grant administration — tainted by fraud, political spoils, and chicanery — the nation would accept nothing less than a man of proven honesty and unswerving devotion to truth and honor. Rutherford Birchard Hayes was such a man.

Hayes' father died shortly before Rud's birth, and he was reared by his mother and her brother, Sardis Birchard, who became Hayes' guardian. Birchard, a flinty transplanted Vermonter, made sure that young Hayes had a proper education. Sophia Hayes, an overly protective mother, and sister Fanny instilled in the future President strong convictions and the expectations of exemplary behavior.

In 1852 Hayes married Lucy Ware Webb, a recent graduate of Cincinnati Wesleyan Women's College. Although Lucy was a strong believer in temperance, it was Rutherford, not Lucy, who refused to allow alcohol in the White House, even at state occasions. Because of her husband's policy, which was politically motivated, later generations would come to know this gracious and beloved First Lady incorrectly as "Lemonade Lucy."

Hayes' path to the White House was through the law and distinguished military service. He began the Civil War as a major and emerged a brevet major general — popular with his men and brave in battle. Stories of his heroism drifted back to Ohio, where he was urged to run for Congress. Refusing to leave active military duty if elected, Hayes replied, "An officer fit for duty who at this crisis would abandon his post to electioneer for a seat in Congress ought to be scalped."

Such feelings were the genesis of his future political attitude, one of absolute integrity and devotion. Such beliefs were destined to carry the former Congressman and three-term Governor of Ohio to the White House.

Rutherford B. Hayes Presidential Center
Fremont, Ohio

I'd rather die in Spiegel Grove than anywhere else.
— Rutherford B. Hayes

Spiegel Grove (Plate 17) is a pleasant, restful wooded estate of twenty-five acres. It is crowned by a stately red brick thirty-three-room house filled with precious antiques and the memory of the President who lived there. Hayes' uncle, Sardis Birchard, built the original structure around 1860. Subsequent additions by Hayes in 1880 and 1889 enlarged the three-story Victorian home to its present dimensions. Sardis Birchard named the grounds Spiegel Grove, using the German word for "mirror" to describe the reflection of pools of water sparkling after a rain.

Sardis Birchard died in January, 1874, willing the estate to his nephew, although Rutherford had already made Spiegel Grove his permanent home in 1873, between his second and third terms as Governor of Ohio. The imposing family residence represents the glory days of Victorian architecture and interior decor. Hayes loved the serene beauty of Spiegel Grove and came back often while Governor and as President.

Sometime between 1909 and 1914, Hayes' descendants presented Spiegel Grove to the State of Ohio, under the condition that the state erect a separate library and museum building to house the President's books and other belongings. Thus, in 1916, the nation's first Presidential library and museum came into existence, housed in a building of classic architecture made from Ohio sandstone. Over the years, the family established several non-profit organizations, which were combined in the mid-1980s to create the Rutherford B. Hayes Presidential Center, its purpose and mandate to administer the Center in conjunction with the Ohio Historical Society.

The museum contains two floors filled with exhibits chronicling the nineteenth President's life and career. Among the more popular highlights are the President's carriage, two dollhouses owned by the President's daughter Fanny, and a display of the unique Hayes White House china. As a major research collection for the post-Civil War period, the library contains 75,000 volumes and 3500 linear feet of manuscript and photographic material, including the President's and Lucy's personal papers.

President and Mrs. Hayes are buried on a wooded knoll near an old Indian trail that winds through the serenity of Spiegel Grove. The peaceful, flower- and tree-filled estate is enclosed by a decorated wrought-iron fence that features six gates brought from the White House. Winding paths allow visitors to enjoy and appreciate the quiet grandeur of a particularly restful and relaxing Presidential retreat.

DIRECTIONS: Fremont is just off the Ohio Turnpike (I–90/I–80). Take Exit 6 (Fremont), and follow the historical markers to the Center (Figure 62).

PUBLIC USE: Season and hours: Monday-Saturday 9 A.M.– 5 P.M. Sundays and holidays Noon – 5 P.M. Closed Thanksgiving, Christmas, New Year's Day. The library is closed Saturdays, Sundays, and all holidays. **Fees:** Adults, $7.50, with discounts for groups, students, and seniors. Admission includes access to the house and the museum. Visits to the house are guided, with tours conducted every 30 minutes. The library is open without charge. Allow 2 hours to enjoy the Rutherford B. Hayes Presidential Center. **Museum shop. For people with disabilities:** The museum is fully accessible. Assistance may be required to enter the house. Please call in advance.

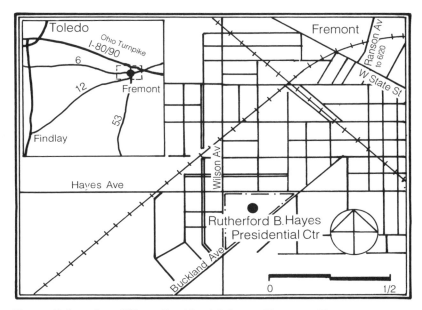

Figure 62. Location of Hayes Presidential Center, Fremont, Ohio.

FOR ADDITIONAL INFORMATION: Contact: Rutherford B. Hayes Presidential Center, Spiegel Grove, Fremont, Ohio 43420–2796, (419) 332–2081. **Read:** (1) *Guide to the Microfilm Edition of the Papers of Rutherford Birchard Hayes — The Nineteenth President of the United States*. 1983. Fremont: The Rutherford B. Hayes Presidential Center. (2) *Hayes Historical Journal*. Winter 1992. Fremont: The Rutherford B. Hayes Presidential Center. (3) Watt P. Marchman. 1988. *The Story of a President: Rutherford B. Hayes and Spiegel Grove*, revised edition. Fremont: Rutherford B. Hayes Presidential Center.

James Abram Garfield

Twentieth President
March 1881 - September 1881

Born November 19, 1831, Orange Township (Moreland
Hills), Ohio
Died September 19, 1881, Elberon, New Jersey

*No man ever started so low that accomplished so much in all
our history . . . not Franklin or Lincoln even.*
— Rutherford B. Hayes, speaking about Garfield

Hayes' rhetoric may have been exaggerated, but Garfield, the
last President born in a log cabin, was quite a man. He was father-

orphaned at two and reared by a tenacious frontier mother who lived long enough to attend the inauguration of her son as President of the United States. Garfield worked early in life, and hard, as a mule driver, farmer, and carpenter. A rough exterior belied his precocious, retentive mind and his rare gift for public speaking. He joined the Union army and rose to the rank of major general, serving with great distinction. He represented his home district in Ohio as congressman for nine terms before being elected to the United States Senate in 1880 by the Ohio Legislature. Before taking office, however, he was nominated for President on the thirty-sixth ballot by a divided Republican nominating convention.

Four months into his term, President Garfield prepared to leave on a summer vacation. On July 2, 1881, in the railroad station in Washington, he was shot by a deranged, frustrated office-seeker, Charles Guiteau. The critically wounded President lingered in the capital for two months, then was moved to the New Jersey shore, where he died on September 19, 1881.

James A. Garfield National Historic Site, "Lawnfield"
Mentor, Ohio

where my boys can learn to work and where I can get some exercise, where I can touch the earth and get some strength from it.

— James Garfield

In 1876, Congressman James A. Garfield bought a run-down farm and 1 1/2-story farmhouse in Mentor, Ohio. The house was the nucleus of what would evolve into a thirty-room Victorian mansion with gables and bay windows (Plate 18). The property was called "Lawnfield" by reporters who camped there during the 1880 Presidential campaign. Garfield preferred to call it his Mentor farm, but he finally gave in to the name "Lawnfield." Garfield was to enjoy his home only briefly.

A great national grief followed Garfield's death, and thousands of citizens concerned for Mrs. Garfield's welfare sent donations. Moved by their emotion and generosity, she decided that the addition of a library to Lawnfield would be the most appropriate tribute to the President, who had appreciated education and loved books.

The library, completed in 1886, is filled with the President's books, as well as mementos, souvenirs, gifts, and other remembrances. Included are Garfield's congressional desk, a funeral wreath sent by Queen Victoria, and the President's Wooton desk with its 122 filing compartments. Garfield's correspondence and other papers are preserved in the Library of Congress.

The Garfield family remained at Lawnfield until the 1930s, when the house and furnishings were donated to the Western Reserve Historical Society. The National Park Service now owns the property and buildings; the Western Reserve Historical Society owns the collections and administers the property. Lawnfield is currently undergoing extensive restoration under the supervision of the National Park Service.

DIRECTIONS: Mentor is a suburb of Cleveland, just off I–90. From I–90 eastbound or westbound, take the Mentor-Kirtland exit (State Route 306); go north on Route 306 for 2 miles to US Route 20 (Mentor Avenue). Bear right on Mentor Avenue and proceed 2 miles to Lawnfield (Figure 63).

PUBLIC USE: Season and hours: Lawnfield is open to the public Saturday and Sunday only and open only for group tours during the week. A conversion of the old carriage barn to a Visitor Center was to be completed by Fall of 1994. After that time the house is to be completely closed until its completion. The opening date is unknown but is projected to be 1996–1997. Call in advance for more specific information. **Fees:** Adults, $3; seniors, $2; children 6–12, $1.50. Allow 1 hour to enjoy Lawnfield. **Gift shop. For people with disabilities:** No special facilities. **Note:** Lawnfield is undergoing a complete restoration. A visitor center has recently opened in the 1893 carriage barn, and the mansion is scheduled to open late in 1998.

FOR ADDITIONAL INFORMATION: Contact: James A. Garfield National Historic Site, "Lawnfield," 8095 Mentor Avenue, Mentor, Ohio 44060, (216) 255–8722. **Read:** Allan Peskin. 1978. *Garfield*. The Kent State University Press.

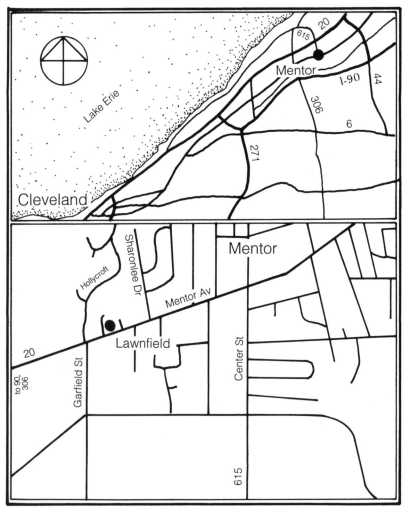

Figure 63. Location of "Lawnfield," Mentor, Ohio.

Chester Alan Arthur

Twenty-first President
1881 – 1885

Born October 5, 1829, Fairfield, Vermont
Died November 18, 1886, New York City, New York

Chet Arthur, President of the United States?
Good God!
— Unknown politician

The people and the politicians will find that Vice President
Arthur and President Arthur are different men.
— Governor Foote of Ohio

Governor Foote was correct. When James A. Garfield of Ohio was nominated for President in 1880, the Republican party picked Chester A. Arthur of New York as his running mate to be a sop to the New York political bosses and to balance the ticket. Arthur was considered a common politico with neither national nor foreign policy experience, but he was destined, by one of those flukes of history, to assume the Presidency of the United States.

Garfield was assassinated only a few months into his term and the country was traumatized, appalled by the thought of an Arthur Presidency. Some politicians suggested he reject the Presidency. Others were more sanguine. One young woman wrote:

> *Rise to the emergency. Disappoint our fears. Force the nation to have faith in you. Show from the first that you have none but the purest aims. It may be difficult at once to inspire confidence, but persevere. In time . . . when you have given reason for it . . . the country will love and trust you. Your name is now on the annals of history. You cannot slink back into obscurity, if you would . . . it is for you to choose whether your record shall be written in black or in gold. For the sake of your country, for your own sake and for the sakes of all who have ever loved you, let it be pure and bright.*

The words were taken to heart. Chester A. Arthur, like other vice presidents, rose to the challenge.

Chester Alan Arthur was the son of a Baptist minister; he was born in rural Vermont, in a parsonage near his father's church. He was brought up in Schenectady, New York, where he attended Union College and earned a law degree. In his early twenties, ambitious to a fault, he traveled to New York seeking fame and fortune, gaining both beyond his wildest dreams. As a member of the New York bar, he distinguished himself as a champion of civil rights for Blacks. He became active in Republican politics, then fell under the control of Senator Roscoe Conkling, who became Arthur's political mentor.

During the Civil War Arthur accepted a generalship in the New York militia, serving as Quartermaster General of the Port of New York, a position of great importance and influence. He conducted the assignment with skill, and it led to his post-war appointment as Collector of Customs of New York. It was a lucrative and blatantly political post, as the Customs House was a dumping ground of political patronage. Once in office, however, President Arthur defied the existing system by striking an early blow at the spoils system that had been endemic to all governmental affairs.

Arthur may have come to the Presidency by a path of political expediency, but once in office, he was capable and incorruptible.

Chester A. Arthur Historic Site
Fairfield, Vermont

William Arthur was a well-educated, albeit impecunious Irish immigrant who arrived in Fairfield as a Baptist minister. His son, Chester, destined to become President of the United States, was born in a tiny, temporary parsonage just down the rocky hill from the Reverend Arthur's church.

The present brick church, which dates from 1830 and was constructed on the site of the original church, is open for visitation. A building was constructed by the state of Vermont in 1953 to represent the original house to which the Arthur family moved in 1830 (Plate 19). The home has two downstairs rooms and an attic or sleeping loft above. It is not furnished as the cramped living space it must have been, but offers instead a pictorial exhibit of President Arthur's life and political career.

DIRECTIONS: Fairfield is in the northwest corner of Vermont, almost to the Canadian border. It can be reached by either Vermont State Route 36 (east-west) or State Route 108 (north-south). The Arthur Historic Site is on a town road 3 1/2 miles east of Fairfield Station; historical markers lead to the site (Figure 64).

PUBLIC USE: Season and hours: June to mid-October, Wednesday-Sunday 9:30 A.M.– 5:30 P.M. **Fees:** $1. Allow 30 minutes to enjoy the site. **Picnic area. For people with disabilities:** Fully accessible.

FOR ADDITIONAL INFORMATION: Contact: Vermont Division of Historic Preservation, 135 State Street, Drawer 33, Montpelier, Vermont 05633–1201, (802) 828–3226. **Read:** George Frederick Howe. 1934. *Chester A. Arthur: A Quarter Century of Machine Politics.* New York: Dodd, Mead and Company.

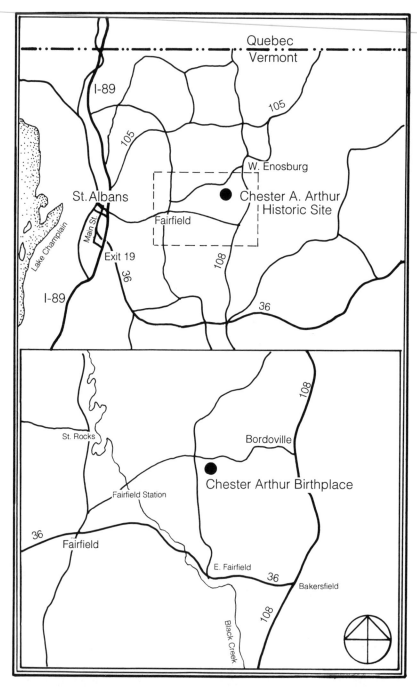

Figure 64. Location of Chester A. Arthur Historic Site, Fairfield, Vermont.

Stephen Grover Cleveland

Twenty-second President
1885 – 1889

Twenty-fourth President
1893 – 1897

Born March 18, 1837, Caldwell, New Jersey
Died June 24, 1908, Princeton, New Jersey

I have tried so hard to do right.
— Grover Cleveland's dying words

Grover Cleveland is a leading trivia President: the only one to serve a term, lose a campaign for reelection, and then make a comeback to win a second term; the only President to hang a man (while sheriff of Buffalo, New York); the only President to be married in the White House; and father of the first baby born in the White House, his daughter Esther.

Cleveland was, naturally, more than a source of trivia, for he was a contributor. He brought to the White House a breath of fresh air after twenty-five years of opposition party rule and the political shenanigans and congressional malfeasance that took place during Reconstruction. He fought New York's Tammany Hall and other special interests who would subvert and manipulate the system for personal gain. To accomplish his goals, he exercised his Presidential veto power more times than had his twenty-one predecessors combined.

Grover Cleveland was an ordinary man of common sense, determined and honest. These were traits taught by pious, devoted parents in the strict atmosphere of Presbyterian parsonages.

Grover Cleveland Birthplace Historic Site
Caldwell, New Jersey

Grover Cleveland was born in the manse of the Caldwell First Presbyterian Church (Plate 20), which his father served as pastor. The simple frame building of 2 1/2-stories was built in 1832 for the sum of $1490. It is similar to many houses of the period, with a gabled roof and clapboard siding.

The Clevelands moved on a few years later to a calling in Fayetteville, New York. The Caldwell manse served the church through many successors until it was purchased and restored as a house museum memorial to the President who had been born within its walls.

Today the house looks as it appeared in the mid-nineteenth century, with artifacts and furniture dating to the Cleveland occupancy. A resident curator is on hand to show visitors the downstairs rooms and to answer questions about Grover Cleveland and his times.

172

DIRECTIONS: From New York City and northern New Jersey, take the Garden State Parkway south to Exit 159 and I–80. Drive west on I–80 to State Route 23 and go south 3 1/2 miles to Bloomfield Avenue. Turn right and go 2 1/2 miles to the Cleveland House. From the Garden State Parkway northbound, take Exit 145 to I–280 and go west to Exit 5B (The Caldwells); then follow South Livingston Avenue 1 mile to Eagle Rock Avenue. Turn right; drive for 1 short block and turn left on Roseland Avenue, proceeding north 2 miles until it dead ends at Bloomfield Avenue. Turn right and go about 2 blocks to the house which is on the north side of Bloomfield Avenue (Figure 65).

PUBLIC USE: Season and hours: Wednesday-Friday 9 A.M.– 6 P.M., Saturday 9 A.M.– 5 P.M., Sunday 1 P.M.– 6 P.M. Closed Noon – 1 P.M. each day. Closed holidays. **Fees:** None. Allow 30 minutes to enjoy the site. **For people with disabilities:** No special facilities.

FOR ADDITIONAL INFORMATION: Contact: Grover Cleveland Birthplace, 207 Bloomfield Avenue, Caldwell, New Jersey 07006, (201) 226–1810. **Read:** Richard E. Welch, Jr. 1988. *The Presidencies of Grover Cleveland.* Lawrence: University Press of Kansas. (American Presidency Series).

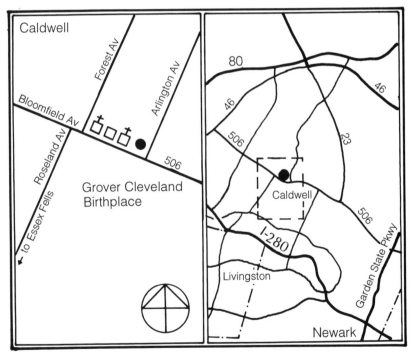

Figure 65. Location of Grover Cleveland Birthplace Historic Site, Caldwell, New Jersey.

173

Benjamin Harrison

Twenty-third President
1889 – 1893

Born August 20, 1833, North Bend, Ohio
Died March 13, 1901, Indianapolis, Indiana

*When a man receives the approbation of his neighbors, he is
indeed blessed.*

— Benjamin Harrison

Plate 1. *Mount Vernon, Mount Vernon, Virginia*

Plate 2. *Adams National Historic Site, Quincy, Massachusetts*

Plate 3. *Monticello, Charlottesville, Virginia*

Plate 4. *Montpelier, Montpelier Station, Virginia*

Plate 5. *Ash Lawn-Highland,
Charlottesville, Virginia*

Plate 6. *The Hermitage,
Nashville, Tennessee*

Plate 7. *Martin Van Buren
National Historic Site,
Kinderhook, New York*

Plate 8. *Berkeley Plantation, Charles City, Virginia*

Plate 9. *Sherwood Forest, Charles City, Virginia*

Plate 10. *Polk Ancestral Home, Columbia, Tennessee*

Plate 11. *Fillmore House Museum, East Aurora, New York*

Plate 12. *The Pierce Manse, Concord, New Hampshire*

Plate 13. *Wheatland, Lancaster, Pennsylvania*

Plate 14. *Abraham Lincoln's Boyhood Home, Knob Creek Farm, Hodgenville, Kentucky*

Plate 15. *Andrew Johnson Birthplace, Raleigh, North Carolina*

Plate 16. *Grant's Birthplace, Point Pleasant, Ohio*

Plate 17. *Rutherford B. Hayes Presidential Center, Fremont, Ohio*

Plate 18. *James A. Garfield National Historic Site, "Lawnfield," Mentor, Ohio*

Plate 19. *Chester A. Arthur Historic Site, Fairfield, Vermont*

Plate 20. *Grover Cleveland Birthplace Historic Site, Caldwell, New Jersey*

Plate 21. *Benjamin Harrison Home, Indianapolis, Indiana*

Plate 22. *National McKinley Birthplace Memorial, Niles, Ohio*

Plate 23. *Sagamore Hill National Historic Site, Oyster Bay, New York*

Plate 24. *William Howard Taft National Historic Site, Cincinnati, Ohio*

Plate 25. *Woodrow Wilson House Museum, Washington, DC*

Plate 26. *President Harding's Home, Marion, Ohio*

Plate 27. *Plymouth Notch Historic District, Plymouth Notch, Vermont*

Plate 28. *Herbert Hoover National Historic Site, West Branch, Iowa*

Plate 29. *Roosevelt Campobello International Park, Campobello Island, New Brunswick*

Plate 30. *Truman Farm Home, Grandview, Missouri*

Plate 31. *The Eisenhower Center, Abilene, Kansas*

Plate 32. *John F. Kennedy National Historic Site, Brookline, Massachusetts*

Plate 33. *Lyndon B. Johnson State and National Historic Parks, Johnson City and Stonewall, Texas*

Plate 34. *The Richard Nixon Library & Birthplace, Yorba Linda, California*

Plate 35. *Gerald R. Ford Library, Ann Arbor, Michigan*

Plate 36. *Carter Presidential Center, Atlanta, Georgia*

Plate 37. *Ronald Reagan Boyhood Home, Dixon, Illinois*

Benjamin Harrison was the grandson of the ninth President and the great-grandson of a signer of the Declaration of Independence. Harrison brought to the White House a family heritage of commitment to service and public responsibility. His own father was a farmer who served two terms in the US Congress. More important, he provided son Benjamin with a wholesome midwestern upbringing and a solid education.

Benjamin served with distinction as a brevet brigadier general in the Civil War, then returned to Indiana to resume his law practice. He was elected to the United States Senate in 1881 and from that powerful political seat was nominated in 1888 as the Republican Presidential candidate. Evincing little interest in the honor, Harrison ran a quiet campaign from his home. He surprised everyone, including himself, by winning the Presidency in the Electoral College, although he polled fewer popular votes than his rival, Grover Cleveland. Four years later, Harrison was defeated by the same opponent.

Benjamin Harrison was a devout and vocal patriot. As President he decreed that the nation's flag should fly from every school and public building, a tradition still honored. Harrison also gave his written approval to Francis Bellamy of Boston, who wrote:

> I pledge allegiance to my flag and the Republic for which it stands; one nation indivisible, with Liberty and Justice for all.

At one point, Harrison commented:

> I did try to make the administration thoroughly American and hope that something was done to develop an increased love of the Flag at home and an increased respect for it abroad.

Benjamin Harrison Home
Indianapolis, Indiana

Great lives do not go out, they go on.
— Benjamin Harrison

General Benjamin Harrison returned to Indianapolis after a distinguished Civil War career. He opened a law office and began construction of a sixteen-room mansion, which was completed in 1875 (Plate 21). The house was of the brick Italianate style, although the addition of a spacious porch reflects the Colonial Revival style that became popular in the 1890s.

Except for his term as President, Harrison lived in Indianapolis until his death in 1901. In 1913 his second wife, Mary, and his daughter Elizabeth moved to New York and leased the house to private tenants; in 1937 they sold it to the Jordan Conservatory of Music to be used as a student dormitory. In 1965, the President Benjamin Harrison Foundation was formed, assumed control of the house, and converted it to its original state. Mrs. Harrison and other family members contributed papers, furniture, and memorabilia to the memorial effort.

Harrison's first wife, Caroline, was a talented, professionally-trained artist who had filled the house with colorful work, including the Harrison White House china of her design: corn tassels on the border, forty-four stars to symbolize the states, and an American eagle representing strength and unity. Her work is still proudly displayed throughout the home. Ten rooms have been fully restored, the third floor serving as a museum gallery for Harrison's personal artifacts and for exhibits delineating his life and political career.

DIRECTIONS: The Harrison home is only 1 block from I–65. Eastbound, exit at Meridian Street but continue straight on 11th Street to Delaware Street, and turn left to the home. Westbound, exit at Pennsylvania Street, immediately turning left and proceeding 1 block to 11th Street, then turning left to go for 1 block to Delaware Street, and left again to the home (Figure 66). There is parking in the rear.

PUBLIC USE: Season and hours: Weekdays 10 A.M.– 3:30 P.M., Sunday 12:30 P.M.– 3:30 P.M. Closed Easter, Thanksgiving, Christmas Eve, Christmas Day, Memorial Day, Labor Day, New Year's Day, and Indianapolis 500 Race Day. Phone for special January hours. **Fees:** Adults, $2, with discounts for groups, students, and AAA members. Guided tours are conducted every 30 minutes. Allow 1 hour to enjoy the Harrison home. A special first-person interpretation, *Live from Delaware Street,* is presented on the first Wednesday of each month (every Wednesday in February) at 9:30 A.M., 11:00 A.M., and 12:30 P.M. **Fees:** $2.50. Picnics on the lawn are permitted by prior arrangement. **Gift shop. For people with disabilities:** There is a ramp to the first floor, but the second floor is not accessible. A videotaped tour of the upper floors is available.

EDUCATIONAL FACILITIES: The Harrison Home is the center for an active educational program including slide shows, videos, and other activities designed for all grade levels. Public programs for adults are also offered.

FOR ADDITIONAL INFORMATION: Contact: President Benjamin Harrison Home, 1230 North Delaware Street, Indianapolis, Indiana 46202–2598, (317) 631–1898. **Read:** (1) Harry J. Sievers, S. J. 1952. *Benjamin Harrison, Hoosier Warrior. 1833–1865.* Chicago: Henry Regnery Company. (2) Harry J. Sievers, S. J. 1959. *Benjamin Harrison: Hoosier Statesman. From the Civil War to the White House, 1865–1888.* New York: University Publishers, Incorporated. (3) Harry J. Sievers, S. J. 1968. *Benjamin Harrison: Hoosier President. The White House and After.* New York: Bobbs-Merrill Co., Inc. (4) Homer E. Socolofsky and Allan B. Spetter. 1987. *Presidency of Benjamin Harrison.* Lawrence: University Press of Kansas.

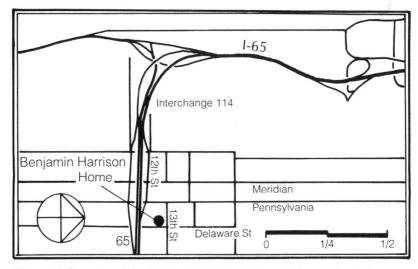

Figure 66. Location of the Benjamin Harrison Home, Indianapolis, Indiana.

William McKinley

Twenty-fifth President
1897 – 1901

Born January 29, 1843, Niles Ohio
Died September 14, 1901, Buffalo, New York

*Up to this time, I'd never really believed that a man could be
a good Christian and a good politician.*
— Attending physician at McKinley's death

William McKinley, the son of an iron foundry owner, was raised in Niles, Ohio. He was forced to leave Allegheny College because of illness and a financial downturn that affected his father's business. The young man volunteered for the Ohio Twenty-third Volunteer Infantry as a private, but his leadership qualities soon surfaced. By the time of the Battle of Antietam he was a commissary sergeant, and his valor that day led to a commission as second lieutenant. He mustered out of the Union army as a brevet major, revered by the troops he had led in engagements that included the Valley campaign of 1864, and respected by his commanding officer, General Rutherford B. Hayes, a man McKinley was destined to follow into the White House.

After leaving the army, McKinley continued his education, turned to the law, and eventually began to practice in the growing Ohio city of Canton. His progress was steady: Stark County Prosecutor, US Congressman for seven terms, Governor of Ohio for two terms. From that lofty and influential position, he proved a formidable national political figure. In 1896, the Republican party nominated him to face William Jennings Bryan for the Presidency.

The Presidential campaign posed awkward personal problems for McKinley because his wife, Ida, suffered from epilepsy and emotional difficulties that had developed after the deaths of their two daughters in the 1870s. Therefore, he and his advisors developed the famous "front-porch" campaign in which politicians and private citizens trekked to Canton to call on the candidate. It was reported that 600,000 people traveled there to see and hear him. The campaign proved successful, as McKinley won with an Electoral College advantage of 271 to 176.

In 1900, McKinley and Bryan faced one another again. The prosperity of the nation led voters to sweep McKinley into a second term. McKinley was inaugurated in March 1901 with many initiatives planned for his second term. After an extended southern and western tour, President and Mrs. McKinley spent August in Canton. Their vacation ended with a Presidential visit to the opening of the Pan-American Exposition in Buffalo, New York, before their scheduled return to Washington. There in Buffalo, on September 6, 1901, William McKinley was shot by anarchist Leon Czolgosz. The President died eight days later, with the words of "Nearer, My God, to Thee" on his lips.

McKinley National Memorial

Canton, Ohio

One of the most impressive and imposing Presidential resting places is the McKinley National Memorial in Canton, Ohio (Figure 67). One hundred eight broad granite steps lead up to a magnificent mausoleum, high above the city that McKinley served with devotion and love. President and Mrs. McKinley and their two infant daughters are entombed in a handsome double-domed building of pink Milford granite. The exterior dome is seventy-five feet in diameter and ninety-five feet high.

At the foot of the steps is a living memorial, the McKinley Museum of History, Science and Industry, which serves the cultural needs of Stark County and the city of Canton with displays and educational programs for all grade levels. One gallery is

Figure 67. The McKinley National Memorial, Canton, Ohio. Photograph by William G. Clotworthy.

devoted exclusively to McKinley: clothing, furniture, photographs, and personal mementos representing his private and public life are the largest collection of McKinley memorabilia in the country. The gallery is dramatized by a tableau of the McKinley living room, fully decorated and featuring life-like wax figures of the McKinleys in full evening dress as if to welcome good friends to their cheery home.

The McKinley Room is only part of the eclectic charm of the museum. A "Street of Shops" contains full-sized reproductions of stores representative of an Ohio town of the 1880s, and an eighty-two-foot HO gauge model train complex follows the Pennsylvania Railroad's route through Canton, Massillon, and points west. Industrial Hall, Discover World — devoted to hands-on science — and a planetarium are three of the other attractions dedicated to the spirit of the great American lying at peace at the top of the hill.

DIRECTIONS: Canton is south of Akron, Ohio, just off I–77. From I–77, use Canton Exit 106 which leads to 13th Street, NW. Proceed east on 13th Street to the bottom of the hill and turn right on Monument Park Drive, which leads directly to the parking area (Figure 68).

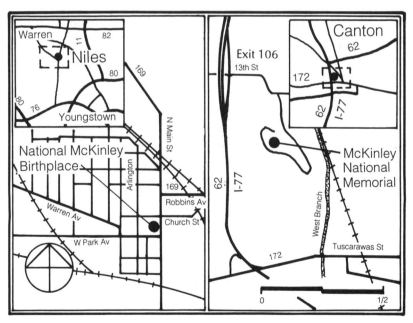

Figure 68. Location of McKinley National Memorial, Canton, Ohio, and National McKinley Birthplace Memorial, Niles, Ohio.

PUBLIC USE: Season and hours: Daily 9 A.M.– 5 P.M., Sunday Noon – 5 P.M. Hours are extended to 7 P.M. during June, July, and August. Closed Thanksgiving, Christmas Eve, Christmas Day, Labor Day, New Year's Day, Memorial Day, and Easter Sunday. Fees: Adults, $5, with discounts for groups, students, and seniors. Allow 2 hours to enjoy the Memorial and the Museum. Picnic area. Gift shop. For people with disabilities: Fully accessible, with the exception of the planetarium.

FOR ADDITIONAL INFORMATION: Contact: Stark County Historical Society, McKinley Museum, 800 McKinley Monument Drive, NW, Canton, Ohio 44703, (216) 455–7043. Read: (1) Edward T. Heald. 1964, 1992. *The Condensed Biography of William McKinley*. Canton: Stark County Historical Society. (2) H. Wayne Morgan. 1963. *William McKinley and His America*. New York: Syracuse University Press.

National McKinley Birthplace Memorial
Niles, Ohio

After William McKinley's death, the city of Niles wished to honor the President who had been born and reared in the community. A successful public subscription campaign exceeded its modest goal and enabled Niles to construct a magnificent marble edifice, the centerpiece of the downtown area and an outstanding example of Greek Classic architecture (Plate 22).

A central outdoor atrium features an Italian marble garden and a larger-than-life statue of McKinley surrounded by sculptured busts of outstanding national and local political figures. The enclosed south side of the building houses the modern Niles Public Library, and the enclosed north wing is a spacious civic auditorium and hall of statuary. On the mezzanine of the auditorium is a collection of McKinley memorabilia and a photographic history of the construction process of the memorial, dedicated by the proud citizens of Niles in 1917.

DIRECTIONS: Niles is 10 miles northwest of Youngstown, Ohio. From I–80, exit to Ohio State Route 46, and proceed north four miles to Niles and the memorial (Figure 68).

PUBLIC USE: Season and hours: Monday-Thursday 8:30 A.M.– 8 P.M., Friday and Saturday 8:30 A.M.– 5:30 P.M. September-May, also open Sunday 1 P.M.– 5 P.M. **Fees:** None. Allow 45 minutes to enjoy the Memorial. **For people with disabilities:** Ramp and restroom facilities.

FOR ADDITIONAL INFORMATION: Contact: McKinley Memorial Library, 40 N. Main Street, Niles, Ohio 44446, (216) 652–1704. **Read:** (1) Joseph G. Butler. 1924. *Life of William McKinley and History of National McKinley Birthplace Memorial.* (2) "McKinley Memorial Library." *Ohio Libraries.* July / August 1990, 12.

Theodore Roosevelt

Twenty-sixth President
1901 – 1909

Born October 27, 1858, New York, New York
Died January 6, 1919, Sagamore Hill, Oyster Bay, New York

At Sagamore Hill we love a great many things . . . birds and trees and books, and all things beautiful, and horses and rifles and children and hard work and the joy of life.
— Theodore Roosevelt

For many years after the death of Abraham Lincoln, America drifted. Presidential power had eroded in an era of bossism, and vice presidents were to be seen and not heard. If they succeeded to the Presidency they became caretakers, their role in office solely to continue existing policies and to tend the country on a temporary basis until the next election.

That attitude changed with the unexpected Presidency of Theodore Roosevelt, one of those "Accidencies" who turned out to be a man of substance and principle, indebted to no one save himself and the citizens of the United States.

Theodore Roosevelt was born in New York City, into a family of wealth and social position. He suffered from asthma as a child and was confined to home and schooled by private tutors. He was blessed, however, with an active mind that sponged up knowledge and with a desire to develop an interest in such special subjects as natural history, zoology, and taxidermy.

Roosevelt, in his autobiography, spoke reverently of his father, who, night after night, walked the floor carrying the pale and suffering young Theodore, tending him with love and concern. He also recalled his father's admonition, "You have the mind, but you haven't got the body. To do all you can with your mind, you must make your body to match it." It was that strong, forceful, and loving advice that compelled Teddy to start a vigorous program of physical exercise and outdoor activity that turned the frail boy into a robust man.

Roosevelt graduated from Harvard, then turned his attention and activities to politics and served from 1882 until 1884 in the New York State Assembly. In 1880 he married Alice Lee, who gave birth to a baby girl, Alice, in 1884. Roosevelt experienced a double tragedy when his mother and his young wife both died on February 14, 1884. Distraught, he fled to Dakota Territory, where he purchased a ranch and attempted to ease his despondency in hard outdoor living. The ranching venture failed, however, and Roosevelt returned to New York, never again to stray far from the political arena.

He held a number of elected and appointed positions, including those of New York City Police Commissioner, from 1895 until 1897, and of Assistant Secretary of the Navy, from 1897 until 1898. He resigned the latter post to organize and lead the Rough Riders to fame in the War with Spain — fame that became a springboard to Roosevelt's 1898–1901 governorship of New York and then to second spot on the 1900 Republican ticket with William McKinley. He assumed the Presidency September 14, 1901, upon McKinley's death; at forty-two, he had become the youngest man to hold the office.

Theodore Roosevelt is considered by historians to have been the first modern Chief Executive. He was certainly the most active, packing many careers into one lifetime: President of the United States; prolific writer; naturalist; conservationist; cowboy; big-game hunter; soldier; Nobel Prize-winner; loving husband and caring father.

Theodore Roosevelt Birthplace National Historic Site

New York, New York

Theodore Roosevelt was born in a narrow, four-story brownstone in midtown New York City, just west of Gramercy Park, a prosperous neighborhood (Figure 69). The Roosevelts lived there until Theodore was fourteen, then moved to a more prestigious address on West 57th Street.

The brownstone house at 28 East 20th Street was demolished in 1916 to make room for a commercial building. After Roosevelt's death in 1919, a group of women formed an association with the purpose of preserving the memory and spirit of the President who had passionately and vigorously moved the nation forward. Their archives describe those efforts:

> *Devotion to a single individual prompted the formation of many early preservation groups, as in the case of the Women's Roosevelt Memorial Association. This organization's intriguing effort is earmarked by several unusual twists. Although the house where he had lived between 1858 and 1872 had been torn down in 1916, the Association was undaunted. In 1919 these concerned women purchased the commercial structure which occupied the site and demol-*

Figure 69. Theodore Roosevelt Birthplace National Historic Site, New York, New York. Photograph courtesy of National Park Service.

ished it. The female architect Theodate Pope Riddle designed a replica brownstone based on adjacent rowhouses and family reminiscences. The Theodore Roosevelt Association administered the reconstructed house museum from its opening in 1923 until its donation to the National Park Service in 1963.

Thanks to that group of dedicated women, we can enjoy a visit to the replicated Roosevelt house, a vivid recollection of prosperous city living in the mid-nineteenth century. Over forty percent of the furnishings are original Roosevelt pieces; the others are of the period. It was in rooms like those of this house that Theodore Roosevelt began his life-long love affair with mental and physical exertion and with the discipline that would make him such an outstanding American leader.

DIRECTIONS: The IRT and BMT subway lines stop at the 23rd Street and 14th Street stations, both within easy walking distance of the Roosevelt house (Figure 70).

PUBLIC USE: Season and hours: Wednesday-Sunday 9 A.M.– 5 P.M. Closed Thanksgiving, Christmas, New Year's Day. **Fees:** $2; under 17, free; 62 and over, free. Allow 1 1/2 hours to enjoy the Roosevelt house. **For people with disabilities:** Not accessible.

FOR ADDITIONAL INFORMATION: Contact: Roosevelt Birthplace National Historic Site, 28 East 20th Street, New York, New York 10003, (212) 260–1616. **Read:** (1) Edmund Morris. 1979. *The Rise of Theodore Roosevelt.* New York: Coward, McCann and Geoghegan. (2) Theodore Roosevelt. 1913. *The Autobiography of Theodore Roosevelt.* New York: Charles Scribner's Sons.

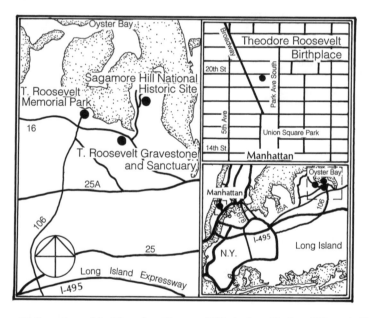

Figure 70. Location of the Theodore Roosevelt Birthplace National Historic Site, New York, New York, and Sagamore Hill National Historic Site, Oyster Bay, New York.

Sagamore Hill National Historic Site
Oyster Bay, New York

*I wonder if you will ever know how much I love Sagamore
Hill?*
> — Theodore Roosevelt, the evening before he died
> at Sagamore Hill.

Two months before he married Alice Lee, Theodore Roosevelt
began to acquire acreage on a promontory overlooking Oyster
Bay, on the northern shore of Long Island. Plans were drawn up
for a house, which was to be named Leeholm, after Alice. Before
construction of the house had begun, however, Alice died.

At the urging of his sister, who convinced him that he needed
a home for his infant daughter, Roosevelt went ahead with plans
for the house. Between 1884 and 1885, he built a rambling Victorian
structure of frame and brick. Its wide, sweeping veranda provided
a panoramic view of Oyster Bay and Long Island Sound. Roosevelt
renamed the property Sagamore Hill (Plate 23) after Indian chief
Sagamore Mohannis, who had signed the land away two hundred
years before.

In December 1886, Roosevelt married Edith Kermit Carow;
they moved to Sagamore Hill the following spring. Eventually the
house resounded with the sounds of more children, a fact that
Roosevelt acknowledged as a source of delight:

> *For unflagging interest and enjoyment, a household of children,
> if things go reasonably well, certainly makes all other forms of
> success and achievement lose their importance by comparison.*

As Roosevelt progressed politically, the house also became a
mecca for public figures: potentates, prize fighters, politicians, and
professors — all associates of the gregarious, inquisitive Roosevelt.
In 1905, Roosevelt added the North Room to the house in order to
provide a formal and roomy space for receiving his guests. The
room, which is popular with today's visitors, was built from exotic
Philippine and American wood and is filled with Roosevelt's
books, paintings, flags, and hunting trophies, as well as with
souvenirs of his public career and world travels.

189

Edith Roosevelt died in 1948. Sagamore Hill and its treasures were acquired by the Theodore Roosevelt Association that year. In 1963 the Association, which also owned the birthplace brownstone in New York City, donated both properties to the federal government for the enjoyment and edification of the American people.

DIRECTIONS: By train: Take the Long Island Railroad from Penn Station in New York City to Oyster Bay. Taxis meet all trains. **By car:** From New York City, take the Long Island Expressway to Exit 41; proceed north on New York State Route 106 to Oyster Bay; then follow the historical markers to Sagamore Hill (Figure 70).

PUBLIC USE: Season and hours: Daily 9:30 A.M.– 4:30 P.M. Hours extended in summer to 5:30 P.M. Closed Thanksgiving, Christmas, New Year's Day. **Fees:** $2. Allow 2 hours to enjoy Sagamore Hill. **Picnic area. Gift shop. For people with disabilities:** The first floor of the mansion is accessible; the second floor is not.

FOR ADDITIONAL INFORMATION: Contact: Sagamore Hill National Historic Site, Oyster Bay, New York 11771, (516) 922–4447. **Read:** (1) Hermann Hagedorn. 1953. *A Guide to Sagamore Hill.* New York: Theodore Roosevelt Association. (2) Hermann Hagedorn. 1954. *The Roosevelt Family of Sagamore Hill.* New York: The Macmillan Company.

Maltese Cross Cabin

Theodore Roosevelt National Park, Medora, North Dakota

> *I never would have been President if it had not been for my experiences in North Dakota.*
> — Theodore Roosevelt

Roosevelt visited the North Dakota badlands in 1883 to hunt buffalo, and he returned in 1884 following the deaths of his mother and his young wife. There he hoped to ease his grief by indulging in the rugged outdoor life of a cowboy.

He became alarmed when he observed the damage being inflicted on the land and wildlife by human intrusion; thus, conservation became an important part of his personal and political agenda. As President he established the National Forest Service,

Figure 71. The Maltese Cross Cabin in Theodore Roosevelt National Park, Medora, North Dakota. Photograph courtesy of National Park Service.

proclaimed eighteen national monuments, and was instrumental in persuading Congress to establish five national parks and fifty-five wildlife refuges.

Theodore Roosevelt was the first "Conservation President," and it was appropriate that a national park bearing his name be established in the rugged land that had inspired his efforts. The Maltese Cross Cabin (Figure 71), named for the ranch where he lived, is simply a rough, shingle-roofed 1 1/2-story cottage of pine logs, with three downstairs rooms and a sleeping loft. It was acquired by the state of North Dakota shortly after Roosevelt's inauguration as President and was transferred to the federal government in 1959.

DIRECTIONS: The Theodore Roosevelt National Park is 135 miles west of Bismarck, North Dakota, on I–94. The cabin is located next to the South Unit Visitors Center in Medora (Figure 72).

PUBLIC USE: Season and hours: The park is open year-round. The Visitor Center is open daily, mid-June through Labor Day, 8 A.M.– 8 P.M. All other months, 8 A.M.– 4:30 P.M. Closed Thanksgiving, Christmas, New Year's Day. **Fees:** $4 per vehicle from May through September. Guided tours of the

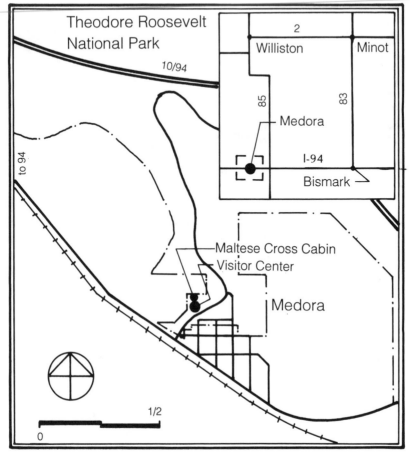

Figure 72. Location of the Maltese Cross Cabin, Theodore Roosevelt National Park, Medora, North Dakota.

Maltese Cross Cabin begin at the Visitor Center and are conducted on a regular schedule, 8:45 A.M.– 4:30 P.M., mid-June-Labor Day. Self-guided tours are available the rest of the year. Allow 30 minutes to enjoy the Maltese Cross Cabin. **Food service:** Picnic and camping areas. **For people with disabilities:** Fully accessible.

FOR ADDITIONAL INFORMATION: Contact: Theodore Roosevelt National Park, Medora, North Dakota 58645, (701) 623–4466. **Read:** (1) Mrs. A. M. Christianson 1955. "The Roosevelt Cabin." *North Dakota History.* July, 117–119. (2) Chester L. Brooks and Ray H. Matison. 1983. *Theodore Roosevelt and the Dakota Badlands.* Medora: Theodore Roosevelt Nature and History Association. (3) Hermann Hagedorn. 1987. *Roosevelt in the Badlands.* Medora: Theodore Roosevelt Nature and History Association.

William Howard Taft

Twenty-seventh President
1909 – 1913

Born September 15, 1857, Cincinnati, Ohio
Died March 8, 1930, Washington, DC

It's great to be great, but it's greater to be human. He was our great fellow because there was more of him to be human. We are parting with three hundred pounds of solid charity to everyone, and love and affection for all his fellow men.
— Will Rogers, eulogizing Taft

One must hark back to the early days of the republic to find a family as devoted to public service as the Tafts of Cincinnati. Only the Adamses and the Harrisons have spawned as many influential activists — both elected and appointed officials in the highest levels of government. Alphonso Taft sat on the federal bench, was twice a member of President Grant's cabinet, and served as minister to Vienna and St. Petersburg. His son, William Howard Taft, became President, and his grandson, Robert, became famous as "Mr. Republican," representing Ohio in the United States Senate for many years.

William Howard Taft is best remembered for his hefty physique and for being the first President to throw out the first ball at the start of the baseball season. His real accomplishments transcended such superficiality, for he had a fine legal mind, a sense of fair play, and unparalleled skill at mediation. A brilliant young attorney, he was appointed Solicitor General of the United States at just thirty-three, then progressed to influential positions as Governor General of the Philippines and as Theodore Roosevelt's Secretary of War.

As President, he was uncharacteristically indecisive, irritable, and procrastinating. Political differences between Taft and Theodore Roosevelt, his predecessor and mentor, split the Republican party in 1912 and enabled Woodrow Wilson and the Democrats to win the White House.

Following his defeat, Taft was named Professor of Constitutional Law at his alma mater, Yale University. He enjoyed academia and the chance to work with young people, but he was not reluctant to leave in 1921 when President Harding offered the one appointment Taft coveted more than any other — Chief Justice of the United States Supreme Court. He filled the post with distinction until shortly before his death.

William Howard Taft National Historic Site
Cincinnati, Ohio

In the mid-nineteenth century Cincinnati was a thriving metropolis of 200,000 scattered along the Ohio River. The arrangement was one that suggested many small towns, rather than one large city. In 1851 attorney Alphonso Taft bought a two-story brick house on Auburn Street (Plate 24) to accommodate his growing family, soon to include a future President. Will Taft was born in a first-floor bedroom, and his mother wrote her sister, "he is perfectly healthy and hearty, and I take real comfort in taking care of him. He is very large for his age, and grows fat everyday."

The Taft house was sturdy and roomy, with Victorian scroll-trimmed eaves and a New England captain's walk. There was a wide verandah and a large, sweeping lawn, a perfect playground for active boys who swam, skated, fought — and loved each other. Will's favorite game was baseball, an interest that continued through his life and culminated with the inauguration of the Presidential custom of throwing out the first ball of the new season.

The Taft home had several owners over the years until 1961, when it was bought by the Taft Memorial Association which, in turn, transferred it to the federal government as a National Historic Site in 1969. The ground floor is fully furnished and appears as it did during the Taft residency. The upper floor contains museum galleries with displays highlighting Taft's career as attorney, diplomat, Chief Executive, professor, and Chief Justice.

DIRECTIONS: The William Howard Taft National Historic Site is close to a major north-south artery, I–71. Southbound on I–71, exit at William Howard Taft Road and proceed west to Auburn Avenue. Turn left and drive 1/2 mile to the house. Northbound, take the left-side exit at Reading-Florence (Exit 2). At the first stoplight, turn left on Dorchester Street and proceed to Auburn Street. Turn right on Auburn. Parking is 1 block away from the house at Southern and Young (Southern is the street north of home) (Figure 73).

PUBLIC USE: Season and hours: Daily 10 A.M.– 4 P.M. Closed Thanksgiving, Christmas, and New Year's Day. **Fees:** None. Allow 1 hour to enjoy the Taft home. **For people with disabilities:** Fully accessible, with an interior elevator to the upper floor.

EDUCATIONAL FACILITIES: A non-profit organization, Friends of the William Howard Taft Birthplace, in association with the National Park Service, conducts a series of special events for both adults and children. To further honor President Taft, the Friends group conducts a yearly contest that culminates in the presentation of a scholarship assistance award.

FOR ADDITIONAL INFORMATION: Contact: Superintendent, William Howard Taft National Historic Site, 2038 Auburn Avenue, Cincinnati, Ohio 45219, (513) 684–3262. **Read:** (1) Henry Fowles Pringle. 1939. *The Life and Times of William Howard Taft.* New York: Farrar and Rinehart. (2) Ishbel Ross. 1964. *An American Family: the Tafts.* Cleveland: World Publishing. (3) Judith Icke Anderson. 1981. *William Howard Taft: An Intimate History.* New York: Norton.

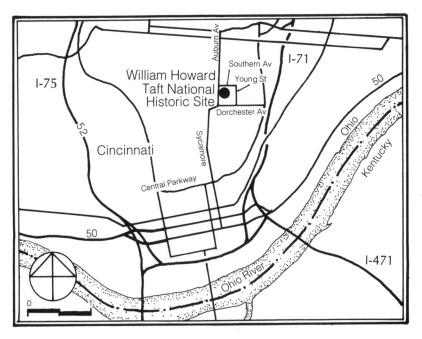

Figure 73. Location of the William Howard Taft National Historic Site, Cincinnati, Ohio.

196

Thomas Woodrow Wilson

Twenty-eighth President
1913 – 1921

Born December 28, 1856, Staunton, Virginia
Died February 3, 1924, Washington, DC

*I am not one of those that have the least anxiety about the
triumph of the principles I have stood for — that we shall
prevail is as sure as God reigns.*

— Woodrow Wilson

"Tommy" Wilson was the son of a Presbyterian minister. The family moved often, but always under pleasant and congenial circumstances. Wilson graduated from Princeton University with the intention of pursuing a career in law until he realized that "law and justice have little to do with one another." He switched to the study of history, especially political, and earned a doctorate with a brilliant dissertation that ensured him of an early, yet solid, reputation in academia.

Wilson had discovered his true calling, teaching and scholarship, and held a number of college teaching posts on his way to becoming president of his alma mater, Princeton. He was the first non-clergyman to be named to that honor. He developed an outstanding record as an administrator, which brought him to the attention of New Jersey's political hierarchy. They urged him to run for the governorship, and he agreed, but only after extracting a commitment of non-interference from the bosses. In 1912, Governor Wilson was nominated for the Presidency of the United States and easily defeated the deeply divided Republicans.

During Wilson's first term, many domestic programs were enacted, and the nation prospered under his vigorous leadership. Wilson had hoped to stay out of the war in Europe, but to no avail. In April, 1917, he proclaimed the joint resolution that enjoined the United States in World War I.

In January, 1918, Woodrow Wilson announced his famous Fourteen Points as a basis for world peace; he hoped that they would be written into the peace treaty at the end of the war. When Armistice was declared on November 11, 1918, he immediately embarked for Europe, where he toured triumphantly before attending the Paris Peace Conference.

In Paris, Wilson pressed for a League of Nations, but was forced home to face questioning from the Senate regarding treaty terms. Any treaty must be ratified by the Senate, and opposition was growing. Nevertheless, Wilson confidently returned to Europe to sign the Versailles Treaty, which included the Covenant of the League of Nations.

Wilson then came back home and began a grueling whistle-stop railroad tour in an attempt to elicit enough public support to force Senate compliance with the treaty. The controversy and rigors of travel exhausted him, however, and he was forced to return to Washington where, on October 26, 1919, he suffered the paralytic stroke that disabled him for the remainder of his life.

The next year encompassed both the lowest and highest points of Woodrow Wilson's career. In March, 1920, the United States Senate rejected the Versailles Treaty, effectively killing Wilson's beloved League of Nations. In December, however, Wilson was awarded the Nobel Peace Prize in recognition of his tireless, idealistic — and unavailing — efforts to bring about a just and lasting peace for all mankind.

Wilson attended the inauguration of Warren G. Harding in 1921, then retired to a comfortable townhouse in an exclusive Washington neighborhood. White-haired and shrunken, he lived until 1924, loved and respected by his neighbors, by every American, and by the citizens of the world.

Woodrow Wilson Birthplace and Museum
Staunton, Virginia

Thomas Woodrow Wilson was born in the manse of the Presbyterian Church where his father served as pastor (Figure 74). It was not a simple parsonage, but a large and imposing townhouse built in the Greek Revival style — a rectangular, brick structure with a two-story, pillared portico reminiscent of Jefferson's Monticello, a particularly attractive exterior. It is framed by sculptured lawns and an unusual rear garden that features boxwoods planted in a distinctive bowknot design, interlaced with brick walks and a staircase leading to the house.

The twelve spacious rooms in the house are filled with such original Wilson furniture and memorabilia as the crib in which infant "Tommy" slept and the family Bible that records his birth in 1856. The Wilsons were in residence for only three years before the Reverend Wilson was transferred to Augusta, Georgia. The house remained a church manse until 1929, when it was deeded to neighboring Mary Baldwin College. Since 1938 it has been maintained by the Woodrow Wilson Birthplace Foundation, which has been responsible for its refurbishing and decoration.

Figure 74. West facade of the Woodrow Wilson Birthplace and Museum, Staunton, Virginia. Photograph by Tommy Thompson; use courtesy of Woodrow Wilson Birthplace and Museum, Staunton, Virginia.

Recently the Foundation purchased an imposing chateau-style mansion two doors away and converted it into a museum of exhibit galleries that graphically represent Wilson's story as student, teacher, university president, governor, President, and world statesman. An attached garage contains a mint-condition Pierce-Arrow touring car, one of the first Presidential limousines.

A visit to the Wilson Birthplace and Museum is a rare experience. The site's ambiance dramatically demonstrates why Wilson returned frequently to visit.

DIRECTIONS: Staunton is west of Charlottesville, Virginia, a few miles west of I–81. Either north- or south-bound, take Exit 57/222, and follow US Route 250 west to US Route 11 in Staunton. Proceed north on Route 11,

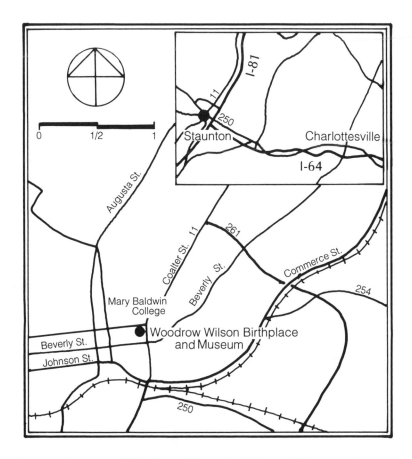

Figure 75. Location of Woodrow Wilson Birthplace and Museum, Staunton, Virginia.

which becomes Coalter Street. The Wilson home and museum are on the left (Figure 75).

PUBLIC USE: Season and hours: Daily 9 A.M.–5 P.M. January and February, Sunday 1 P.M.–5 P.M. Closed Thanksgiving, Christmas, New Year's Day. **Fees:** Adults, $6, with discounts for groups, students, and seniors. Allow 1 1/2 hours to enjoy the home and museum. **Gift shop. For people with disabilities:** Museum galleries and lower and first floors of Birthplace fully accessible.

FOR ADDITIONAL INFORMATION: Contact: Woodrow Wilson Birthplace and Museum, 1824 Coalter Street, Staunton, Virginia 24401, (703) 885–0897. **Read:** Katharine L. Brown. 1991. *The Woodrow Wilson Birthplace*, 2nd edition, revised. Staunton: Woodrow Wilson Birthplace Foundation, Inc.

201

Woodrow Wilson Boyhood Home
Augusta, Georgia

The Reverend Joseph R. Wilson accepted the pulpit of the First Presbyterian Church of Augusta in 1858 and moved into an old parsonage with his wife, two daughters, and infant son, "Tommy." Two years later the church purchased a new house in order to provide more suitable and spacious accommodations for its pastor. The Wilsons lived in the new manse at 7th and Telfair for ten years.

The house (Figure 76) was not fancy. It was an ordinary brick building of 2 1/2 stories, with a separate outside structure used both as kitchen and as servants' quarters. A rear porch extended the full width of the house, and a stable was located in the northwest corner of the lot.

Woodrow Wilson once recalled that his first conscious memory was of an event that took place when he was living in Augusta: while playing outside, he heard that Lincoln had been elected President and that there was to be a war. He ran inside to ask his father what the news meant.

Figure 76. Woodrow Wilson Boyhood Home, Augusta, Georgia. Photograph courtesy of Historic Augusta, Inc.

The Civil War began when Wilson was four years old and ended when he was nine, and it made an important impression on him. Augusta was a crossroads and a major urban center of 20,000 people. Although the city was never invaded, much war-related activity, including constant troop movement, took place there. A US arsenal, the Confederate Powderworks, and factories for cotton goods were located in Augusta. Joseph Wilson's church was used for a time as a stockade for federal prisoners. Later, like every other public building in the city, it was used as a hospital.

In later years, Wilson remembered many of these things, including the hardships — the scarcity of food and other essentials. Surely these experiences influenced the undeveloped psyche of the person who was destined, many years later, to lead his nation through "the war to end all wars."

Joseph Wilson was called to Columbia, South Carolina, in 1870, and a new pastor moved into the Augusta manse. Changes and renovations were effected over the years — installation of water closets, overhaul of decayed woodwork, painting, the addition of mantels to the dining and living rooms, and significant repairs following a tornado in 1911. The house was sold by the church to a private party and changed hands several times. In 1979, the home was listed on the National Register of Historic Places, but its condition declined until 1991, when it was bought at auction by Historic Augusta, Inc., a non-profit organization whose mandate is to preserve historically and architecturally significant sites and structures in Augusta. Renovation of the house is under way; the home is open only to groups by advance reservation.

DIRECTIONS: Augusta is 150 miles east of Atlanta, Georgia, just off I–20. Exit at Washington Road and proceed east. (Washington Road becomes Calhoun Expressway, then Green Street.) Turn right on 7th Street; the house is at the end of the block on the right, 419 7th Street (Figure 77).

PUBLIC USE: Season and hours: Open by appointment only. **Fees:** Adults, $2, with discounts for students and seniors. Allow 45 minutes to enjoy the home. **For people with disabilities:** No special facilities.

FOR ADDITIONAL INFORMATION: Contact: Woodrow Wilson Boyhood Home, Historic Augusta, 111 10th Street, PO Box 37, Augusta, Georgia 30903, (706) 724–0436. Read: August Heckscher. 1991. *Woodrow Wilson.* New York: Maxwell Macmillan International.

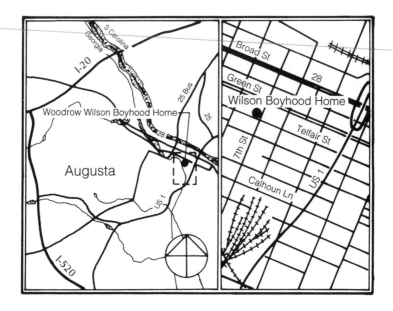

Figure 77. Location of the Woodrow Wilson Boyhood Home, Augusta, Georgia.

Woodrow Wilson Boyhood Home
Columbia, South Carolina

"Tommy" Wilson spent three important teenage years in Columbia — a southern town occupied by federal troops — a town attempting to rebuild after the conflagration of war — a town trying to survive the trauma of Reconstruction.

Wilson's father was Professor of Theology at the Columbia Theological Seminary and served as pastor of the First Presbyterian Church. Neither post provided housing. Being financially able, the Wilsons built a house, the first they had ever owned. The building is conservative — reflecting the lifestyle of the owners and the era in which they lived — with bay windows, arched doorways, iron mantels painted to resemble marble, and gas lighting.

The house (Figure 78) was saved from demolition in 1928 by a state-wide fund-raising drive conducted by the American Legion.

Figure 78. The Woodrow Wilson Boyhood Home, Columbia, South Carolina. Photograph courtesy of Historic Columbia Foundation.

It was open to the public for many years, but again fell into decline until its most recent rescue by the Historic Columbia Foundation. Under the Foundation's direction, the Wilson house has been restored to the spirit of the 1870s — the clapboard siding repainted and the interior restored, according to the curator, "to the flair the Wilsons and their contemporaries loved. Sentimental clutter mingles in the rooms with trademarks of the age: the antimacassar, the lambrequin, the ottoman." The house also contains the bed in which Wilson was born in Staunton, as well as his mother's four-volume set of the Bible, a gift from her husband. The pretty little front garden is graced by a large tea olive tree and several magnolias planted by Mrs. Wilson.

During their stay in Columbia, Woodrow joined his father's church, and he often remarked on his affection for South Carolina. It was apparent that the faith he accepted and the political and human chaos he witnessed there contributed to his developing philosophy and his compassionate attitude.

DIRECTIONS: Columbia, South Carolina's capital, is served by two major highways. From I–26, exit to US Route 126 and continue into Columbia, where Route 126 becomes Elmwood Avenue. At the end of Elmwood, turn right on Bull Street and proceed 4 blocks to Blanding Street. Go left on Blanding to Henderson Street. Go right on Henderson and continue 1/2 block to the parking area for four historic homes, including the Wilson house. From I–20, take the exit marked "277" to Columbia. State Route 277 becomes Bull Street. From there follow the above directions to the parking area, where specific directions to the Visitor Center are posted (Figure 79).

PUBLIC USE: Season and hours: Tuesday-Saturday 10 A.M.– 3:15 P.M., Sunday 1 P.M.– 4:15 P.M. Guided tours are conducted at quarter past each hour. Closed mid-December to January 2 and on major holidays. **Fees:** The Wilson Boyhood Home is one of four historic houses within a five-block area. The Visitor Center for all four facilities is located in the Robert Mills House, where individual home tickets costing $3, or combination tickets costing $10, may be purchased. Discounts for groups, AAA members, and students are available. Allow 45 minutes to enjoy the Wilson Home. **Gift shop. For people with disabilities:** There is a ramp to the first floor of the Wilson house. The upper floor is not accessible.

FOR ADDITIONAL INFORMATION: Contact: Robert Mills House, 1616 Blanding Street, Columbia, South Carolina 29201, (803) 252–1770.

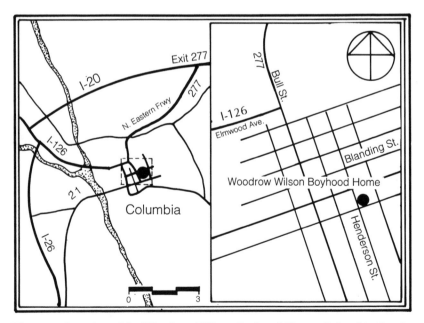

Figure 79. Location of the Woodrow Wilson Boyhood Home, Columbia, South Carolina.

Woodrow Wilson House Museum
Washington, DC

Woodrow Wilson moved from the White House to a handsome, four-story red brick townhouse (Plate 25) in an exclusive Washington neighborhood. There he passed away in 1924. His widow, Edith Bolling Wilson, remained in the house until 1961 and carefully preserved its furnishings and ambiance. Upon her death the house was bequeathed to the National Trust for Historic Preservation, which converted it to a house museum, dedicated to the life and career of one of America's greatest leaders and its first great internationalist.

Each room, from the fully-stocked kitchen to the cheery solarium overlooking a formal walled garden, reflects the variety of Wilson's life and the honesty and simplicity of his values. Large and light, the rooms are rich with souvenirs, gifts, and other possessions that highlight Wilson's career as professor, administrator, governor, President, and international statesman. Visitors are intrigued by the collection of Presidential memorabilia: his inaugural Bible, his typewriter, a framed mosaic presented by the pope, and many others. They are moved by the closet where his clothes still hang, the bed in which the invalid former President spent so much time, and the fully equipped nurse's room. In this house one gains an intimate understanding of how difficult Wilson's last months were, both on him and on those who loved and cared for him.

Yet the house is not unhappy. It is pleasant, cheerful, and friendly, testimony to the indomitable spirit of the man who led his nation through a great world war and into the modern era of international responsibility.

DIRECTIONS: From downtown Washington, DC, take the Metro Red Line subway to Dupont Circle and use the Q Street exit. Proceed northwest on Massachusetts Avenue for 7 blocks to S Street. Turn right up a hill to #2340 (Figure 15).

PUBLIC USE: Season and hours: January-December, Tuesday-Sunday, 10 A.M.– 4 P.M. Closed Thanksgiving, Christmas, New Year's Day. **Fees:** Adults, $4, with discounts for groups, students, and seniors. Groups are urged to make advance reservations. Guided tours take about 45 minutes and begin with a short orientation film. **For people with disabilities:** First floor fully accessible. A small elevator can accommodate some disabled visitors, but those requiring assistance are requested to call ahead.

EDUCATIONAL FACILITIES: A series of four educational programs for elementary and secondary school students are available through the school year. Tours deal with specific aspects of Wilson's Presidency or private life. Educators are encouraged to call the house for further information.

FOR ADDITIONAL INFORMATION: Contact: Woodrow Wilson House, 2340 S Street, NW, Washington, DC 20008, (202) 387–4062. **Read:** Henry Bragdon. 1967. *Woodrow Wilson: The Academic Years.* Cambridge: Belknap Press of Harvard University Press.

Warren Gamaliel Harding

Twenty-ninth President
1921 – 1923

Born November 2, 1865, Corsica (Blooming Grove), Ohio
Died August 2, 1923, San Francisco, California

Government is not of super-men, but of normal men, very much like you and me.

— Warren G. Harding

Here was a man whose soul was seared by a great disillusion-ment. We saw him gradually weaken, not only from physical exhaustion, but also from mental anxiety. Warren Harding had a dim realization that he had been betrayed by a few of the men whom he believed were his devoted friends. That was the tragedy of Warren Harding.

— Herbert Hoover at 1931 convocation
honoring Harding

Harding's tragedy was, of course, the nation's. Both were bruised and damaged by Teapot Dome, the greatest financial scandal in the country's history.

It has been said that any President, insulated as he is, is often the worst-informed man in Washington. Such may well have been the case with Harding, who was not a "hands-on" executive to begin with. In addition, at the time of Teapot Dome Harding was distracted by his wife's illness, as well as his own.

Harding's friendly, gregarious nature and trusting character brought fatal consequences. Yet his accomplishments were varied and contributed positively to post-World War I adjustments, as America entered a new era of world influence and cooperation.

President Harding's Home
Marion, Ohio

Warren Harding was born in the tiny hamlet of Corsica, now Blooming Grove, Ohio, and was reared and schooled in nearby Caledonia and at Ohio Central College in Iberia. His father was a country doctor and farmer who worked hard to support a family with eight children. The family eventually moved to the larger community of Marion where, still in his teens and with his father's financial help, Warren purchased the *Marion Star*. He remained editor and publisher of the *Marion Star* until he left Marion for the White House.

Harding was a gregarious booster, joiner, and back-slapper who drifted into local politics, never dreaming where his sunny personality and innate speaking ability would lead. There are some who would say that neither was the biggest influence on his career but that the greatest influence was his wife, Florence. She worked with Harding at the *Star* and unquestionably was an important factor in his life — personal, professional, and political.

Shortly after their marriage in 1891, the Hardings moved into a newly completed Victorian house (Plate 26) — their home until their deaths. The house was typically midwestern and contemporary and reflected the popular architecture and styling of the day: it was 2 1/2 stories, painted green with white trim, with pots of petunias and geraniums found seasonally on the rotunda porch. The house became famous as the site of Harding's famous "front-porch" campaign of 1920 when 600,000 people visited Marion to see and hear the candidate. It was a campaign similar to William McKinley's two decades earlier.

Mrs. Harding bequeathed the house and furnishings to the Harding Memorial Association, and four rooms were opened to the public in 1926. In 1965 the Association embarked on a total renovation, restoring the house to appear as it had at the time of Harding's residency. Ceiling light fixtures were replaced by the original gas fixtures, the Hardings' wallpaper was duplicated, and the furniture was returned to its original arrangement. Personal effects were left as they were found, and the house feels as if Warren Harding had just stepped out for a stroll, leaving his straw hat and cane in the hall.

In 1920, Harding built a small outbuilding in back of the house, to be used as headquarters by the National Press Corps covering the Presidential campaign. It has been converted into a Visitor Center, which includes a small museum. Just outside, in a neatly trimmed garden, is a sundial mounted on a marble base. Inscribed in the marble are words spoken by Warren Harding in 1916 and paraphrased by another President almost fifty years later:

> In this great fulfillment we must have a citizenship less concerned about what the government can do for it and more anxious about what it can do for the nation.

Ironic words from a President with a tarnished reputation and an administration that did not heed those words of wisdom.

President and Mrs. Harding are entombed under a monument of white marble situated in the center of ten acres of landscaped parkland about a mile from the house. It is a pleasing, inspiring, and peaceful place.

President Harding's home is currently owned and operated by the Ohio Historical Society.

DIRECTIONS: Marion is 50 miles north of Columbus, Ohio, just off US Route 23. Take the Ohio State Route 95 exit and proceed west on Route 95, which becomes Mount Vernon Avenue in Marion. Follow the historical markers to the Harding home (Figure 80).

PUBLIC USE: Season and hours: Memorial Day-Labor Day, Wednesday-Saturday 9:30 A.M.– 5 P.M., Sunday, Noon – 5 P.M. April, May, September, October, open for tours by appointment only. **Fees:** Adults, $2.50; discounts for groups, students, and seniors. Tours are guided. Allow 1 hour to enjoy the Harding home. **Gift shop. For people with disabilities:** There is partial accessibility to the first floor, but only with advance notice.

FOR ADDITIONAL INFORMATION: Contact: President Harding's Home, 380 Mount Vernon Avenue, Marion, Ohio, 43302 (614) 387–9630. **Read:** (1) Randolph Downes. 1970. *The Rise of Warren Gamaliel Harding, 1865–1920.* Ohio State University Press. (2) Robert K. Murray. 1969. *The Harding Era.* Minneapolis: University of Minnesota Press.

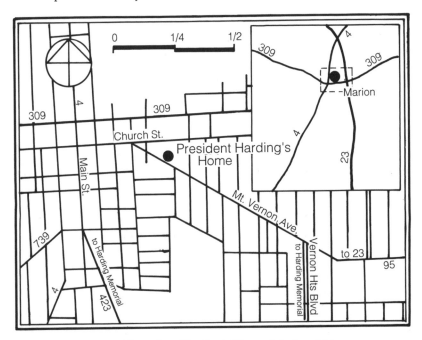

Figure 80. Location of President Harding's Home, Marion, Ohio.

John Calvin Coolidge

Thirtieth President
1923 – 1929

Born July 4, 1872, Plymouth Notch, Vermont
Died January 5, 1933, Northampton, Massachusetts

We draw our Presidents from the people. It is a wholesome thing for them to return to the people. I came from them. I wish to be one of them again.

— Calvin Coolidge

Before Calvin Coolidge was born, generations of Coolidges had lived and worked in tiny Plymouth Notch, population 432. Calvin's father was a farmer and the owner of a general store; he believed in the simple values of hard work, public service, and love of God and family. Calvin certainly learned those lessons well and carried them through his own career and into the White House.

He was known as "Silent Cal," a sobriquet that stereotyped him as ineffective and indecisive. More's the pity, for he was another of our vice presidents who rose to the occasion of the unexpected death of a President and fulfilled the high office with competence, diligence, and probity.

Coolidge had not been tarnished by the scandals of the Harding administration, and the country responded to his native honesty and taciturn personality, perhaps best exemplified by the often-told story of the Washington hostess who gushed at dinner that she had bet that she could get more than two words out of him, and Coolidge coolly replied, "You lose!"

Coolidge personified that which is good about his native Vermont, the "Green Mountain State": reticence and depth of thought, followed by careful action, are characteristic of its citizens, who live in the quietude of the deep and silent hills. The people of America appreciated those qualities as well, and Coolidge rode their best wishes, and a robust post-war economy, to his own election for a full term in 1924.

Plymouth Notch Historic District

Plymouth Notch, Vermont

It was here that I first saw the light of day. Here I received my bride; here my dead lie pillowed on the loving breast of our everlasting hills.

— Calvin Coolidge

Calvin Coolidge was the only President born on the fourth of July; the event took place in a tiny bedroom in the back of his father's general store. The house in which he grew up is across the street — the house made famous in 1923 when Vice President

214

Calvin Coolidge was sworn in as thirtieth President of the United States by his notary public father.

The Coolidge homestead remains as it was on that early morning in August, as does the hamlet of Plymouth Notch — a late-nineteenth/early-twentieth century rural village in a perfect state of preservation (Plate 27). Plymouth Notch has been called a "Yankee Brigadoon," unchanged for the last hundred years. In 1970, the entire community was recognized as important to our heritage and entered into the National Register of Historic Places. The State of Vermont, Division for Historic Preservation, made a strong commitment to preserve the original characteristics of the town and its lifestyle. The Plymouth Notch Historic District was formed, and the homes of Coolidge's family and neighbors, the community church, the one-room schoolhouse, and the general store are all preserved as they were in the early part of the century.

Calvin Coolidge left Plymouth and Vermont to seek his fortune in neighboring Massachusetts, where he worked as an attorney and became interested in politics. He served as mayor of Northampton, as state senator, as lieutenant governor, and as governor before entering the national political arena as Harding's vice president.

Coolidge may have left Vermont physically, but Plymouth Notch remained home in his heart. He returned to visit and vacation frequently and, in 1933, he returned for eternity. The President and Mrs. Coolidge lie in the village cemetery, along with six generations of family members. His grave is noble in its simplicity, Calvin Coolidge pillowed forever on the loving breast of the everlasting hills.

DIRECTIONS: Plymouth Notch is on Vermont State Route 100A, 6 miles south of US Route 4, midway across the state (Figure 81).

PUBLIC USE: Season and hours: Late May to mid-October, daily 9:30 A.M.– 5:30 P.M. **Fees:** Adults, $4, with discounts for registered groups of 15 or more. Children under 14, free. Allow 2 hours to enjoy Plymouth Notch. **Food service:** The Wilder House Restaurant is open for lunch. **Gift shops:** One in the Visitor Center, another in the General Store. **For people with disabilities:** The Visitor Center and restaurant are fully accessible. Portions of the village are accessible.

EDUCATIONAL FACILITIES: Teacher's packets are available, and school trips are welcome.

FOR ADDITIONAL INFORMATION: Contact: Plymouth Notch Historic District, Box 247, Plymouth, Vermont 05056, (802) 672–3773. **Read:** (1) Calvin Coolidge. 1929. *The Autobiography of Calvin Coolidge*. New York: Cosmopolitan Book Corporation. (Reprinted by the Calvin Coolidge Memorial Foundation, Plymouth, Vermont, 1989) (2) Donald R. McCoy. 1967. *Calvin Coolidge: The Quiet President*. New York. (Reprinted by University Press of Kansas, Lawrence, Kansas, 1988.) (3) Ishbel Ross. 1962. *Grace Coolidge and Her Era*. New York. (Reprinted by the Calvin Coolidge Memorial Foundation, Plymouth, Vermont.) (4) Jane Curtis, Will Curtis, and Frank Lieberman. 1985. *Return To These Hills: Calvin Coolidge in Vermont*. Woodstock: Lieberman Books.

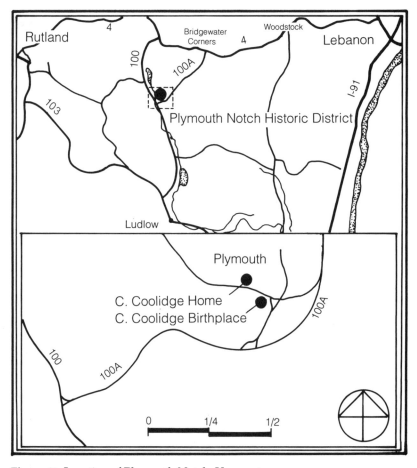

Figure 81. Location of Plymouth Notch, Vermont.

Herbert Clark Hoover

Thirty-first President
1929 – 1933

Born August 10, 1874, West Branch, Iowa
Died October 20, 1964, New York, New York

But I prefer to think of Iowa as I saw it through the eyes of a ten year-old boy . . . and the eyes of all ten year-old Iowa boys are or should be filled with the wonders of Iowa's streams and woods, of the mystery of growing crops. His days should be filled with adventure and great undertakings, with participation in good and comforting things.

— Herbert Hoover

"Bert" Hoover, the son of a blacksmith, was born in the tiny Quaker village of West Branch, Iowa; he was the first President born west of the Mississippi. Quakers live by the principles of hard work, honesty, and responsibility to the less fortunate, and Herbert Hoover grew to exemplify those characteristics.

Herbert's father died when the boy was six, and his mother passed away three years later. When he was eleven he was sent to live in Newberg, Oregon, with his Uncle Henry and Aunt Laura Minthorn, who had recently lost a son.

At age 15 he began working for the Oregon Land Company in Salem, Oregon, and later worked his way through Stanford University, joining its first graduating class, the class of 1895. Degree in hand, he launched an industrial and business career that sent him around the globe on various mining ventures. America's entry into World War I found him in London, where the American ambassador pressed him into service to assist thousands of stranded Americans in returning home. That task completed, he was asked to coordinate European relief efforts, a job so well conducted that he was appointed to post-war duty as Director General of Post War Relief and Rehabilitation. The monumental effort saved hundreds of thousands of lives and became the model for World War II's Marshall Plan.

Hoover returned to the United States in 1921, to be named Secretary of Commerce by President Harding. He was retained in that job by President Coolidge, and when Coolidge declined to run for reelection in 1928, the Republicans nominated Herbert Hoover as their candidate for President.

Hoover's successful business and political career, as well as his positive contributions to the nation and to the world, will always be overshadowed by the fact that he was President at the time of the 1929 stock market crash, the beginning of the Great Depression. He was, however, a unique and talented man. He lived another thirty-one years, made productive by his service on many important governmental commissions and by his prolific writing — he was the author of forty books. He provided valuable advice to those who followed him into the White House.

Herbert Hoover National Historic Site
West Branch, Iowa

The Herbert Hoover National Historic Site comprises almost two hundred acres and is divided into three distinct areas. A modern Visitor Center opens to the restored portion of mid-nineteenth century West Branch, which includes Hoover's birthplace cottage, the first schoolhouse in West Branch, the Quaker meeting-house, and a blacksmith shop similar to Hoover's father's (Plate 28).

The birthplace cottage is a tiny frame house, fourteen by twenty feet, built by Jesse Hoover in 1871. It consists of a single bedroom and a kitchen/living room flanking a central chimney. The bedroom contains a rope bed with feather ticking and a trundle bed that was pulled from beneath for the children. When it was cold, the living room served as a kitchen, with the stove used for both cooking and heating. In warmer weather the stove was moved to the back porch summer kitchen.

The Hoover Presidential Library is one of nine administered by the National Archives. The library is archival, serving as a research center for scholars and historians interested in Hoover's role in the history of the United States. The museum, containing exhibits, displays, memorabilia, documents, and photographs, covers Hoover's ninety years of life and his decades of service to the public welfare. Most visitors are charmed by the reproduction of his retirement office in New York's Waldorf Towers, amused by an exhibit of Roaring 20s souvenirs, and moved by a display chronicling Hoover's monumental work in feeding Europe after World War I, an effort that earned him the sobriquet, "The Great Humanitarian."

The memorial site, where the graves of President and Mrs. Hoover are marked by simple marble slabs, is a grassy knoll overlooking the village of West Branch.

DIRECTIONS: West Branch is 10 miles east of Iowa City, Iowa, just off I–80. From either direction, take Exit 254 and follow the historical markers 1/2 mile north to the Visitor Center (Figure 82).

PUBLIC USE: Season and hours: Daily 9 A.M.– 5 P.M. Closed Thanksgiving, Christmas, New Year's Day. Library hours may vary. **Fees:** Adults $2, with discounts for seniors and golden eagle passports. No charge for those 15 and under, or for organized groups from recognized educational institutions. Allow 2 hours to enjoy the Hoover Historic Site. **Museum shop. For people with disabilities:** Fully accessible with the exception of the schoolhouse.

EDUCATIONAL FACILITIES: The Library-Museum and the Historic Site sponsor educational programs and activities for all ages.

FOR ADDITIONAL USE: Contact: Herbert Hoover National Historic Site, West Branch, Iowa 52358, (319) 643–2541 (Historic Site), (319) 643–5301 (Library-Museum). **Read:** Herbert Hoover. 1951–1952. *The Memoirs of Herbert Hoover*, 3 volumes. New York: The Macmillan Company.

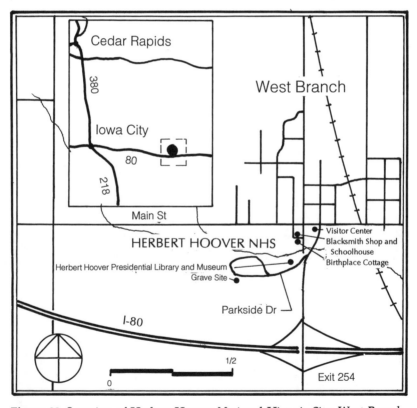

Figure 82. Location of Herbert Hoover National Historic Site, West Branch, Iowa.

Hoover-Minthorn House
Newberg, Oregon

After the untimely deaths of his parents, eleven-year-old Herbert Hoover moved to Oregon to live with his maternal uncle, Dr. Henry Minthorn, a physician and educator. The Minthorn House (Figure 83) was ordinary: a white two-story frame building with a big cellar that Hoover called "Aunt Laura's social security," filled as it was with preserved fruits, vegetables, jams, and jellies. The house had been constructed in 1881 by Jesse Edwards, the Quaker founder of Newberg. Dr. Minthorn purchased it in 1885 when he moved to town to become superintendent of the Friends Pacific Academy and to act as physician to the pioneer farming community. Mrs. Minthorn became principal of the grammar school. Hoover found himself surrounded by a community of people devoted to high principles, a living experience that augured well for the lifetime of service that lay ahead. Even today, a visit to the Minthorn house and a walk through the streets and quiet neighborhoods of small-town Newberg engender admiration for the solid Quaker values imbued in our nation's thirty-first President.

Figure 83. The Hoover–Minthorn House, Newberg, Oregon. Photograph courtesy of Hoover-Minthorn House.

The Minthorn house was purchased by the Herbert Hoover Foundation, friends and colleagues of President Hoover, in 1953. It was opened as a museum in 1955, on Hoover's eighty-first birthday. In 1982 the Foundation presented the home to the National Society of Colonial Dames of Oregon. Restoration efforts have accurately followed the room plans recalled by President Hoover. Most of the furnishings are of the period, although the furniture in Hoover's bedroom is the actual set he used as a boy.

DIRECTIONS: Newberg is 23 miles southwest of Portland, Oregon, on State Route 99W. When entering Newberg, watch for and use the left turn lane from Route 99W to South River Street. The Hoover-Minthorn House is 1 block south (Figure 84).

PUBLIC USE: Season and hours: March-November, Wednesday-Sunday 1 P.M.– 4 P.M. December and February, Saturday and Sunday 1 P.M.– 4 P.M. Closed in January. Fees: Adults, $1.50, with discounts for groups, students, and seniors. Allow 45 minutes to enjoy the home. **Picnic area. For people with disabilities:** No special facilities.

FOR ADDITIONAL INFORMATION: Contact: Hoover-Minthorn House, 115 South River Street, Newberg, Oregon 97132, (503) 538–6629.

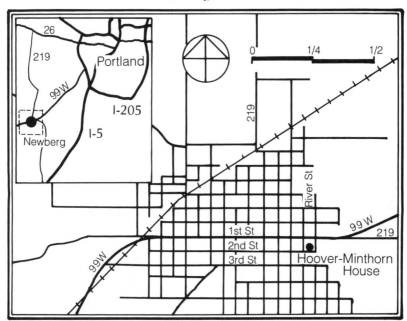

Figure 84. Location of Hoover-Minthorn House, Newberg, Oregon.

Franklin Delano Roosevelt

Thirty-second President
1933 – 1945

Born January 30, 1882, Hyde Park, New York
Died April 12, 1945, Warm Springs, Georgia

The only limit to our realization of tomorrow will be our doubts of today. Let us move forward with strong and active faith.

— Roosevelt's last written words

On March 4, 1933, Franklin Delano Roosevelt was sworn in as the thirty-second President of the United States. The country was in desperate financial straits. Millions of citizens were unemployed; banks were either failing or foreclosing on family homes and farms. The future was uncertain.

The nation had wisely chosen the right man for the hard times. Roosevelt's strong and confident voice rallied the country with words of hope tempered with a dose of common sense and sacrifice:

> let me assert my firm belief that the only thing we have to fear is fear itself . . . terror which paralyzes needed efforts to convert retreat into advances . . . .

The people responded as Roosevelt, by personal and moral persuasion, increased the power of the Presidency — using it, but not abusing it, for the well-being of all citizens.

Roosevelt, like a few other modern Presidents, was akin to our first Presidents, those Virginia aristocrats with private education and an inner mandate to serve and protect their fellows. Roosevelt, too, was born to the gentry. He was educated abroad and by tutor at home and matriculated at Groton. Although Roosevelt wished to go to Annapolis, he attended Harvard's law school at his father's urging, but he did not receive his degree. He did receive a law degree from Columbia University and was admitted to the bar in 1902, but he was a less-than-avid attorney, interested more in politics than in practicing law. He enjoyed an almost casual career in both elected and appointive offices until 1921, when he was stricken with infantile paralysis. He used a wheelchair for the rest of his life. Somehow galvanized by the adversity, Roosevelt willed himself to greater efforts and accomplishments. Martin Tupper's words challenged him:

> Never give up . . . if adversity presses,
> Providence wisely has mingled the cup,
> And the best counsel in all your distresses,
> Is the stout watchword of "Never Give Up!"

Roosevelt's greatest success lay ahead, in his roles as governor of New York and as President. To Americans everywhere he was a modern George Washington — beloved in war and peace, content in the love and approbation of his countrymen.

Franklin D. Roosevelt National Historic Site
Hyde Park, New York

This is the house in which my husband was born and brought up. . . . He always felt that this was his home, and he loved the house and the view, the woods, special trees . . . .
— Eleanor Roosevelt

Franklin Roosevelt was born in 1882 in a seventeen-room clapboard house (Figure 85) built between 1800 and 1826. The house was called "Brierstone" when his father purchased it in 1867; the name was changed later to Springwood. Roosevelt spent much of his life at Springwood — now recognized familiarly by the name of Hyde Park, the town in which it is situated. Here Roosevelt was shaped into a man; here he brought his bride; here he recuperated from the psychological, physical, and emotional trauma of infantile paralysis.

In 1914, with an eye to the future, Roosevelt initiated extensive alterations and renovations at Springwood. A small tower was removed to make room for a complete third floor of bedrooms,

Figure 85. Entrance to Franklin D. Roosevelt National Historic Site, Hyde Park, New York. Photograph courtesy of New York State Department of Economic Development.

nurseries, and maid's quarters. The clapboard siding was stuccoed, two native blue-stone wings were added, and the exterior blossomed with a classic columned portico. The renovations were completed in 1915.

The heavy Victorian decor of the interior remained unchanged, although seven more bathrooms were installed, and the addition of a paneled living room and library lent a dignity to the house that it had not enjoyed previously. The library features Roosevelt's governor's chair and his beloved books, as well as two massive fireplaces and a Gilbert Stuart portrait of Roosevelt's great-great-grandfather. The library opens to a screened porch overlooking the lawn and a dramatic view of the Hudson Valley. It is a scene that makes visitors reflect, as did Frances Perkins in her book, *The Roosevelt I Knew:*

> *He particularly admired the beautiful view, as did everyone. . . . Roosevelt looking off down the river at the view he admired, with a book, often unopened, in one hand, and a walking stick in the other; dogs playing nearby, and the children romping a little further down the lawn. The scene was like a Currier and Ives print of Life along the Hudson.*

Until 1939, Presidential papers were considered private property to be retained by the President after leaving office — sometimes saved, but often lost forever. Franklin Roosevelt, ever cognizant of his place in history, arranged to perpetuate it by building the Franklin D. Roosevelt Library, using private funds, then turning it over to the National Archives. His action ensured that his records would become the property of the people, a decision honored by all subsequent Chief Executives.

The Roosevelt Library is a building of Dutchess County native blue fieldstone. A museum section was opened to the public in 1941; the library portion was opened to research scholars in 1946. The original arrangement of displays in the museum was personally supervised by the President. The exhibits provide an intimate glimpse into Roosevelt's life and the historical period that he dominated. Most visitors smile when they see Roosevelt's specially-equipped Ford roadster, which he loved to drive over the country roads around Hyde Park. His White House desk and many other artifacts are on display.

The Hyde Park estate — the Library, the Springwood mansion, and the spacious grounds — creates an atmosphere of relaxation and nostalgia. Guests contemplate Roosevelt's historical contributions in the museum — a truly evocative experience, culminated by viewing the exquisite Rose Garden, situated between the house and library. It is there that President and Mrs. Roosevelt lie at rest, their graves as simple as the President had specified: "a plain white monument — no carving or decoration . . . ." Simple they may be, but they are adorned forever with the love and respect of millions of Americans.

DIRECTIONS: The town of Hyde Park is on US Route 9, 5 miles north of Poughkeepsie, New York. Historical markers guide visitors to the National Historic Site (Figure 86).

PUBLIC USE: Season and hours: April 1-November 1, daily 9 A.M.– 5 P.M.; November 1-April 1, closed Tuesdays and Wednesdays. Closed Thanksgiving, Christmas, New Year's Day. The library, reserved for research, is open Monday-Friday 9 A.M.– 4:45 P.M. and is closed all holidays. **Fees:** Adults, $4; ages 16 and under, free; ages 62 and over, free. (For museum, 62 and over, $1.) Guided tours of the home of FDR are available from November to April. From April to October 30, tours are self-guided. Groups over 10 must make reservations. Allow 2 hours to enjoy the Roosevelt National Historic Site.

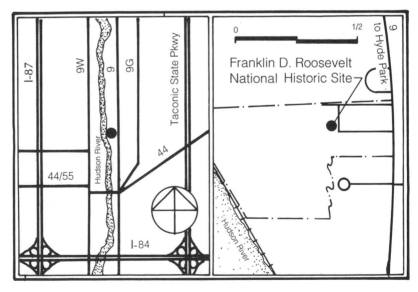

Figure 86. Location of Franklin D. Roosevelt National Historic Site, Hyde Park, New York.

Museum shop: Run by the Roosevelt-Vanderbilt Historical Association in the garage stable behind the home. **Gift shop:** run by the National Archives in the basement of the Library. **For people with disabilities:** The first floor of the home is accessible; the second floor is not. An album of second-floor photographs is available by request. The museum is fully accessible.

FOR ADDITIONAL INFORMATION: Contact: FDR National Historic Site, 529 Albany Post Road, Hyde Park, New York 12538, (914) 229–9115 (Home of FDR), (914) 229–8114 (Museum). **Read:** (1) *Eleanor Roosevelt. Franklin D. Roosevelt and Hyde Park.* (A handbook, available through Hyde Park Historical Association.) Washington, DC: US Government Printing Office. (2) Franklin D. Mares and Richard Cheek. 1993. *Springwood.* Hyde Park: Hyde Park Historical Association.(3) Geoffrey C. Ward. 1985. *Before the Trumpet.* New York: Harper and Row.

Roosevelt Campobello International Park
New Brunswick, Canada

It is most fitting that the memory of so gallant and illustrious an American should be so honored on the Canadian Island which he loved.
— England's Queen Mother, at dedication, 1967

Campobello Island, lying off the coast of Maine, was purchased by a group of American investors in the late nineteenth century and promoted as a summer resort for the wealthy. Franklin Roosevelt's father bought four acres and a partially built house in 1883 and completed the house in 1885. The family enjoyed summers of sailing, hiking, swimming, and picnicking at Campobello (Plate 29).

In 1910, Roosevelt's mother purchased a Dutch Colonial cottage nearby and presented it to Franklin and Eleanor as a wedding gift. The young Roosevelts and their active children visited the island regularly to enjoy its isolation, bracing climate, and relaxing atmosphere. It was at Campobello in 1921, after a cold swim, that Franklin Roosevelt was stricken with infantile paralysis — polio.

The Roosevelt Campobello International Park was established in 1964 by agreement between the governments of the United States and Canada; it was opened officially in 1967. The Roosevelt cottage is maintained as it was during the President's final visit in 1933. The rooms are furnished with original Roosevelt possessions and reminders of the vigorous personality who vacationed there: a family telescope, Franklin Junior's crib, the large frame chair used to carry the disabled President, even a megaphone used to hail boats — or to call children to dinner.

The park itself contains landscaped gardens of the Roosevelt era. Manicured paths lead to woods, fields, and glorious views of the islands and shores of Passamaquoddy and Cobscook bays in Canada and Maine.

DIRECTIONS: Take US Route 1 north to Maine Route 189, which crosses the Roosevelt Memorial Bridge at Lubec, Maine, and becomes Canadian Route 774. The park is 1 1/2 miles past Canadian Customs (Figure 87).

PUBLIC USE: Season and hours: From Memorial Day, for 20 consecutive weeks, daily 9 A.M.– 5 P.M. **Fees:** None. Allow 1 hour to enjoy the Roosevelt Cottage. **Picnic areas. For people with disabilities:** The first floor of the cottage is accessible, with a filmed presentation of the second floor.

FOR ADDITIONAL INFORMATION: Contact: Roosevelt Campobello Park Commission, Box 97, Lubec, Maine 04652, (506) 752–2922. **Read:** (1) "At Home on Campobello Island." *Country Living.* May 1991, 92–97. (2) "Historic Houses: Campobello." *Architectural Digest.* March 1985, 220–228. (3) Roosevelt Campobello International Park Commission Annual Report. Lubec, Maine.

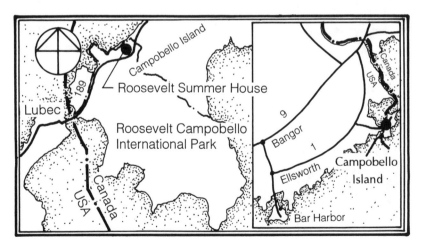

Figure 87. Location of Roosevelt Campobello International Park, Campobello Island, New Brunswick.

FDR's Little White House
Warm Springs, Georgia

Franklin Roosevelt, searching for relief from the debilitating physical effects of polio, first traveled to Warm Springs in 1924. Delighted with the rejuvenating waters and relaxing atmosphere, he returned to Warm Springs again and again, eventually building his own six-room bungalow situated among whispering Georgia pines and surrounded by azaleas, dogwood, and mountain laurel (Figure 88).

The bucolic aura encouraged contemplation. Warm Springs was the crucible for ideas manifested in Roosevelt's activities as President, especially in those social programs affecting the weak, the poor, and the disenfranchised. It was his experience in Warm Springs and his interaction with other patients that inspired the organization of the March of Dimes, the premier charitable group devoted to stamping out polio.

The Warm Springs cottage reflected Roosevelt's desire and need for privacy, comfort and the restorative environment of Georgia. Ironically, it was on a visit to Warm Springs that he

Figure 88. FDR's Little White House, Warm Springs, Georgia. Photograph courtesy of the State of Georgia.

230

collapsed and died, while sitting for a portrait. As tribute, a decision was made to preserve the cottage as it was on the day of his death, and it remains so, Elizabeth Shoumatoff's unfinished portrait still on its easel.

Thousands of visitors flocked to Warm Springs following Roosevelt's death, and in January, 1946, the State of Georgia formed a special commission to administer the property. In order to make the site comfortable and more attractive for the public, the State built a Visitor Center and Museum, in which are displayed many of Roosevelt's treasures. Visits to Warm Springs begin at the Visitor Center with the screening of a twelve-minute film, *A Warm Springs Memoir of Franklin Delano Roosevelt*. Guests then proceed to the Little White House cottage along a path called "Stones and Flags of the States." All of the fifty states, as well as the District of Columbia, have contributed a specimen of native stone; the stones are embedded along the sides of the path, with each state's flag flying above its memorial.

DIRECTIONS: From Atlanta, Georgia, take I–85 south to the second Newnan exit (Exit 8) and proceed south on US Route 27A to Warm Springs. Follow the historical markers to the Little White House (Figure 89).

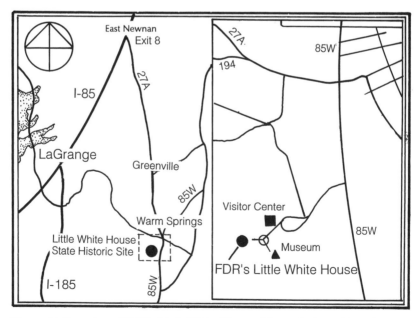

Figure 89. Location of FDR's Little White House, Warm Springs, Georgia.

PUBLIC USE: Season and hours: Daily 9 A.M.–5 P.M. The museum closes at 4:30 P.M. Site closed Thanksgiving, Christmas, New Year's Day. **Fees:** Adults, $4, with discounts for groups and students. Allow 1 1/2 hours to enjoy the Little White House. **Food service:** Snack bar. **Gift shop. For people with disabilities**: Fully accessible.

FOR ADDITIONAL INFORMATION: Contact: FDR's Little White House, Route 1, Box 10, Warm Springs, Georgia 31830, (706) 655–5870. **Read:** (1) Geoffrey C. Ward. 1989. *A First Class Temperament: The Emergence of Franklin Roosevelt.* New York: Harper & Row. (2) Hugh Gregory Gallagher. 1985. *FDR's Splendid Deception.* New York: Dodd, Meade, & Co. (3) Turnley Walker. 1953. *Roosevelt and the Warm Springs Story.* New York: A. A. Wyn.

Harry S. Truman

Thirty-third President
1945 – 1953

Born May 8, 1884, Lamar, Missouri
Died December 26, 1972, Kansas City, Missouri

I learned from [history] that a leader is a man who has the ability to get other people to do what they don't want to do, and like it.

— Harry S. Truman

Where does America find men who — in time of national trauma — step into the most difficult job in the world and perform with aplomb, intelligence, and force of character? Where does America find men like Harry Truman?

Truman was Franklin Roosevelt's third vice president. He inherited the Presidency when the country, deeply traumatized by Roosevelt's death, needed a man of strength, experience, and vision. The nation wondered — the whole world wondered — how an obscure, midwestern machine politician could successfully terminate World War II and prepare his country for difficult post-war adjustments at home and abroad.

Truman often said that he got his strength from the people, and perhaps that's so. It's more likely that he inherited common sense from his parents and learned the virtues of hard work and honesty in a hard Missouri boyhood. Faced with horrendous decisions as President — whether to drop the atomic bomb, how to face the Korean conflict, and how to approach the task of rebuilding Europe — this common man from the heartland of America handled them with courage and determination. He was a man of the people, who called him "Mr. Citizen," a nickname he loved and appreciated more than any worldly honor.

Harry S Truman Birthplace State Historic Site
Lamar, Missouri

On May 8, 1884, in the downstairs bedroom of a 1 1/2-story house in Lamar, Missouri, Mrs. Martha Ellen Truman gave birth to a healthy boy christened just plain "Harry." Truman later added the S, as he felt it appeared more dignified, and claimed it did not stand for any one name but was a compromise between the names of his grandfathers, Anderson Shipp Truman and Solomon Young. Truman, perhaps joking, once told newspaper reporters that there should not be a period after the S. There is still controversy over the use of the period, even though Truman used it himself on many existing documents.

John and Martha Truman purchased the small birth house and lot a year before Harry was born, for $685. The house had four

Figure 90. Harry S Truman Birthplace State Historic Site, Lamar, Missouri. Photograph by Rita Embry.

rooms downstairs and two upstairs; a smokehouse and a well stood outside (Figure 90). The Trumans lived in Lamar briefly; they finally settled in Independence in 1890.

The United Auto Workers of America purchased the birthplace house in 1957. They restored it, decorated it with furnishings from the time of the Truman occupancy, and turned it over to the State of Missouri. The house is now a State Historic Site maintained by the Missouri Department of Natural Resources, Division of Parks and Recreation. President Truman was present at the dedication of the house in 1959. In his speech he said:

> *They don't do this for a former President until he's been dead fifty years. I feel like I've been buried and dug up while I'm alive and I'm glad they've done it to me today.*

DIRECTIONS: Lamar is 100 miles south of Kansas City, Missouri, at the intersection of US Route 71 (north-south) and US Route 160. Proceed east on Route 160 to Truman Street; turn left on Truman and continue to the house (Figure 91).

PUBLIC USE: Season and hours: Monday-Saturday 10 A.M.– 4 P.M., Sunday Noon – 4 P.M. **Fees:** None. Allow 30 minutes to enjoy the Truman house. **Gift shop. For people with disabilities:** No special facilities.

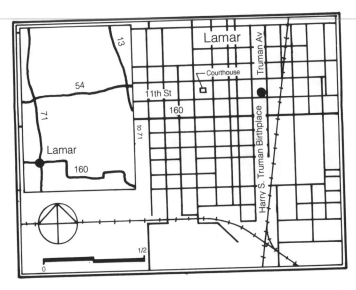

Figure 91. Location of Harry S Truman Birthplace State Historic Site, Lamar, Missouri.

FOR ADDITIONAL INFORMATION: Contact: Harry S Truman Birthplace, 1009 Truman Avenue, Lamar, Missouri 64759 (417) 682–2279. **Read:** Harry S. Truman. 1960. *Mr. Citizen.* New York: Bernard Geis Associates.

Truman Farm Home

Grandview, Missouri

Shortly after Harry Truman's birth, the Trumans moved to Independence, where they lived in a succession of houses as their fortunes ebbed and flowed. They were living on Waldo Street at the time Harry graduated from high school, with hopes of going on to college. It was not to be, as his father made a disastrous investment in grain futures that wiped out the family's savings, as well as Harry's dream of college. His parents were forced to move to Grandfather Young's farm in Grandview while Harry remained in Independence, where he accepted a series of jobs — bank clerk, theater usher, piano player — until his father asked him to help manage the farm.

Truman lived and worked on the farm in Grandview (Plate 30) for ten years preceding his World War I service; he later described the experience as "the best years of my life." His days were filled with hard physical activity, his nights with public life as a soldier, Mason, postmaster, and school board member — a life of hard work and service that established a pattern for his future political career. Somehow in his busy agenda he found time to travel to Independence frequently to court and eventually win the heart of Bess Wallace — the future Mrs. Truman.

Harry Truman commanded an artillery battery in France during World War I and was mustered out of the army as a major. He did not return to Grandview, although the farmhouse and land remained in the Truman family until 1981, when it was purchased by the Truman Farm Home Foundation. They restored it as a tribute to the "grass roots boy" who had left Grandview as a simple farmer and gone on to become one of the world's most influential and beloved leaders. On May 8, 1994, the Truman Farm Home became part of the Harry S Truman National Historic Site, administered by the National Park Service.

The farmhouse is of the pre-World War I era: a two-story frame with six rooms and an outside well. It has been furnished with period furniture.

DIRECTIONS: Grandview is just south of Kansas City, Missouri. Take I-435 south to US Route 71, still proceeding south. Exit at Blue Ridge Boulevard; turn right and continue 1/2 mile to the farm, which is on the left, just past the Truman Corners Shopping Center (Figure 92).

PUBLIC USE: Season and hours: May through August, Friday, Saturday and Sunday, 9 A.M.– 4 P.M. **Fees:** None. Allow 30 minutes to enjoy the Truman farm. **For people with disabilities:** No special facilities.

FOR ADDITIONAL INFORMATION: Contact: Harry S Truman National Historic Site, 219 North Main Street, Independence, Missouri 64050, (816) 254–2720. **Read:** (1) Harry Truman and Merle Miller. 1973, 1974. *Plain Speaking.* New York: Berkley. (2) Robert H. Ferrell. 1991. *Harry S. Truman: His Life on the Family Farms.* Worland: High Plains Publishing Company.

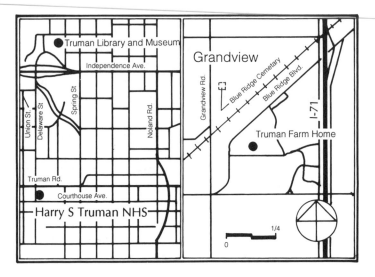

Figure 92. Location of Truman Farm Home, Grandview, Missouri, and Harry S Truman National Historic Site, Independence, Missouri.

Harry S Truman National Historic Site
Independence, Missouri

I always came back to Independence every chance I got because the people in Independence, the people in Missouri had been responsible for sending me to Washington. And that's why when I ended up in the White House, after I had finished the job, I came back here. This is where I belong.
— Harry S. Truman

Harry Truman not only belonged, he was Independence — representing the basic, good, and honest values nurtured in all of the small towns, neighborhoods, and farms of middle America.

The Truman home at 219 North Delaware Street (Figure 93) is the center of an historic district that has been described by Truman biographer Jonathan Daniels:

Figure 93. Harry S Truman National Historic Site, Independence, Missouri. Photograph courtesy of National Park Service.

> *Truman the man matches the sturdy Midwestern character of North Delaware Street and the neighborhood which, more than any other, suggests the life and career of the former Chief Executive.*

It was a neighborhood with a distinctive assortment of architectural styles, representing every decade since the mid-nineteenth century; a neighborhood where President Truman took his famous constitutionals; a neighborhood of solid citizens who were proud of but not intimidated by their famous neighbor.

Harry Truman married Bess Wallace in 1919. They returned from their honeymoon to live at 219 North Delaware with Bess' widowed mother. Except for their time in Washington, the house in Independence was the Truman home until Mrs. Truman's death in 1982.

The house is a fourteen-room Victorian, completed in 1885 by Mrs. Truman's grandparents. It has seven bedrooms, a high-ceilinged parlor, a music room, and a large dining room. The interior reflects prosperity — tiled fireplaces, heavy mahogany and walnut furniture, windows with colored glass borders, and a pleasant screened porch leading to a small, heavily-bordered rear yard and a two-car garage. The exterior is decorated with the exaggerated jigsaw trim typical of the late nineteenth century.

Harry Truman was not a man for change, and the house received minimal modernization over the years — central heating, electricity, telephone, and radio. Thus the house has remained, as one visitor remarked, "Harry Truman Comfortable," a home in the best sense — warm and charming — a true reflection of the people who lived within its walls. During Truman's Presidency, the house hosted world leaders, and afterwards it became a popular tourist attraction when the ex-President resided there. President Truman once said:

> *In all the years since I left the White House, I have wondered why so many people come from so far away and take so much trouble to look at the house where I live. Perhaps it's because once a man has been President he becomes an object of curiosity like those other notorious Missouri characters, Mark Twain and Jesse James.*

It is more likely that they came, and still come, in tribute to the humble little man who led the country with dignity and courage through days of peril and turmoil.

Mrs. Truman bequeathed the Truman home to the nation, and 219 North Delaware Street was declared a National Historic Site to be maintained by the National Park Service. A Visitor Center is located on Main Street, just five blocks away, where tickets are available for guided tours of the house. That is only one of many attractions in Independence associated with President Truman. Maps are available for those who wish to make a Truman neighborhood walking tour, and the Jackson County Courthouse is nearby, as is the Missouri-Pacific Railroad station where Truman's famous "whistle-stop" campaign of 1948 ended.

DIRECTIONS: From Kansas City, Missouri, take I–70 east to I–435; proceed north on I–435 to the Truman Road Exit. Proceed 3 miles on Truman Road to Main Street. The Visitor Center is on the corner, with adequate parking across the street. The home itself, at 219 North Delaware Street, is 5 blocks west of the Visitor Center (Figure 92, page 240).

PUBLIC USE: Season and hours: Visitor Center open daily 8:30 A.M.– 5 P.M. Tours of the home conducted daily from Memorial Day through Labor

Day. Closed Mondays during the rest of the year. Also closed Thanksgiving, Christmas and New Year's Day. The first tour leaves at 9 A.M.; after that tours leave every 15 minutes, in groups of 8. **Fees:** Adults, $2; 16 and under, free on first-come, first-served basis. Allow 1 hour to enjoy the site. **Gift shop:** At the Visitor Center. **For people with disabilities:** Accessible.

FOR ADDITIONAL INFORMATION: Contact: Harry S Truman National Historic Site, 219 North Main Street, Independence, Missouri 64050, (816) 254–9929.

Harry S. Truman Library and Museum
Independence, Missouri

The pride and joy of President Truman's retirement was the Harry S. Truman Library and Museum (Figure 94), which is administered by the National Archives and Records Administration. He spent many hours in its planning and retained an office there until his death. The building is noble in its simplicity, reflecting the sincerity and common sense of "a most uncommon man."

A retrospective in the museum covers Truman's remarkable career, from his school days in Independence to his congressional service, his Presidential ascendancy, and the monumental issues

Figure 94. The Harry S. Truman Library and Museum, Independence, Missouri. Photograph courtesy of National Park Service.

he dealt with as President: the Atom Bomb, the Korean conflict, the Marshall Plan, and the formation of the United Nations. There is a replication of the Oval Office as it appeared in the early 1950s; in addition, the museum gallery exhibits the table upon which the United Nations Charter was signed on June 26, 1945. Many state gifts are displayed, the most imposing being a massive dining room suite of carved Philippine ebony presented to President Truman by Philippine President Quirino.

A large picture window has been installed, enabling visitors to stand in the courtyard and look into President Truman's office, kept as it was at the time of his death. The courtyard holds the plain graves where Harry and Bess Truman rest peacefully in the soil of the town, the state, and the nation they loved and served with dedication.

> *The President — whoever he is — has to decide. He can't pass the buck to anyone. No one else can do the deciding for him. That's his job.*
>
> — Harry S. Truman

DIRECTIONS: From Kansas City, Missouri: Take I–70 east to I–435 north to US Highway 24 and the Winner Road exit. Proceed east 3 miles on US 24 to the Truman Library exit (Figure 92).

PUBLIC USE: Season and hours: The library portion consists of research materials, primarily archival holdings, which are available to historians and other scholars. The museum is open to the general public daily 9 A.M.– 5 P.M. Closed Thanksgiving, Christmas and New Year's Day. Tours of the museum are self-guided. **Fees:** $2 for each visitor over 15 years of age, except students in organized tour groups for whom application has been made in advance. Allow 2 hours to enjoy the Truman Museum. **Museum shop. For people with disabilities:** Fully accessible.

FOR ADDITIONAL INFORMATION: Contact: Harry S. Truman Library and Museum, US Highway 24 and Delaware Street, Independence, Missouri 64050, (816) 833–1400. **Read:** (1) David McCullough. 1992. *Truman.* New York: Simon and Schuster. (2) Jonathan Daniels. 1950. *The Man of Independence.* Philadelphia: J. B. Lippincott Company. (3) *Public Papers of the Presidents of the United States, Harry S. Truman, 1945–1953.* 8 volumes. 1961–1966. Washington, DC: US Government Printing Office. (4) Raymond H. Geselbracht, et al., comp. 1991. *Guide to Historical Materials in the Harry S. Truman Library.* Independence: Harry S. Truman Library.

Little White House Museum
Key West, Florida

Before Camp David, there was no official Presidential weekend or vacation retreat, and it was not unusual for the President to remain in the White House. There were no "flights to the ranch," as Johnson and Reagan made, nor "hops to the Cape," like those made by Kennedy, but only long trips by train, car, buggy, or horseback to isolated homes, farms, and plantations.

Harry S. Truman, however, was the only President to get away from it all at a naval base. In 1946, Truman was unable to shake a severe cold, and his physician ordered him to take a vacation in the sun. Admiral Chester W. Nimitz, Chief of Naval Operations, suggested the Commandant's home (Figure 95) at the submarine base in Key West, Florida, where the President would have the privacy, security, and sunshine he needed. Truman was so pleased with the arrangements that he returned to Key West ten times during his term for a total of 175 days. In 1949 he wrote home to his wife:

Figure 95. The Little White House Museum, Key West, Florida. Photograph by Oscar Thompson.

*Dear Bess, you should see the house! . . . the place is all
redecorated, new furniture and everything. I've a notion to
move the capital to Key West and just stay.*

It wasn't until the fifth visit, however, that he could persuade Mrs. Truman to join him. Daughter Margaret has said that Mrs. Truman felt that "it was a stag place and that he would have a better time beyond her critical eye." Mrs. Truman enjoyed her infrequent visits, but her point was well taken. The President and his cronies, lubricated with bourbon and branch water, relaxed with nightly poker sessions.

The submarine base closed in 1974, and the property was sold in 1986 to a real estate investor, who transferred the Little White House title to the State of Florida. Careful study of naval records and of the 1949 redecoration plans enabled restorers to replicate the look that the house had during the time that Truman worked and played there. Most of the furniture is original, including the famous poker table with the mahogany top that hid evidence of cards and poker chips from the press and public during the day.

The Little White House Museum presents the public with an opportunity to discover a personal side of Harry Truman and to understand how his no-nonsense personality was balanced by his ability to relax and shake off the tremendous pressure of high office away from Washington.

DIRECTIONS: Key West, Florida, is the southern terminus of US Route 1, 150 miles south of Miami. Follow Route 1 to Whitehead Street; turn right and proceed several blocks to Caroline Street. Walk 1 block through the Presidential Gates to the Little White House Museum (Figure 96).

PUBLIC USE: Season and hours: Daily 9 A.M.– 5 P.M. **Fees:** Adults, $6, with discounts for groups and students. Allow 1 hour to enjoy the museum. **Gift shop. For people with disabilities:** First floor fully accessible.

FOR ADDITIONAL INFORMATION: Contact: The Little White House Museum, 111 Front Street, Key West, Florida 33040, (305) 294–9911. **Read:** (1) Arva Moore Parks. 1991. *Harry Truman and the Little White House in Key West.* Miami: Centennial Press. (2) Margaret Truman. 1972. *Harry S. Truman.* New York: William Morrow and Company. (3) Wright Langley and Sharon Wells. n.d. *A Study for the Preservation and Interpretation of Presidents: Harry Truman's Little White House.* Key West: Florida Keys Preservation Board.

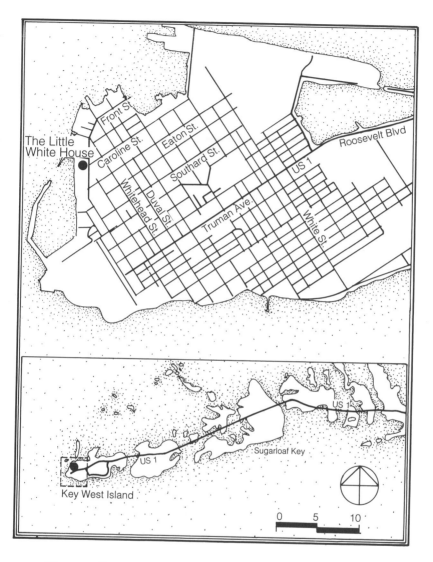

Figure 96. Location of The Little White House, Key West, Florida.

Dwight David Eisenhower

Thirty-fourth President
1953 – 1961

Born October 14, 1890, Denison, Texas
Died March 28, 1969, Washington, DC

*The mission of this Allied Force was fulfilled at 0241, local
time, May 7, 1945.*
— Eisenhower, first report noting the end
of World War II in Europe.

Dwight David Eisenhower, like Truman, came from the great American middle west. Like Truman, he was reared by strong parents who had to struggle but who never lost sight of the homely values of hard work and honesty tempered by faith in God. Eisenhower once remarked:

> *I have found out in later years we were very poor, but the glory of America is that we didn't know it then. . . . if each of us in his own mind would dwell more upon those simple virtues — integrity, courage, self-confidence and unshakable belief in his Bible — would not some of [our] problems tend to simplify themselves?*

Eisenhower's decision to attend West Point was based on the family's economic situation as much as his own youthful exuberance and combative nature. Through his army career he was assigned to a number of posts, including a stint as Douglas MacArthur's aide in the Philippines. At the beginning of World War II, when he was a staff colonel in Texas, his organizational skill caught the eye of General George C. Marshall, the Army Chief of Staff. Marshall picked Eisenhower to lead the Allied invasion of North Africa. Eisenhower's notable success led to his promotion to the position of Supreme Allied Commander for the Allied invasion of Europe and the subsequent defeat of the Axis powers.

He returned to the United States in triumph and served a term as Army Chief of Staff before resigning to accept the presidency of Columbia University. However, the nation again called for his military and diplomatic skills when President Truman appointed him Commander of NATO forces in Europe. While he was fulfilling that commitment the Republican party nominated him for President, and he returned to campaign and then defeat Adlai E. Stevenson in the 1952 general election.

Eisenhower had much in common with Ulysses S. Grant: they were the only West Point graduates to achieve the Presidency; they were both commanders of victorious armies; neither had political experience before being nominated for President. The similarities end there. Unlike Grant, Eisenhower used his military command skills effectively as President and prevented the rampant fraud that was endemic in Grant's administration.

Eisenhower Birthplace State Historic Park
Denison, Texas

I am the most intensely religious man I know. Nobody goes through six years of war without faith.
— Dwight D. Eisenhower

When Dwight Eisenhower entered West Point he put down Tyler, Texas, as his birthplace. Fifty years later, at the height of his military fame, an elderly schoolteacher in Denison, Texas, recalled an Eisenhower family and a baby boy she'd rocked to sleep in 1890. A phone call to General Eisenhower's mother confirmed that Dwight had indeed been born in Denison, where his father had come to work with the railroad.

After World War II, a group of Denison citizens formed the Eisenhower Birthplace Foundation, which purchased the old house at the corner of Lamar and Day (Figure 97). It was renovated, and the city converted the entire block around the house into a restful city park. A bedroom quilt is the sole remaining Eisenhower possession on display, but the house is furnished in the style of the

Figure 97. Eisenhower Birthplace State Historic Park, Denison, Texas. Photograph courtesy of Eisenhower Birthplace State Historic Park.

1890s, the period when "Ike" was born. One of the rooms has been converted to an exhibit area featuring newsreel footage of President Eisenhower's military and political career.

The Foundation dissolved in 1958 and turned the property over to the Texas Parks and Wildlife Department, which is responsible for its long-term maintenance. Daily administration has been handled by Texas Rural Communities, Inc. since February, 1993. The site has been expanded to include a new Visitor Center, which features a gift shop, a video room, and artifacts from the 1940s, 1950s, and 1960s. A hiking trail, the Red Store Conference Center, and the old railroad station — Eisenhower's father worked for the railroad — have been opened. Further expansion of the site is in the developmental stages and includes refurbishing two turn-of-the-century buildings.

DIRECTIONS: Denison is 75 miles north of Dallas, Texas, on US Route 75 where it intersects with US Route 69. Follow the historical markers to the Eisenhower birthplace (Figure 98).

PUBLIC USE: Season and hours: Daily 9 A.M.– 5 P.M. Closed major holidays. **Fees:** Adults, $2; children 612, $1; under 6, free. Tours of the house are guided. Bus tours are welcome; reservations can be made but are not required. Allow 1 hour to enjoy the Eisenhower house. **Gift shop. For people with disabilities:** No special facilities.

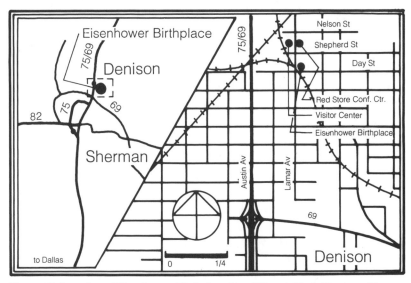

Figure 98. Location of Eisenhower Birthplace State Historic Park, Denison, Texas.

FOR ADDITIONAL INFORMATION: Contact: Eisenhower Birthplace State Historic Park, 208 East Day Street, Denison, Texas 75020, (903) 465–8908. **Read:** (1) Kenneth S. Davis. 1945. *Soldier of Democracy: A Biography of Dwight Eisenhower.* Garden City, New York: Doubleday & Co.(2) Laura Black. "Texas Remembers Ike." *Texas Highway Magazine.* October 1990, 16. (3) Sherrie S. MacLeRoy "Ike's Birthplace: Our 34th President Came from Humble Beginnings." *Texas Parks and Wildlife Magazine.* January 1989, 34–37.

The Eisenhower Center

Abilene, Kansas

The proudest thing I can claim is that I am from Abilene . . . through this world it has been my fortune or misfortune to wander at considerable distance. Never has this town been outside my heart or my memory.

— Dwight D. Eisenhower

General of the Army, President of the United States, world leader, and graduate of Abilene High School, class of 1909. Abilene will never let the memory of Dwight Eisenhower fade, proud as it is of its most famous son. To perpetuate his memory, Abilene, in association with the Eisenhower Foundation, initiated and built a magnificent tribute, The Eisenhower Center (Plate 31). The Center is a five-building complex surrounding a handsome downtown park.

A visit to The Eisenhower Center starts at the Visitor Center with screening of a film that reviews the life of President Eisenhower. A self-guided tour continues at the adjacent museum, which was dedicated on Veterans Day, 1954. Five major galleries within the museum contain items associated with Eisenhower's history, including childhood artifacts, high school memorabilia, military souvenirs, and Presidential gifts from heads of state and from ordinary citizens.

Next door to the museum stands Eisenhower's boyhood home, a small two-story frame house with an attic. His mother lived in it until her death in 1946, when it was willed to her sons. Eventually they donated it to the Eisenhower Foundation for inclusion in the Center. Left as it was at Mrs. Eisenhower's death, it contains original furnishings, including the upright piano the boys learned to play and the big double beds in which they slept.

The Dwight D. Eisenhower Library, across the park, was established to preserve the President's papers and other related historical material. The library is administered by the National Archives as an integral part of our system of national record-keeping. Like the other Presidential Libraries, it is archival and not open to the general public.

President Eisenhower requested to be buried in Abilene and his wishes were observed. President and Mrs. Eisenhower and their infant son, Doud, are entombed in The Place of Meditation, a steepled sanctuary located at the head of the mall centering the park. Etched above their marble sarcophagi are the memorable words spoken by General Eisenhower at London's Guildhall on July 12, 1945:

> *Humility must always be the portion of any man who receives acclaim earned in blood of his followers and sacrifices of his friends.*

DIRECTIONS: Abilene is 85 miles west of Topeka, Kansas, just off I–70. From either eastbound or westbound, take Exit 275 and proceed south on State Route 15 for 2 miles to Abilene. Historical markers guide visitors to The Eisenhower Center (Figure 99).

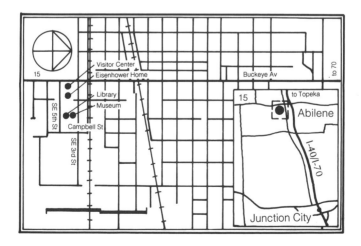

Figure 99. Location of The Eisenhower Center, Abilene, Kansas.

PUBLIC USE: Season and hours: Daily 9 A.M.– 4:45 P.M., with extended hours in the summer. Closed Thanksgiving, Christmas, New Year's Day. **Fees:** For the museum: Ages 16 – 61, $2; 62 and over, $1.50; 15 and under, free. All other attractions are free. Allow 2 hours to enjoy the Eisenhower Center. **Gift shop. For people with disabilities:** Fully accessible.

FOR ADDITIONAL INFORMATION: Contact: The Eisenhower Center, Abilene, Kansas 67410, (913) 263–4751. **Read:** Stephen E. Ambrose. 1990. *Eisenhower: Soldier and President.* New York: Simon and Schuster.

Eisenhower National Historic Site

Gettysburg, Pennsylvania

When I die, I am going to leave a piece of ground better than I found it.

— Dwight D. Eisenhower

In 1915, Second Lieutenant Dwight David Eisenhower graduated from West Point. Eisenhower was a captain in 1918 when Camp Colt, in Gettysburg, Pennsylvania, was set up as a Tank Training Center. He was promoted to the rank of Lieutenant Colonel (temporary) to command the army's fledgling tank corps. He was frustrated by serving stateside duty while a war was being fought in Europe; nonetheless, he fell in love with Gettysburg, a pretty rural town in the foothills of the Appalachians.

Thirty-three years later, General of the Army Dwight D. Eisenhower and his wife bought a ramshackle farm and its run-down house (Figure 100) on the outskirts of Gettysburg. It was a dream come true for an army couple who had spent a lifetime moving from one army post to another, and from one rental to another, to find permanence and pride of ownership at last. They had the house partially razed and replaced it with "Mamie's Dream House," a twenty-room Georgian that was completed in 1955.

The house contains eight bedrooms, eight baths, a living room, a dining room, a kitchen, and a porch. The living room is filled with Mrs. Eisenhower's treasures — an accumulation of furniture,

Figure 100. Eisenhower National Historic Site, Gettysburg, Pennsylvania. Photograph courtesy of National Park Service.

family pictures, and decorative objects collected over thirty-nine years of marriage — as well as with gifts the couple received from friends and admirers from around the world. To the Eisenhowers, the heart of the house was the sun porch. Mrs. Eisenhower once said, "We lived on the porch," and it is easy to see why. The comfortable furniture and casual atmosphere were perfect for informal entertaining and relaxation. The view from the sun porch looks out to the east, to the Gettysburg battlefield.

Just outside the porch is the most famous conversation piece — Ike's putting green and sand trap, installed by the Professional Golfer's Association in the 1950s as a thank-you gift to America's most famous duffer.

The farm consists of three main buildings — the house, a barn, and a guest house — plus a reception center. Visitors are transported to the farm by bus from the Eisenhower Tour Information Center, which is located in the lower level of the National Park Service Visitor Center in downtown Gettysburg. Tours of the house and grounds are self-guided, with points of interest marked by red and white five-star signs. In addition, visitors interested in walking may take a half-mile walking tour of the farm, using a brochure as a guide, or they may walk to the skeet range, where an exhibit explains Eisenhower's interest in the shooting sports.

During the Eisenhower Presidency the Gettysburg farm was an essential retreat from the pressures of Washington. It once served as temporary White House while the President recuperated from his first heart attack. Thus it was host to many national and world leaders. Charles DeGaulle, upon visiting the Eisenhower farm, wrote:

> *Place, agreeable.*
> *Site, interesting.*
> *Host, charming.*

In 1967, the Eisenhowers presented the farm to the federal government, but they remained in residence until Ike's death in 1969, and Mrs. Eisenhower's in 1979. In 1978 she had remarked, "We had only one home ... our farm."

DIRECTIONS: Gettysburg is 35 miles southwest of Harrisburg, Pennsylvania, at the junction of US Routes 15 and 30. Follow the signs to the National Park Service Visitor Center (Figure 101).

PUBLIC USE: Season and hours: April-October, daily 9 A.M.– 4:15 P.M.; November 1-March 31, Wednesday-Sunday 9 A.M.– 4 P.M. Closed Thanks-

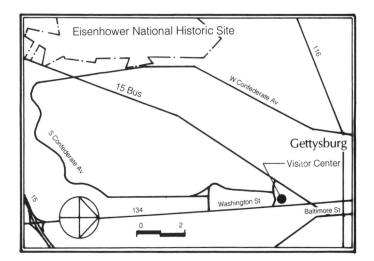

Figure 101. Location of Eisenhower National Historic Site, Gettysburg, Pennsylvania.

giving, Christmas and New Year's Day and for 4 weeks from mid-January to mid-February. **Fees:** Adults, $3.60; children 13–16, $1.60; 6–12, $1.05. Educational groups and holders of Golden Eagle, Age or Access Passes receive reduced rates. All visits begin at the Eisenhower Tour Information Center located in the National Park Service Visitor Center. Visits can be made only by shuttle bus. Allow 2 hours to enjoy the Eisenhower Farm. **Gift shops:** One at the Farm, one at the Visitor Center. **For people with disabilities:** Arrangements should be made at the Eisenhower Tour Information Center.

EDUCATIONAL FACILITIES: The Visitor Center serves the Eisenhower Farm and the Gettysburg National Military Park, site of the Civil War's most famous battle. The Gettysburg National Cemetery is across the street from the Visitor Center.

FOR ADDITIONAL INFORMATION: Contact: Superintendent, Eisenhower National Historic Site, 97 Taneytown Road, Gettysburg, Pennsylvania 17325, (717) 338–9114. **Read:** (1) Dwight D. Eisenhower. 1967. *At Ease: Stories I Tell to Friends.* New York: Doubleday. (Reprinted by Eastern Acorn Press, 1981, 1989.) (2) Dwight D. Eisenhower. 1969. *In Review: Pictures I've Kept.* New York: Doubleday.

John Fitzgerald Kennedy

Thirty-fifth President
1961 – 1963

Born May 29, 1917, Brookline, Massachusetts
Died November 22, 1963, Dallas, Texas

*And so, my fellow Americans, ask not what your country
can do for you: ask what you can do for your country.*
— John F. Kennedy, 1961

John F. Kennedy was the first President born in the twentieth century and the youngest ever elected. Despite doubts about his inexperience and fears of his Roman Catholicism, he prevailed to win the Presidency; he captured the imagination of the world and the nation with his idealism, his youthful vigor, and his vision of a modern Camelot. He envisioned a "New Frontier of renewal as well as change," to be led by a young generation brought up in a fast-paced world of instant communication and expanding global responsibility.

Just short of three years into his term, Kennedy was felled by an assassin's bullet, his dream for America unrealized. His memory still lives, however, in the hearts, minds, and actions of those left behind, those dedicated to fulfilling that dream.

> *We in this country, in this generation, are, by destiny rather than choice, the watchmen on the walls of world freedom. We ask, therefore, that we may exercise our strength with wisdom and restraint, and that we may achieve in our time and for all time the ancient vision of "peace on earth, good will toward men." That must always be our goal . . . and the righteousness of our cause must always underlie our strength. For as was written long ago: Except the Lord keep the city, the watchman waketh but in vain.*
>
> — Kennedy's last written words, 1963

John F. Kennedy National Historic Site
Brookline, Massachusetts

John Kennedy was born into rather modest circumstances, in a small frame house (Plate 32) on a quiet, tree-lined street in a middle-class suburb of Boston. His father was an up-and-coming young executive but had not as yet accumulated fortune, notoriety, or political influence. Joseph and Rose Kennedy had moved into the house on Beals Street in 1914. The addition of four children to the family made for cramped living, necessitating a move to a larger house in the same neighborhood, on Naples Road, in 1921. They remained there until 1927.

The Kennedy family re-purchased the six-room Beals Street house in 1966. Matriarch Rose Kennedy supervised a restoration project, and the house was furnished and decorated to its earlier appearance. It was designated a National Historic Site in 1967 when the family donated it to the federal government.

Four sites important to the early Kennedy years are within easy walking distance of Beals Street: the Naples Road residence to which the family moved from Beals Street, St. Aidan's Church, The Dexter School, and the Edward Devotion School — the latter three attended by John and his older brother, Joseph. None of these sites is open to the public, but many visitors enjoy the historic walk and the ambiance of the friendly neighborhood that spawned and nurtured one of our most beloved Presidents.

DIRECTIONS: Brookline is a suburb of Boston, Massachusetts. From Boston: **By car:** Take the Massachusetts Turnpike west and exit at Allston/Cambridge, which flows into Cambridge Street. After 3/4 mile, turn left on Harvard Street. Proceed over two sets of trolley tracks; Beals Street is the sixth street after the second set of tracks. Turn left on Beals and go to #83, a green house with a flagpole. Parking is on the street. **By Rapid Transit:** Take the C line of the Green Line to the Coolidge Corner station. Follow the historical markers for a ten-minute walk to the home (Figure 102).

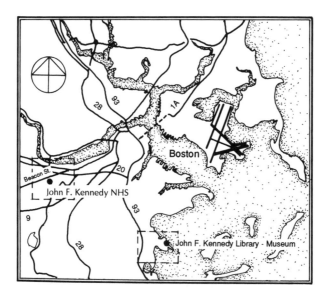

Figure 102. Location of John F. Kennedy National Historic Site, Brookline, and the John F. Kennedy Library and Museum, Boston, Massachusetts.

258

PUBLIC USE: **Season and hours:** Visitor Center open May through October, Wednesday-Sunday, 10 A.M.– 4:30 P.M. House shown by guided tour only at 10:45, 11:45, 1:00, 2:00, and 3:00. From 3:30 to 4:30 P.M. the house is open for self-guided tours. **Fees:** Adults, $2. Children 16 and under, free. Allow 1 hour to enjoy the Kennedy Birthplace. **Museum shop. For people with disabilities:** No special facilities.

FOR ADDITIONAL INFORMATION: Contact: JFK National Historic Site, 83 Beals Street, Brookline, Massachusetts 02146, (617) 566–7937. **Read:** (1) Arthur M. Schlesinger, Jr. 1965. *A Thousand Days: John F. Kennedy in the White House.* Cambridge: Houghton Mifflin, Riverside Press. (2) *Victorian Homes Magazine.* April 1993.

John Fitzgerald Kennedy Library and Museum
Boston, Massachusetts

One man can make a difference and every man should try.
— John F. Kennedy

The Kennedy Library (Figure 103) — stark, striking, and imposing — stands beside the sea that President Kennedy loved. The park-like surroundings and the unique view of Boston's historic skyline and harbor provide a beautiful setting. The interior of the Library, with huge picture windows and spacious galleries, is an aesthetic experience in perfect harmony with Kennedy's interest in the arts. The building was designed by the internationally renowned architect, I. M. Pei, who captured the modernity and vision of the man it honors.

Like the other Presidential libraries, the Kennedy Library is a research archive. In addition to Kennedy's personal and Presidential papers, the Library houses The Ernest Hemingway Collection and an extensive collection of oral history interviews.

The museum section represents the life of President Kennedy. The office of the President is illustrated by a combination of films, videotapes, audio recordings, photographs, letters, speeches, and artifacts. One exhibit area focuses on key Kennedy administration issues such as the Cuban Missile Crisis, the development of the Peace Corps, and the Space Program. The intention of the museum is to place the Kennedy story into the broad perspective of world

Figure 103. The John F. Kennedy Library and Museum, Boston, Massachusetts. Photograph courtesy of John F. Kennedy Library.

and American history. The Library's own description of the museum expresses the hope that "visitors will take from the museum a deeper appreciation of our system of government and a greater awareness of the benefits and responsibilities of living in a free society."

DIRECTIONS: By car: From the south of Boston: Take the Southeast Expressway (I–93) to Dorchester, then take Exit 14 to Morrissey Boulevard. Follow the historical markers to the Library. From the north and Boston: Take the Southeast Expressway to Exit 15, then follow the historical markers (Figure 102). **By Rapid Transit:** Take the MBTA Red Line to the JFK/UMass station, where shuttle buses transport visitors to the Library. The free shuttle buses run every 30 minutes between 9 A.M. and 5 P.M.

PUBLIC USE: Season and hours: Daily 9 A.M.– 5 P.M. Closed Thanksgiving, Christmas, New Year's Day. **Fees:** Adults, $5, with discounts for groups, students, and seniors. Allow 2 hours to enjoy the Library. **Food service:** There is a cafe, open from 10 A.M.– 3 P.M. Picnics are allowed on the grounds. **Gift shop. For people with disabilities:** Fully accessible.

FOR ADDITIONAL INFORMATION: Contact: John Fitzgerald Kennedy Library, Columbia Point, Boston, Massachusetts 02125, (617) 929–4523. **Read:** (1) Ronald E. Whealan, ed. 1993. *Historical Materials in the John Fitzgerald Kennedy Library.* Boston: John F. Kennedy Library. (2) Thomas Rose. "Problem Solving Approach Creates a Monumental Library." *Building Design and Construction.* December 1979, 110–115. (3) William Davis and Christina Tree. 1980. *The Kennedy Library.* Exton: Schiffer Publishing Co.

The John F. Kennedy Hyannis Museum
Hyannis, Massachusetts

I always come back to the Cape and walk the beach when I have a tough decision to make. The Cape is the one place I can think and be alone.

— John F. Kennedy

The John F. Kennedy Hyannis Museum (Figure 104), which opened in the summer of 1992, was founded by a private foundation, the Committee of the JFK Hyannis Museum, and is administered by the Hyannis Chamber of Commerce. The objective for the museum is to provide visitors with an opportunity to explore and appreciate President Kennedy's deep affection for Cape Cod and the lifestyle he enjoyed there. The exhibits, including over eighty photographs and a video narrated by Walter Cronkite, are a reflection of the Kennedy years in Hyannis and a celebration of the individual man, his family, and his friends in the context of a place he loved. The museum is located in the old Barnstable town hall.

DIRECTIONS: From US Route 6 (the road to the Cape), take Exit 6 and proceed on Massachusetts State Route 132 to Hyannis. At the Airport rotary,

Figure 104. The John F. Kennedy Hyannis Museum, Hyannis, Massachusetts. Photograph by David Still, *The Barnstable Patriot.*

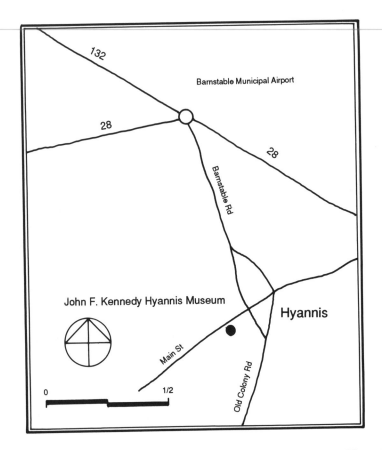

Figure 105. Location of the John F. Kennedy Hyannis Museum, Hyannis, Massachusetts.

take Barnstable Road to Main Street and go right (one-way) to the Old Town Hall, which houses the museum (Figure 105).

PUBLIC USE: Season and hours: Summer hours, Monday-Saturday, 10 A.M.– 4 P.M.; Sunday, 1 P.M.– 4 P.M. Call for off-season hours. **Fees:** Ages 16 and over, $1; under 16, free. Allow 45 minutes to enjoy the museum. **For people with disabilities:** Fully accessible.

FOR ADDITIONAL INFORMATION: Contact: JFK Hyannis Museum, 397 Main Street, Hyannis, Massachusetts 02601, (508) 790–3077. **Read:** J. Julius Fanta. 1968. *Sailing with President Kennedy, the White House Yachtsman.* New York: Sea Lore.

Lyndon Baines Johnson

Thirty-sixth President
1963 – 1969

Born August 27, 1908, Stonewall, Texas
Died January 22, 1973, Johnson City, Texas

I will do my best. That is all I can do. I ask your help, and God's.

— Lyndon Johnson

Lyndon Johnson was the eighth vice president to succeed to the nation's highest office upon the death of a President. He was undoubtedly the best prepared, as President Kennedy had entrusted Johnson with important responsibilities and kept him informed of administration policies and problems. Before becoming vice president, Johnson had enjoyed a long and effective career in Congress, the last several years of which he had been Senate majority leader. While the nation was shocked and horrified by the assassination of Kennedy, it was reassured by the strong and forceful image of Johnson as he assumed office.

Johnson maintained continuity by pressing forward with Kennedy's New Frontier agenda. In 1964, he was elected President in his own right by garnering the highest number of popular votes ever recorded. Having that new mandate, he began to press his own agenda. He negotiated remarkable success in the areas of civil rights, education, and environmental legislation. His administration saw the establishment of the Clean Air and Clean Water Acts, the Wilderness Act, and the National Trails Act. More national park lands were set aside during Johnson's term of office than in any previous administration.

By 1968, however, Johnson's Presidency had bogged down in the morass of Vietnam, and he chose not to run for reelection. Thus he perpetuated the tradition of no vice president's ever having been elected to two full terms of his own.

Lyndon B. Johnson State and National Historic Parks

Johnson City and Stonewall, Texas

The Johnson State and National Parks (Plate 33) represent a unique cooperative effort to memorialize a famous American. The scope of the effort reflects both Johnson's stature and that of the vast Texas hill country he loved.

The National Park consists of two distinct areas, miles apart. The famous LBJ Ranch is in Stonewall, fourteen miles west of Johnson City. A Visitor Center is located in the Texas State Historical Park just across the Pedernales River from the ranch. National

Park Service tour buses leave from the Visitor Center regularly, stopping at the LBJ Ranch house, the one-room schoolhouse where Johnson began his education, a reconstructed birthplace house, and the Johnson family cemetery, final resting place for the active, larger-than-life President. In his eulogy at Johnson's funeral, John Connally remarked on the appropriateness of the place:

> along the stream and under the trees he loved he will now rest. He first saw light here. He last felt life here. May he now find peace here.

The Johnson Settlement is a complex of restored structures in Johnson City that trace the evolution of the hill country from the days of the rugged, open-range cattle kingdoms to those of modern ranching and farming. In 1913, when Lyndon Johnson was five, his family moved into a comfortable house in Johnson City. The vernacular house on 9th Street has been restored and furnished to represent the period of Johnson's youth. Johnson lived there off and on until 1937, when he gave his first political speech — declaring his candidacy for Congress — from the front porch of the house.

DIRECTIONS: Johnson City is 50 miles west of Austin, Texas. From Austin, take US Route 290 and proceed west to Johnson City (Figure 106).

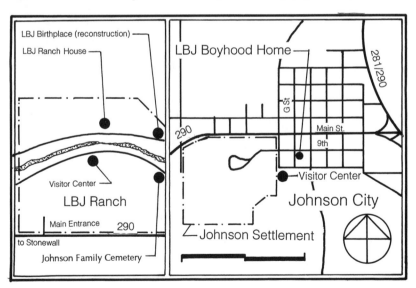

Figure 106. Location of the Lyndon B. Johnson State and National Historic Parks at Johnson City and Stonewall, Texas.

PUBLIC USE: Season and hours: Johnson City-daily 8:45 A.M.– 5 P.M.; LBJ Ranch-daily 8 A.M.– 5 P.M. **Fees:** Johnson City, free. LBJ Ranch, $3; children under 6, free. **Picnic areas:** Both parks. **Gift shop:** Both sites. **For people with disabilities:** Designated sites in Johnson City are accessible.

FOR ADDITIONAL INFORMATION: Contact: LBJ National Historic Site, Box 329, Johnson City, Texas 78636, (210) 868–7128. **Read:** (1) Robert Dallek. 1991. *Lone Star Rising.* New York: Oxford University Press. (2) Glen E. Carls and Gwendolyn A. Gardner. 1986. *Cultural Landscape Report, Lyndon B. Johnson National Historical Park.* College Station: Texas A&M University.

Lyndon B. Johnson Library and Museum
Austin, Texas

It's all here, the story of our time . . . with the bark off.
— Lyndon B. Johnson, at the dedication of
the Johnson Library and Museum

The Johnson Library and Museum (Figure 107), like the other Presidential facilities built since Roosevelt's, consists of two divi-

Figure 107. Lyndon B. Johnson Library and Museum, Austin, Texas. Photograph courtesy of National Park Service.

sions. The Library, used mainly by scholars and researchers, contains 35 million historical documents; the Museum provides public exhibits of historical and cultural interest. Sequential displays enable visitors to follow the political life of Lyndon Johnson — from his tenure as a young congressman to his term as President of the United States — author of some of the most sweeping and far-reaching legislation in our history, and victim of the division caused by the war in Vietnam.

DIRECTIONS: The Library is on the campus of the University of Texas in Austin, 1 block from I–35. Exit I–35 at 26th Street and proceed west to Red River; go left on Red River and continue to the Library (Figure 108).

PUBLIC USE: Season and hours: Daily 9 A.M.– 5 P.M. Closed Christmas. **Fees:** None. Allow 2 hours to enjoy the Johnson Library and Museum. Gift shop. **For people with disabilities:** Fully accessible.

FOR ADDITIONAL INFORMATION: Contact: Lyndon B. Johnson Library, 2313 Red River Street, Austin, Texas 78705, (512) 482–5279. **Read:** (1) Connie Shirley. 1992. "Powerful Pages of History." *Texas Highways.* October, 40–45. (2) *A White House Diary: The Exhibition.* 1985. Austin: Lyndon Baines Johnson Library. (Other exhibition catalogs are also available from the Museum.) (3) *Historical Materials in the Lyndon Baines Johnson Library.* 1988. Austin: Lyndon Baines Johnson Library.

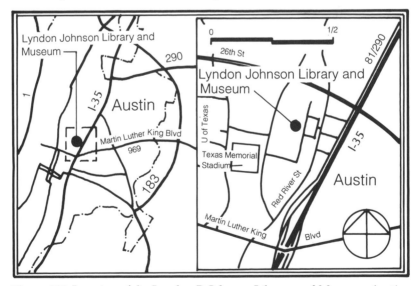

Figure 108. Location of the Lyndon B. Johnson Library and Museum, Austin, Texas.

Richard Milhous Nixon

Thirty-seventh President
1969 – 1974

Born January 9, 1913, Yorba Linda, California
Died April 22, 1994, New York, New York

*We think that when someone near us dies, we think that
when we lose an election, we think that when we suffer a
defeat that all is ended. Not true. It is only a beginning,
always.*

— Richard Nixon, 1974

*I believe in the American Dream, because I have seen it come
true in my own life.*

— Richard Nixon

Richard Nixon's dream became a nightmare as he was forced from the Presidency by the scandal of Watergate, a national trauma that overshadowed the real accomplishments in domestic and world affairs by this unusual politician and statesman. Completing the full circle of his life, President Nixon's final resting place is only a few steps from the house in which he was born, near what is called "The First Lady's Garden." There he and his wife, Pat, lie at peace.

Nixon exemplified the American dream — rising from hardship and political obscurity to the Presidency — but his positive attributes were often offset by a pugnacious and unforgiving nature. He entered politics after service in World War II and rose steadily in elected office and among the ranks of the Republican party.

While Nixon was a United States Senator from California, General Eisenhower picked him to be his running mate in 1952. He was falsely accused of having a secret expense account during the campaign, but he survived the attack and went on to be a dutiful and effective vice president. He was defeated in his own bid for the Presidency in 1960, then lost a race for the governorship of California. Most experts considered Nixon a political dinosaur, but he rose from the ashes of oblivion to win the Republican nomination in 1968 and to defeat Hubert Humphrey for the White House.

Richard Nixon's Presidential successes included initiation of the War on Cancer, the beginning of the Environmental Protection Agency, the dramatic opening of relations with Red China, the ending of the Vietnam War, and SALT I, the first nuclear arms limitation agreement signed with the Soviet Union. He was assured of greatness.

Until Watergate.

> *I let the American people down. And I have to carry that burden with me for the rest of my life.*
>
> — Richard Nixon

The Richard Nixon Library & Birthplace
Yorba Linda, California

What you will see here, among other things, is a personal life — the influence of a strong family, of inspirational ministers, of great teachers. You will see a political life — running for Congress, running for the Senate, running for governor, running for President three times. And you will see the life of a great nation — 77 years of it. A period in which we had unprecedented progress for the United States. And you will see great leaders — leaders who changed the world, who helped to make the world what it is today.

> — Richard Nixon at Dedication of the Nixon
> Library and Birthplace, 1990

Richard Nixon was born in a small farm house that has been restored on the exact spot where his father built it in 1913. The house (Plate 34) is now part of a nine-acre complex of gardens and buildings showcasing the career of Richard Nixon. The birth house stands at one end of the distinctive Formal Garden, which features seasonal plantings and a 130-foot-long reflecting pool of quiet beauty.

At the other end of the garden and pool is the magnificent Main Gallery, which houses archives, a motion-picture theater and amphitheater, and fourteen thousand square feet of museum galleries holding exhibits that highlight Nixon's political career and legacy.

Tours of the museum and birthplace home are self-conducted; through the magic of electronics visitors see and hear the former President describe his personal, governmental, and diplomatic experiences. The pistol presented to the President by Elvis Presley, the telephone used to talk with the Apollo 11 astronauts on the moon, and priceless gifts of state are a few of the hundreds of fascinating artifacts on display. Perhaps the most dramatic exhibit is a statuary hall featuring life-sized figures of the great world leaders of Nixon's era: Charles DeGaulle, Winston Churchill, Konrad Adenauer, Golda Meir, Anwar Sadat, and others. President Nixon said of these people:

leaders of Nixon's era: Charles DeGaulle, Winston Churchill, Konrad Adenauer, Golda Meir, Anwar Sadat, and others. President Nixon said of these people:

> *They are leaders who have made a difference. Not because they wished it, but because they willed it.*

Two other exhibits are of particular interest. The Lincoln Sitting Room in the White House has been replicated. It was Nixon's favorite room in the White House; he used it for relaxation, speech writing, and contemplation. Of course, everyone is fascinated by a Watergate display at which visitors listen to White House tapes and view a photo montage of President Nixon's last day in office.

> *I have insisted that the Nixon Library not be a monument to the career of one man, but a place where visitors and scholars will be able to recall the events of the time I served as President and to measure and weigh the policies my administration pursued. I hope it will be a vital place of discovery and rediscovery, of investigation and contemplation, of study, debate, and analysis.*

> — Richard Nixon

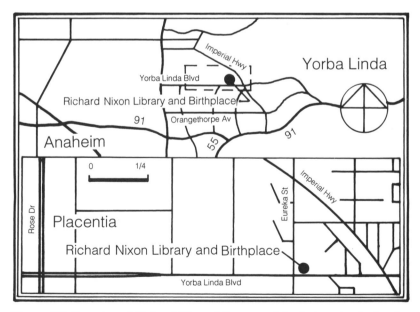

Figure 109. Location of Richard Nixon Library and Birthplace, Yorba Linda, California.

271

DIRECTIONS: Yorba Linda is 45 minutes from downtown Los Angeles. From Los Angeles, take I-10 East to I-57 South to Yorba Linda Boulevard. Turn left and proceed to the Library (Figure 109).

PUBLIC USE: Season and hours: Daily 10 A.M.– 5 P.M., Sunday 11 A.M.– 5 P.M. Closed Thanksgiving, Christmas. **Fees:** Adults, $5.95; discounts for groups, students, and seniors. Children under 8 free. Allow 2 hours to enjoy the Nixon Museum and Birthplace. **Gift shop. For people with disabilities**: Fully accessible.

FOR ADDITIONAL INFORMATION: Contact: Richard Nixon Library & Birthplace, 18001 Yorba Linda Boulevard, Yorba Linda, California 92686, (714) 993–3393. **Read:** (1) David Landis. 1993. "Nixon: Rewriting the Book on Presidential Libraries." (Reprinted by The Richard Nixon Library and Birthplace from *USA Today* "Travel" section, June 10.) (2) Leon Whiteson. 1990. "The Design [of the Nixon Library]." *Los Angeles Times,* special "Nixon Library" section, July 17, 12–13. (3) Richard M. Nixon. 1978. *The Memoirs of Richard Nixon.* New York: Grosset and Dunlap. (4) Stephen E. Ambrose. 1987. *Nixon,* 3 volumes. New York: Simon and Schuster. (5) Susan Spano. 1993. "Nixon Library: The Making of the Man." (Reprinted by The Richard Nixon Library and Birthplace from *The New York Times,* National Edition, May 30.)

Gerald Rudolph Ford

Thirty-eighth President
1974 – 1977

Born July 14, 1913, Omaha, Nebraska

My fellow Americans, our long national nightmare is over.
Our Constitution works; our great republic is a government
of laws and not of men. Here the people rule.
                                        — Gerald R. Ford, 1974

Gerald R. Ford holds a unique place in America's constitutional history; he is the only person appointed to replace both a resigned vice president and a resigned President.

Gerald Ford was born in Omaha, Nebraska, as Leslie Lynch King, Jr., in 1913. A year later the Kings were divorced, and Mrs. King took the baby to Grand Rapids, Michigan, to her parents' home. The young mother remarried in 1917, and the lad was adopted by his stepfather and given his name, Gerald R. Ford. He was not aware of the truth of his birth until he was seventeen years of age. Ford's childhood was pleasant and uneventful, his biography including a football scholarship to the University of Michigan, World War II naval duty, and graduation from Yale Law School, after which he experienced the lumps and bumps of marriage, fatherhood, and the establishment of a law practice in Grand Rapids.

Ford gravitated to politics and was elected to Congress in 1948; he climbed steadily if not spectacularly up the ladder of congressional seniority, leadership, and influence. Known for quiet, dogged, and honest determination, he was a logical and popular choice to replace the disgraced Spiro Agnew as vice president in 1973. In that post Ford served President Nixon with distinction.

The Watergate scandal and Nixon's dramatic resignation of the Presidency elevated Ford to the White House at a dark and difficult moment in America's political history. Wearied and disillusioned by the scandals and constant revelations of misdeeds at the highest levels of government, America welcomed the comfortable and honest Jerry Ford to the Oval Office.

Ford's administration, albeit honest to the core, was beset by an economic recession, by Ford's controversial pardon of Richard Nixon, and by his questionable decisions on foreign policy. Ford barely edged out California Governor Ronald Reagan in a bruising battle for delegates at the Republican convention in 1976. That was a hollow victory, as it was the precursor to a narrow defeat by Jimmy Carter in the general election.

Gerald R. Ford Library
Ann Arbor, Michigan

Unlike other Presidential libraries and museums, the components of President Ford's are in different cities, although they are considered one institution under a single administration. The library building (Plate 35) is in Ann Arbor on the North campus of Ford's alma mater, the University of Michigan. A two-story structure of brick and glass, the Library was built by the University in 1981 with funds raised privately for that purpose. It is now maintained and administered by the National Archives, which holds it under a perpetual lease.

The Library is archival. It is intended as a place for collecting, preserving, and promoting public use of materials pertaining to the Ford Presidency or related to public issues and events. Housed in the Library are nearly twenty million manuscript and audiovisual records that were moved from the White House in a convoy of nine semitrailer trucks immediately upon Jimmy Carter's inauguration in 1977. The records remained in storage in Ann Arbor until the Library was completed.

DIRECTIONS: Ann Arbor is 35 miles west of Detroit. From Detroit, take I–94 west to US Route 23 and turn north on Route 23, exiting at Plymouth Road in Ann Arbor. Go west on Plymouth Road and continue 1 mile to Beal Avenue. Turn south on Beal (University of Michigan North Campus); continue 1/2 mile to the Library (Figure 110).

PUBLIC USE: Season and hours: Monday-Friday 8:30 A.M.– 4:45 P.M. Closed federal holidays. **Fees:** None. Researchers under age 16 must be accompanied by an adult. **For people with disabilities:** Fully accessible.

EDUCATIONAL FACILITIES: Special talks and tours are available to groups by advance reservation and include screening of the Ford Museum film, *The Presidency Restored*. In association with other organizations, the Library hosts conferences and other events that focus upon public policies, government affairs, and civic education.

FOR ADDITIONAL INFORMATION: Contact: Gerald R. Ford Library, 1000 Beal Avenue, Ann Arbor, Michigan 48109, (313) 741–2218. **Read:** (1) Gerald R. Ford. 1979. *A Time to Heal.* New York: Harper & Row. (2) David A.

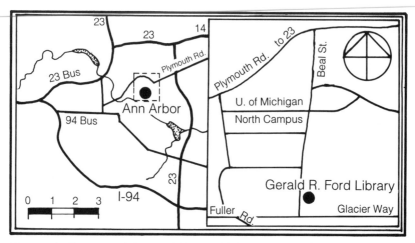

Figure 110. Location of the Gerald R. Ford Library, Ann Arbor, Michigan.

Horrocks 1994. "Access and Accessibility at The Gerald R. Ford Library." *Government Information Quarterly.* Winter. (3) David A. Horrocks. 1993. *Guide to Historical Materials in The Gerald R. Ford Library.* Ann Arbor: Gerald R. Ford Library.

Gerald R. Ford Museum
Grand Rapids, Michigan

The Gerald R. Ford Museum (Figure 111) is a handsome triangular building on the west bank of the Grand River, appropriately only a few blocks from downtown Grand Rapids, the city that Ford represented in Congress for twenty-five years. The museum was dedicated in 1981, with Presidents Reagan and Ford, the Prime Minister of Canada, and the President of Mexico in attendance.

Visitors enter the museum via a park, past a panel from the Berlin Wall, and under a representation of an American astronaut in full space gear that seems to float above the entrance. Ford's years of public service in the Congress and the Presidency coincided with many dramatic moments in our history, and the exhibits reflect them vividly and honestly. The SS *Mayaguez* crisis, the

Figure 111. Gerald R. Ford Museum, Grand Rapids, Michigan. Photograph courtesy of National Archives.

Watergate scandal, Mrs. Ford's involvement with the Equal Rights Amendment, and her battle with cancer are all fully represented. Hundreds of photographs and documents trace Ford's boyhood in Grand Rapids, his marriage, his law career, his congressional years, and his Presidency. A favorite exhibit is a replication of Ford's first campaign office — in a Quonset hut. His Oval Office is also replicated. President Ford has expressed his pleasure with the museum:

> *The exhibits convey so much of the texture and substance of this nation's experiment in self-government.*

DIRECTIONS: Grand Rapids is in western Michigan, 75 miles west of the state capital, Lansing. From Lansing, take I–96 to I–196; use the Ottawa Street exit in Grand Rapids and continue south to Pearl Street. Turn right on Pearl and proceed 3 blocks to the Museum. From Kalamazoo in the south, take US Route 131 North, and exit at Pearl Street. Turn right on Pearl and continue directly to the Museum, which is on the left (Figure 112).

PUBLIC USE: Season and hours: Daily 9 A.M.– 5 P.M. Closed Thanksgiving, Christmas, New Year's Day. **Fees:** Adults, $2, with discounts

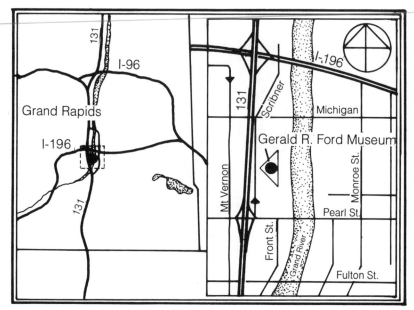

Figure 112. Location of the Gerald R. Ford Museum, Grand Rapids, Michigan.

for seniors. Children under 16, free. Allow 2 hours to enjoy the museum. **Museum shop. For people with disabilities:** Fully accessible.

EDUCATIONAL FACILITIES: An award-winning documentary film, *Gerald R. Ford: The Presidency Restored,* is shown in the auditorium every hour. Throughout the year the Museum sponsors special events ranging from seminars and discussion groups to school lectures catering to all educational levels.

FOR ADDITIONAL INFORMATION: Contact: Gerald R. Ford Museum, 303 Pearl Street, Grand Rapids, Michigan 49504, (616) 451–9290.

James Earl Carter, Jr.

Thirty-ninth President
1977 – 1981

Born October 1, 1924, Plains, Georgia

My name is Jimmy Carter and I'm running for President.
— Jimmy Carter, accepting the Democratic
nomination for President, 1976

It was a little shocking that someone we knew wanted to be
President, but if Jimmy wanted to be President, why not?
— Maxine Reese, Plains resident

Buoyed by a firm belief in what experts considered to be a quixotic cause, Jimmy Carter came from nowhere to win the White House in 1976. He had no national political base, although he had been a successful governor of Georgia. What he did have was tremendous energy and absolute integrity, something the nation was seeking after the experience of Watergate.

Before Carter, only Presidents Grover Cleveland and Woodrow Wilson had achieved the Oval Office with neither the benefit of previous civilian service in Washington nor the prestige of having been a commanding general. The lack of insider advantage and legislative experience proved difficult if not fatal for Carter. While he was indebted to no one, neither was Congress indebted to him; his effectiveness and his popularity dwindled steadily throughout his term of office.

In spite of the difficulties, the Carter administration accomplished a number of significant goals. These included a comprehensive energy program overseen by a new Department of Energy; major educational programs led by a new Department of Education; deregulation in energy, transportation, communications, and finance; and important environmental protection legislation, including the Alaska Lands Act.

International affairs provided both the high and low points of the Carter Presidency. Acting as peacemaker between the leaders of Egypt and Israel, Carter effected the Camp David Accords. His administration also accomplished the SALT II treaty with the Soviet Union, the Panama Canal Treaties, and the establishment of official diplomatic relations with the People's Republic of China. At the other end of the spectrum, Carter's Presidency suffered irreparable damage when the revolutionary government of Iran seized the American embassy in Teheran and held its staff hostage for fourteen months. Jimmy Carter brought to the office business acumen, a deep religious belief, and a probity that was forged in American small-town values; none of these qualities, however, seemed strong enough to overcome the actions of militants half a world away.

Jimmy Carter National Historic Site
Plains, Georgia

The rural southern culture of Plains revolves around farming, church, and school — all deep, lasting influences on the character of Jimmy Carter. The Jimmy Carter National Historic Site (Figure 113) was established not only to interpret his life but to preserve the history and heritage of a tiny rural southern community.

Jimmy Carter was born in Plains Hospital — he was the first President to have been born in a hospital — and grew up in the nearby community of Archery. His father was a farmer and a businessman, his mother a registered nurse.

Carter was educated in the Plains public schools, attended Georgia Southwestern College and the Georgia Institute of Technology, and received a bachelor's degree in engineering from the United States Naval Academy in 1946. His naval tour after graduation included an assignment to the staff of the famed Admiral Hyman Rickover, who oversaw the development of the first nuclear submarine. While working with Admiral Rickover, Carter attained the rank of lieutenant, senior grade.

Figure 113. The Jimmy Carter National Historic Site, Plains, Georgia. Photograph courtesy of National Park Service.

281

When Carter's father died in 1953, Carter resigned his commission to the Navy and returned to Plains, where he worked his own farm and continued his father's fertilizer and farm supply business. He soon became involved in civic affairs; he became chairman of the county school board and the first president of the Georgia Planning Association. His performance in such positions led to Carter's election as Georgia state senator and, later, as governor of Georgia. His accomplishment in state office eventually brought him national attention.

The Jimmy Carter National Historic Site covers seventy-seven acres, and the Plains Historic Preservation District encompasses most of Plains. The famous Seaboard Railroad depot, the location of Jimmy Carter's 1976 campaign headquarters, serves as a Visitor Center and houses a small museum and bookstore. The Visitor Center offers a sixteen-minute video in which President and Mrs. Carter give a tour of their home in Plains. The home is not open to the public, however, and is protected by the Secret Service.

The National Park Service is currently renovating Plains High School, with the intention of converting it into an improved Visitor Center and Carter Museum. Completion of the renovation is scheduled for 1995. Just three blocks from the depot, Plains High School is where both Jimmy and Rosalynn Smith attended school from the first through the eleventh grade. The museum will be filled with papers, memorabilia, and other material pertaining to Carter's upbringing in a small, rural, southern community.

The Jimmy Carter National Historic Site also includes Jimmy Carter's boyhood home in Archery; eventually it will include the Carters' current residence. Other attractions, not open to the public, are the Plains Hospital, Carter's mother Lillian's house, and the church where Jimmy Carter and Rosalynn Smith were married.

Self-guided driving and walking tours are available; there is also a private bus tour company. A tour of Plains, with its ordinary homes and friendly, industrious people, is a walk bearing witness to the real spirit and community of America.

DIRECTIONS: From Atlanta, Georgia, take I–75 south to US Route 19; follow Route 19 southwest to Americus and turn west on US Route 280 to go to Plains (Figure 114).

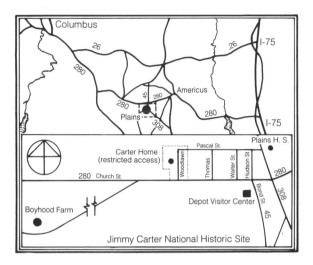

Figure 114. Location of Jimmy Carter National Historic Site, Plains, Georgia.

PUBLIC USE: Season and hours: Visitor Center, daily 9 A.M.– 5 P.M. Closed Christmas and New Year's Day. **Fees:** None. Allow several hours to enjoy Plains. **Gift shop. For people with disabilities:** No special facilities.

FOR ADDITIONAL INFORMATION: Contact: Jimmy Carter National Historic Site, PO Box 392, Plains, Georgia 31780, (912) 824–3413; The Georgia Welcome Center, Plains, Georgia 31780, (912) 824–7477. **Read:** Jimmy Carter. 1988. *An Outdoor Journal.* New York: Bantam Books.

Carter Presidential Center
Atlanta, Georgia

The Carter Presidential Center (Plate 36) is a sprawling complex of inter-connected modern buildings set in a grove of Georgia pines and flowering plants and affording a breathtaking view of the Atlanta skyline. The centerpiece of the Center is the Jimmy Carter Library, which houses the personal papers and state documents of the Carter administration for use by researchers and historians. A public museum within the Library highlights the personal aspects of the Carter Presidency and displays the gifts

presented to the Carters during their stay in the White House —
gifts from heads of state as well as hand-made gifts from the
American people. Prominent among the former are a silver falcon,
gift of the Kingdom of Saudi Arabia; a gold evening purse with
diamonds, rubies, and green onyx, a gift from the Kingdom of
Morocco; and an oil portrait of President Carter, presented by
President Lopez Portillo of Mexico.

"Town Hall" is an interactive video display by which modern
technology allows visitors to ask President Carter questions ranging from "What did Amy do all day in the White House?" to "Why
did you choose Camp David as the site for the Sadat-Begin talks?"
Also popular with visitors are the replicated Oval Office and a
formal dinner setting from the White House. A visit to the Museum of the Jimmy Carter Library provides a glimpse of the
American Presidency and the profound impact that Presidential
decision-making has on all citizens.

In addition to the Jimmy Carter Library, the Carter Center
houses the offices of the Task Force for Child Survival, Global 2000,
and the Carter Center for Emory University, all causes close to the
heart of the still-active former President.

DIRECTIONS: Take I–75/I–85 to Exit 96. Follow the Freedom Parkway 1 1/2
miles east to the Carter Center parking lot (Figure 115).

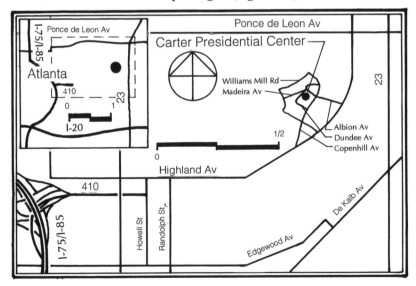

Figure 115. Location of the Carter Presidential Center, Atlanta, Georgia.

PUBLIC USE: **Season and hours**: Monday-Saturday 9 A.M.– 4:45 P.M., Sunday Noon – 4:45 P.M. Closed Thanksgiving, Christmas, New Year's Day. **Fees**: Adults, $4; senior citizens, $2; children ages 16 and under, free. Allow 2 hours to enjoy the Carter Center. **Food service**: Full-service restaurant. **Museum shop**. **For people with disabilities**: Fully accessible.

FOR ADDITIONAL INFORMATION: **Contact**: Carter Presidential Center, One Copenhill Avenue, Atlanta, Georgia 30307, (404) 331–3900. **Read**: (1) "Design for a President: The Carter Presidential Center." *Interior Design*. May 1987. (2) Donald B. Schewe. 1989. "Establishing a Presidential Library: The Jimmy Carter Experience." *Prologue*. Summer. (3) Erwin C. Hargrove. 1988. *Jimmy Carter as President: Leadership and the Public Good*. Baton Rouge: Louisiana State University Press. (4) Robert F. Hanson. 1988. "The Carter Presidential Center and Library." *Georgia Journal*. Summer.

Ronald Wilson Reagan

Fortieth President
1981 – 1989

Born February 6, 1911, Tampico, Illinois

When people tell me that I became President on January 20, 1981, I feel I have to correct them. You don't become President of the United States. You are given temporary custody of an institution called the presidency, which belongs to our people.

— Ronald Reagan

Ronald Wilson Reagan was born in the homespun Illinois farming town of Tampico, the son of a strong mother and a charming rogue of a father who suffered from what Reagan later called the "Irish Disease." The family moved frequently as the elder Reagan lost or changed employment, eventually settling in Dixon, Illinois.

Reagan's boyhood in Dixon was pleasant, albeit uneventful, and his youthful exuberance and good looks made him very popular. Small-town influences and Mrs. Reagan's strength of character helped instill in Ronald solid mid-western values. He developed an ebullient personality and charming presence, a presence easily translated into radio, television, and motion picture success. It was not a great leap, then, to transfer it to the political arena, especially in the age of television and instant communication. As President, Ronald Reagan led the nation into an era of good feeling and prosperity.

Although Reagan was elected as a conservative Republican, his political roots were those of a New Deal Democrat; his political hero was Franklin D. Roosevelt. As early as 1952, Reagan expressed reservations about the direction of the Democratic Party, but he was reluctant to switch his affiliation due to a corporate commitment to General Electric and union activities on behalf of the Screen Actors Guild. After fulfilling those commitments, he switched parties in 1962, some observers speculating that the impetus to switch was Reagan's desire to run for office — with the Democratic party controlled by the Kennedys, chances of immediate success lay with the Republicans. To the critics, Nancy Reagan responded, "Remember when Churchill left the Liberal party to join the Conservatives? He said, 'Some men change their party for the sake of their principles; others their principles for the sake of their party.' Ronnie feels that way about becoming a Republican."

Reagan had little else in common with Churchill, but he did share dramatic life coincidences with his hero, Roosevelt. Without question, they were two of the most persuasive American orators of the twentieth century. Both survived assassination attempts, each was an eternal optimist, and each led the United States with dignity and enthusiasm through a period of economic ennui and political misgivings. One, the privileged scion of wealth, led the nation to victory against the forces of fascism. The other, a product of the Great Depression, led the country when communism fell, the final victory in what was known as the Cold War.

The two leaders differed in background and political philosophy, yet both were forceful champions for change — their lives, their similarities, and especially their differences symbolized the glory of our form of free and representative government.

Scandal touched the Reagan presidency, but his charisma enabled him to retain the confidence and admiration of most of the American people.

Ronald Reagan Birthplace
Tampico, Illinois

John Reagan has been calling thirty-seven inches a yard and giving seventeen ounces for a pound this week at Pitney's store, he has been feeling so jubilant over the arrival of a ten pound boy Monday.
— *The Tampico Tornado*, February 10, 1911

Ronald Reagan was born in the cramped bedroom of a walk-up apartment (Figure 116) situated above a bakery on the main street of Tampico, a tiny midwestern farming community. The apartment consisted of six small but comfortable rooms. The Reagans remained in the apartment only a short time; they moved at least twice in Tampico before moving to Dixon, Illinois, in 1920.

The birthplace apartment has been restored to approximate its 1911 appearance and includes period furnishings and pictures. The lower floor, which once housed the bakery, has been converted to a gift shop and small museum.

DIRECTIONS: Tampico is 100 miles west of Chicago, 15 miles south of I–88. From I–88, take the Sterling exit; proceed south on Illinois State Route 88 to State Route 172, then follow the historical markers to Tampico (Figure 117).

PUBLIC USE: Season and hours: Summer months, daily 10 A.M.– Noon, 1 P.M.– 4 P.M. All other times by appointment. **Fees:** $1. Guided tours of the apartment are conducted by the owner, Mrs. Paul Nicely. Allow 1 hour to

Figure 116. The Ronald Reagan Birthplace, Tampico, Illinois. Photograph by William G. Clotworthy.

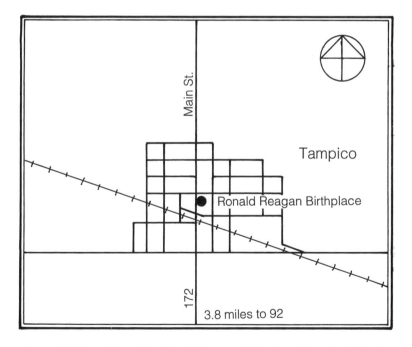

Figure 117. Location of the Ronald Reagan Birthplace, Tampico, Illinois.

enjoy the Reagan Birthplace. **Gift shop. For people with disabilities:** Not accessible.

FOR ADDITIONAL INFORMATION: Contact: Reagan Birthplace, 111 Main Street, Tampico, Illinois 61283, (815) 438–2815. **Read:** Lou Cannon. 1991. *President Reagan: The Role of a Lifetime.* New York: Simon and Schuster.

Ronald Reagan Boyhood Home
Dixon, Illinois

The Reagans moved to Dixon in 1920 when Ronald was nine; he spent important formative years in the lively community, which afforded plenty of activities devoted to the development of young bodies, minds, and spirits. The city library, the First Christian Church, and the YMCA all had programs designed to advance the growth of healthy, solid values.

The Reagan home (Plate 37) was a modest, two-story frame building of seven rooms — middle-class and comfortable. Ronald and his older brother, Neil, shared one upstairs bedroom and their parents another. The third was a sewing room for Mrs. Reagan, who took in sewing to supplement income. Downstairs was a parlor, a sitting room, and a dining room, in addition to a kitchen with a Jewel gas stove and a top-loading icebox. Outside was a barn where the boys raised rabbits, and a large vegetable garden.

Shortly after Reagan's nomination for President in 1980, a local letter carrier noticed that the old Reagan house was for sale. He rushed to the real estate office and made a $250 down payment, an act that initiated a community fundraising drive to preserve the house. The movement was coordinated by the Ronald Reagan Home Preservation Foundation, a non-profit organization of over one hundred volunteer citizens, many of whom continue to serve as tour guides, interpreters, and maintenance personnel.

The Foundation acquired the house next door to the Reagans' home and converted it into a Visitor Center. Recently they purchased the abandoned South Central School, where President Reagan attended elementary school. The ultimate goal of the Foundation is to create The Dixon Historical Center.

DIRECTIONS: Dixon is 100 miles west of Chicago, just off I–80. Take the Dixon exit and follow the historical markers to the house (Figure 118).

PUBLIC USE: Season and hours: March-November, Monday-Saturday 10 A.M.– 4 P.M., Sunday 1 P.M.– 4 P.M.; December-February, Saturday 10 A.M.– 4 P.M., Sunday 1 P.M.– 4 P.M. Closed some holidays. **Fees:** Donations accepted. Tours of the house are guided. Allow 1 hour to enjoy the Reagan Boyhood Home. **Gift shop. For people with disabilities:** The Visitor Center, next door to the Home, is accessible.

FOR ADDITIONAL INFORMATION: Contact: Ronald Reagan Boyhood Home, 816 South Hennepin Avenue, Dixon, Illinois 61021, (815) 288–3404. **Read:** (1) Anne Edwards. 1987. *Early Reagan.* New York: Morrow. (2) Norman E. Wymbs. 1987. *A Place to Go Back To: Ronald Reagan in Dixon, Illinois.* New York: Vantage Press, Inc.

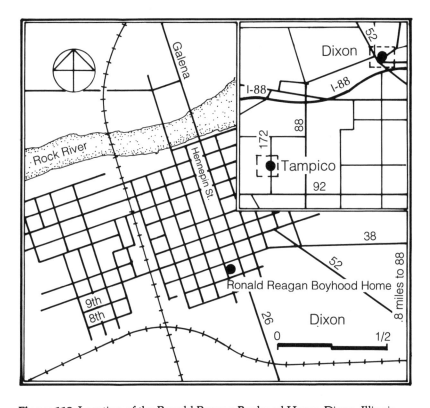

Figure 118. Location of the Ronald Reagan Boyhood Home, Dixon, Illinois.

Ronald Reagan Presidential Library
Simi Valley, California

This land, its people, the dreams that unfold here and the freedom to bring it all together . . . these are what makes America soar . . . up where you can see hope billowing in those freedom winds.

— Ronald Reagan

The Reagan Library (Figure 119) stands high in the rugged mountains of Southern California and commands a spectacular and sweeping view of the Simi Valley and its surrounding foothills. It is a Spanish mission-style complex of 153,000 square feet — the largest library in the Presidential Library system, and the first opened under the terms of the Presidential Records Act. It will eventually house all of President Reagan's papers and records related to his administration.

The library portion of the complex, as in other Presidential Libraries, is archival, with use restricted to scholars and historians.

Figure 119. Ronald Reagan Presidential Library, Simi Valley, California. Photograph by Donald W. Clotworthy.

A public exhibit area includes gifts from world leaders and displays recounting President Reagan's personal and political history. Visitors are always intrigued by the replicated Oval Office, accurate to the pictures on the walls and the knick-knacks on the President's desk.

A wide rear verandah overlooks the valley and is dramatized by a section of the Berlin Wall that was presented to President Reagan by the people of Germany in 1990. Its commemorative plaque reads ". . . for his unwavering dedication to humanitarianism and freedom over communism throughout his Presidency."

DIRECTIONS: From Los Angeles, take Ventura Freeway (US Route 101) west, turning north on State Route 23. Exit at Olsen Road and proceed north for 2 miles to Presidential Drive and the entrance to the Library (Figure 120).

PUBLIC USE: Season and hours: Monday-Saturday 10 A.M.– 5 P.M., Sunday Noon – 5 P.M. Open until 6 P.M. during daylight savings time. Closed Thanksgiving, Christmas, New Year's Day. **Fees:** Adults, $2, with discounts for groups, students, and seniors. Allow 2 hours to enjoy the Reagan Library. **Gift shop. For people with disabilities:** Fully accessible.

FOR ADDITIONAL INFORMATION: Contact: Ronald Reagan Presidential Library, 40 Presidential Drive, Simi Valley, California 93065, (805) 522–8444. **Read:** (1) Garry Wills. 1987. *Reagan's America: Innocents at Home.* New York: Doubleday. (2) Ronald Reagan. 1990. *An American Life.* New York: Simon and Schuster.

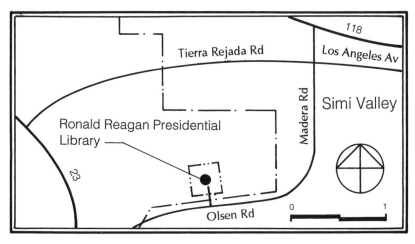

Figure 120. Location of Ronald Reagan Presidential Library, Simi Valley, California.

George Herbert Walker Bush

Forty-first President
1989 – 1993

Born June 12, 1924, Milton, Massachusetts

America is never wholly herself unless she is engaged in high moral principle. We have such a purpose today. It is to make kinder the face of the nation and gentler the face of the world.
— George Bush, inaugural address

The public career of George Bush recalls the tradition of the nation's early leaders, those men of substance and wealth who believed in public service as a way of life and accepted responsibility to their fellow citizens as a matter of natural course. George Bush was scion of an aristocratic New England family. He was educated at prestigious Phillips Exeter Academy and at Yale University, where he earned Phi Beta Kappa honors in economics. His college career was interrupted by World War II, in which he served as the Navy's youngest commissioned pilot and flew fifty-eight combat missions in the Pacific. After the war he eschewed his father's investment banking business and opted to enter the oil business in Texas.

He represented Texas in Congress briefly but was unsuccessful in two campaigns for the United States Senate. However, his solid Republican credentials earned his appointment as Ambassador to the United Nations. Later he was named Republican National Chairman, the head of the United States liaison office in China, and, finally, Director of the Central Intelligence Agency.

In 1980, Bush contested Ronald Reagan for the Republican Presidential nomination but was defeated. He accepted Reagan's offer of the vice presidency, a post he held for eight years with ability and dedication. He ran for President in 1988 and handily defeated challenger Michael Dukakis.

The Bush Presidency was marked by wild swings of success and failure. In 1990 Bush promulgated Operation Desert Storm, a war to rescue the Kingdom of Kuwait from the subjugation of Iraq, its neighbor in the Middle East. Bush cobbled together an international force under the aegis of the United Nations; the war was brilliantly conceived and fought, an unqualified diplomatic and military success.

Bush's domestic policies, on the other hand, were unsuccessful. The nation was in a deep recession and could not seem to recover from its economic decline. The President tried to persuade the voters that his policies were sound, but he was defeated for reelection in 1992 by Bill Clinton.

George Bush's most famous home is the family vacation mansion at Kennebunkport, Maine. It remains in the family and is not open to the public. Plans are well under way, however, for the George Bush Presidential Library, to be located on the campus of

Texas A&M University. Construction is scheduled to begin in 1995, with a completion date sometime in 1997.

FOR ADDITIONAL INFORMATION: Contact: Bush Presidential Library Center, Texas A&M University, College Station, Texas 77843–1145, (409) 862–2251. **Read:** (1) Fitzhugh Green. 1989. *George Bush: An Intimate Portrait.* New York: Hippocrene Books. (2) Nicholas King. 1980. *George Bush: A Biography.* New York: Dodd, Mead.

William Jefferson Clinton

Forty-second President
1993 –

Born August 19, 1946, Hope, Arkansas

All I am or ever will be came from [Hope, Arkansas].
— Bill Clinton

Bill Clinton was only thirty-four when he lost his bid for reelection as governor of Arkansas in 1980, thus earning the dubious distinction of becoming the youngest ex-governor in history. "The people sent me a message," he later wrote, " and I learned my lesson."

He learned it well. In 1982, the still-youthful Clinton swept back into the Little Rock statehouse, and he ultimately served five terms as governor. His successes in that office included balanced budgets, a scandal-free, efficient administration, and an innovative, albeit controversial, program to upgrade the state's weak educational system. Clinton also served as chairman of the Democratic Leadership Council, the National Governors' Association, the Education Commission of the States, and the Lower Mississippi Delta Development Commission.

To the surprise of many, Clinton eschewed an attempt for the Presidency in 1988; however, he ran an almost perfect primary campaign in 1992 to win the Democratic nomination from a formidable field of candidates. He went on to defeat George Bush and Ross Perot in a rancorous general election.

Bill Clinton was born in the small town of Hope, Arkansas, as William Jefferson Blythe, IV. His father was killed in an automobile accident three months before Bill's birth; Bill was left in the care of his grandparents in Hope while his mother went to New Orleans to train for nursing, a career she maintained for the rest of her life. The bright and personable boy was reared by his grandparents and other relatives until 1950, when his mother married Roger Clinton, a car salesman. Bill changed his name to Clinton when his younger half-brother, Roger Clinton, Junior, started school, so that they would both have the same name.

Hoping for a more secure financial situation, the Clintons moved from Hope to Hot Springs when Bill was seven. Clinton family life was not easy, as Roger Clinton, Senior, was a hard drinker subject to frequent rages. Through the turmoil, Bill became exceptionally responsible in school, church, and home. His half-brother Roger has said, "My brother took over the leadership role in our family when he was just a kid."

Adversity powered ambition as well, as Clinton progressed to an exemplary career. He received a Bachelors degree from Georgetown University in 1968 and a law degree from Yale University Law School in 1973. From 1968 to 1970 he studied in England at Oxford University as a Rhodes Scholar. He returned to his home state to teach at the University of Arkansas law school and to begin a private law practice in Little Rock.

Clinton was defeated in his first attempt at public office, in 1974, by a popular sitting congressman. Two years later he was elected Arkansas' Attorney General and served a single term before being elected Governor in 1978.

Bill Clinton's gregarious nature, his wit, his oratorical ability, and his unerring political instincts enhanced his record of initiating and developing solid programs of reform and progress to enable him to achieve the highest office in the land. Asked by journalist Garry Wills during the 1992 Presidential campaign why he thinks of himself as a successful politician, Clinton replied:

> I like people, and like to help them. I can get them together, organize them, help them reach their goals.

The town of Hope has developed the "Clinton Loop," consisting of the two houses in which he lived, the site of the hospital — since razed — where he was born, Miss Mary Perkins' School for Little Folks — now a hairdressing salon — and the Edith Brown Elementary School where Clinton attended first and second grades when it was Brookwood Elementary School. None is open to the public, but there are interpretive markers at each site. Hot Springs, Arkansas, where he completed his secondary education, is planning a similar tour that will include his home and high school.

FOR ADDITIONAL INFORMATION: Contact: Hope Advertising and Promotion Commission, Box 596, Hope, Arkansas 71801, (501) 777–7500; Hot Springs Chamber of Commerce, Box K, Hot Springs, Arkansas 71902, (800) 543–1433. Read: Garry Wills. "Beginning of the Road." *Time*. July 20, 1992, 33–34, 55–59.

The White House
Washington, DC

One of the enduring symbols of our government is the White House, home and office to our Presidents since 1800. George Washington initiated and approved its design but never lived in it. He was inaugurated in New York City, which was capital of the United States for one year before the President's headquarters were moved to Philadelphia and finally to Washington. The executive office and mansion in New York was a three-story brick building at 3 Cherry Street, close to what is now the Manhattan foot of the Brooklyn Bridge. The private home used as a temporary executive residence in Philadelphia was similar in design to the New York home. It was on High Street, near Independence Hall. Unfortunately, neither of those early Presidential homes has been saved.

In 1790, Congress passed the Residence Act, which authorized a house for Congress and a house for the President as part of a "Grand Columbian Federal City," which was to be built "at some place on the Potomac between the mouth of the Eastern branch and the Conogocheague." Thus was the District of Columbia conceived.

Major Pierre L'Enfant was commissioned to design the major government buildings in the city, but he was dismissed in 1792. The design of the President's House was opened to an architectural competition, won by Irish-born James Hoban, who based his winning entry on the Dublin home of the Duke of Leinster.

The cornerstone was laid in 1792, but eight years passed before President John Adams moved into the still-unfinished house. Despite such inconveniences as inadequate firewood and the lack of running water, Mrs. Adams managed to make six rooms livable.

Thomas Jefferson was the next occupant. Working with Benjamin Latrobe, he made many changes and improvements, as might have been expected from such an architectural tinkerer. The west colonnade, which now faces the Rose Garden, is a legacy of Jefferson's Presidency.

During the design competition years earlier, Jefferson had championed a design featuring a red brick facade. If he had prevailed, we might be referring to the Brick House or the Red House — proving, perhaps, that Thomas Jefferson was fallible, after all. The house was instead made of stone, which was whitewashed in 1798; the appellation "the white house" eventually followed. The house was torched by the British on August 14, 1814, during the War of 1812, and only the outer walls were left intact. When the house was finally rebuilt, white paint was used to cover the scorched stone. The "White House" did not become the official name until the Presidency of Theodore Roosevelt.

From the time of Thomas Jefferson, Presidents have redecorated, personalized, restored, or expanded The White House, some more dramatically than others, but each leaving his imprint in some way. During Andrew Johnson's tenure of office, his daughter and hostess, Martha Johnson Patterson, supervised as the house was refurbished from its post-Civil War shambles. President Taft, who desired more office space, had the first Oval Office built. Rutherford B. Hayes, a man of wealth and taste, redecorated extensively, but with an eye to enhancing tradition rather than eliminating it. On the other hand, Chester Arthur got rid of much of the house's historic furniture and hired Louis Comfort Tiffany to furnish the house in lavish Victorian style. With Franklin Roosevelt's

Presidency, The White House received an indoor swimming pool, a wheelchair ramp, and the East and West Wings as we know them.

The grounds, too, have undergone changes, having begun with sixty acres and grown smaller and more private through the years. Extensive conservatories have given way to the gardens of today.

In the late 1940s, an engineering study found that the White House was structurally unsound — it was literally falling down — and a major renovation effort was initiated. Thus did The White House arrive at its present-day form under Harry Truman.

Seat of government, home to Presidents, center of the free world. All these phrases have been used to describe The White House — the house that hosts more tourists than any other, the house that all Americans view with respect. Men battle to move into it but sometimes discover that living in it can be less than rewarding. Harry Truman called it a "glamorous prison." Gerald Ford said it was "the best public housing I've ever seen," and Mary Todd Lincoln referred to it as "that white sepulcher." Most of its residents have decried the lack of privacy, one exception being Barbara Bush, who noted, "and about those tourists . . . we love them. George and I often walk the dogs down to the gates to chat with the people who come to see this beautiful place."

The White House has been home to newlyweds and old married folks, widowers, and one bachelor. Proposals, marriages, births, and christenings have taken place under its roof. It has known the experiences of Teddy Roosevelt's children roller-skating across the floor, the pillow fights of the Garfield boys, and the courtship of Lynda Johnson in the third floor solarium. In short, the White House is little different from homes all across the nation, for it is the home — temporary and less private, perhaps — of a genuine American family. Home, also, to the dreams, aspirations, and faith of an entire nation of people. It is the President's home — and ours.

The White House is open to the public for self-guided tours, although some areas, such as the Oval Office and the family living quarters, are closed. Tours begin in the East Wing and proceed by the Library and the Vermeil Room, then up the staircase to the

State Floor, where visitors may see the East Room, the Green, Red, and Blue Rooms, the State Dining Room, and the Entrance Hall.

DIRECTIONS: The White House is located on Pennsylvania Avenue, between 15th and 16th streets, and is most easily reached via the Metro subway system. The White House is a short three-block walk from the Farragut North, McPherson Square, and Metro Center stations, all stops on the Blue and Orange lines. Metro Center station is also served by the Red Line (Figure 121).

PUBLIC USE: Season and hours: Tuesday-Saturday 10 A.M.– Noon. Hours extended during the peak tourist season. **Fees:** None. Allow 1 hour to enjoy the White House. **For people with disabilities:** Fully accessible.

FOR ADDITIONAL INFORMATION: Contact: The White House, 1600 Pennsylvania Avenue, Washington, DC, Tours: (202) 456–7041 or 472–3669. **Read:** (1) *The White House: An Historic Guide.* 1991. Washington, DC: The White House Historical Association. (2) William Kloss, et al. 1992. *Art in the White House: A Nation's Pride.* Washington, DC: The White House Historical Association. (3) William Seale. 1992. *The White House: The History of an American Idea.* Washington, DC: The American Institute of Architects. (4) William Seale. 1986. *The President's House: A History,* 2 volumes. Washington, DC: The White House Historical Association.

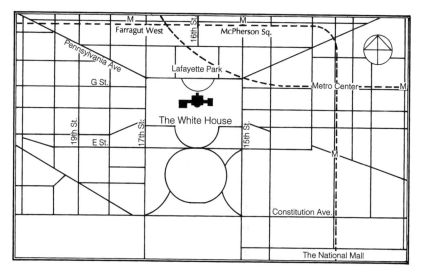

Figure 121. Location of the White House, Washington, DC.

Camp David
Maryland

In 1942, Franklin Roosevelt, searching for relief from the summer heat and humidity of Washington, established a retreat in the Catoctin Mountains of Maryland. He called the place "Shangri-La," the name of the perfect mountain kingdom described by James Hilton in his novel, *Lost Horizon*. It was re-named Camp David by President Eisenhower in honor of his grandson, and it has been the official Presidential retreat ever since. The camp has an office for the President, living quarters for the First Family, staff, and guests, and recreational facilities of all kinds, including a putting green and swimming pool.

Regular government business is conducted at Camp David, where Presidents have hosted important international conferences and negotiations. President Roosevelt met with Prime Minister Churchill during World War II, and President Eisenhower conferred with Premier Khrushchev of the Soviet Union in 1959. In the most famous meeting, President Carter used the privacy and informality of Camp David to host peace talks between President Anwar el-Sadat of Egypt and Prime Minister Menachem Begin of

Israel. A major agreement resulted, known to the world as the Camp David Accords.

Camp David is administered by the Military Office of the White House and operated by the United States Navy. It is protected by the United States Marines and is not open to the public.

Section III
Additional Information about Presidential Sites

Birthplaces of the Presidents

George Washington: Popes Creek Plantation, Virginia. Open to the public.

John Adams: Braintree (now Quincy), Massachusetts. Open to the public.

Thomas Jefferson: Goochland County, Virginia. Historical marker.

James Madison: Port Conway, Virginia. Historical marker.

James Monroe: Westmoreland County, Virginia. Historical marker.

John Quincy Adams: Braintree (now Quincy), Massachusetts. Open to the public.

Andrew Jackson: The Waxhaws, South Carolina. Historical marker.

Martin Van Buren: Kinderhook, New York. Historical marker.

William Henry Harrison: Charles City, Virginia. Open to the public.

John Tyler: Charles City, Virginia. Private property.

James K. Polk: Pineville, North Carolina. Replicated farm.

Zachary Taylor: Orange County, Virginia. Historical marker.

Millard Fillmore: Locke, New York. Historical marker.

Franklin Pierce: Hillsborough, New Hampshire. Open to the public.

James Buchanan: Cove Gap, Pennsylvania. Historical marker.

Abraham Lincoln: Hardin (now Larue) County, Kentucky. Open to the public.

Andrew Johnson: Raleigh, North Carolina. Open to the public.

Ulysses S. Grant: Point Pleasant, Ohio. Open to the public.

Rutherford B. Hayes: Delaware, Ohio. Historical marker.

James A. Garfield: Orange Township (now Moreland Hills), Ohio. Historical marker.

Chester A. Arthur: Fairfield, Vermont. Open to the public.

Grover Cleveland: Caldwell, New Jersey. Open to the public.

Benjamin Harrison: North Bend, Ohio. Historical marker.

William McKinley: Niles, Ohio. Historical marker.

Theodore Roosevelt: New York, New York. Open to the public.

William Howard Taft: Cincinnati, Ohio. Open to the public.

Woodrow Wilson: Staunton, Virginia. Open to the public.

Warren G. Harding: Blooming Grove, Ohio. Historical marker.

Calvin Coolidge: Plymouth Notch, Vermont. Open to the public.

Herbert Hoover: West Branch, Iowa. Open to the public.

Franklin D. Roosevelt: Hyde Park, New York. Open to the public.

Harry S. Truman: Lamar, Missouri. Open to the public.

Dwight D. Eisenhower: Denison, Texas. Open to the public.

John F. Kennedy: Brookline, Massachusetts. Open to the public.

Lyndon B. Johnson: Stonewall, Texas. Open to the public.

Richard M. Nixon: Yorba Linda, California. Open to the public.

Gerald R. Ford: Omaha, Nebraska. Historical marker.

Jimmy Carter: Plains, Georgia. Hospital, closed to tourists.

Ronald Reagan: Tampico, Illinois. Open to the public.

George Bush: Milton, Massachusetts. Private property.

William J. Clinton: Hope, Arkansas. Historical marker.

Burial Sites of the Presidents

George Washington: Mount Vernon, Virginia.

John Adams: United First Parish Church, Quincy, Massachusetts.

Thomas Jefferson: Monticello, Charlottesville, Virginia.

James Madison: Montpelier, Orange, Virginia.

James Monroe: Hollywood Cemetery, Richmond, Virginia.

John Quincy Adams: United First Parish Church, Quincy, Massachusetts.

Andrew Jackson: The Hermitage, Nashville, Tennessee.

Martin Van Buren: Kinderhook Cemetery, Kinderhook, New York.

William Henry Harrison: North Bend, Ohio.

John Tyler: Hollywood Cemetery, Richmond, Virginia.

James K. Polk: State Capitol, Nashville, Tennessee.

Zachary Taylor: Family Graveyard, Springfield, Kentucky.

Millard Fillmore: Forest Lawn Cemetery, Buffalo, New York.

Franklin Pierce: Old North Cemetery, Concord, New Hampshire.

James Buchanan: Woodward Hill Cemetery, Lancaster, Pennsylvania.

Abraham Lincoln: Oak Ridge Cemetery, Springfield, Illinois.

Andrew Johnson : Andrew Johnson National Cemetery, Greeneville, Tennessee.

Ulysses S. Grant: Grant's Tomb, New York City, New York.

Rutherford B. Hayes: Hayes Presidential Center, Fremont, Ohio.

James A. Garfield: Lakeview Cemetery, Cleveland, Ohio.

Chester A. Arthur: Rural cemetery, Albany, New York.

Grover Cleveland: Old Princeton Cemetery, Princeton, New Jersey.

Benjamin Harrison: Crown Hill Cemetery, Indianapolis, Indiana.

William McKinley: McKinley Memorial, Canton, Ohio.

Theodore Roosevelt: Youngs Memorial Cemetery, Oyster Bay, New York.

William Howard Taft: Arlington National Cemetery, Arlington, Virginia.

Woodrow Wilson: Washington National Cathedral, Washington, DC.

Warren G. Harding: Harding Memorial, Marion, Ohio.

Calvin Coolidge: Plymouth Cemetery, Plymouth, Vermont.

Herbert Hoover: National Historic Site, West Branch, Iowa.

Franklin D. Roosevelt: The Rose Garden, Roosevelt National Historic Site, Hyde Park, New York.

Harry S. Truman: Truman Library, Independence, Missouri.

Dwight D. Eisenhower: Eisenhower Center, Abilene, Kansas.

John F. Kennedy: Arlington National Cemetery, Arlington, Virginia.

Lyndon B. Johnson: National Historic Site, Stonewall, Texas.

Richard M. Nixon: Richard M. Nixon Library and Birthplace, Yorba Linda, California.

Museums and Other Sites of Interest

Washington Monument
The National Mall
Washington, DC

The 555-foot obelisk, designed by Robert Mills, is the dominating feature of the nation's capital. It was dedicated in 1850.

Valley Forge National Historical Park
Box 953
Valley Forge, Pennsylvania 19481
(215) 783–1077

Site of the Continental Army's winter encampment, 1777–1778. The historical park encompasses over three thousand acres containing monuments, markers, earthworks, Washington's headquarters, reconstructed barracks, and other buildings.

Fort Necessity National Battlefield
RD 2, Box 528
Farmington, Pennsylvania 15437
(412) 329–5512

In 1754, Washington led Virginia militiamen and South Carolina regulars against the French and Indians. This was Washington's first military campaign and one of the first skirmishes of the French and Indian War. The fort has been reconstructed, with entrenchments and earthworks.

Colonial National Historic Park
Box 210
Yorktown, Virginia 23690
(804) 887–1776

Site of the Yorktown battlefield, where independence was finally achieved with the surrender of the British army to General Washington. There is a visitor center, museum, and monument.

Jefferson Memorial
South Bank of the Tidal Basin
The National Mall
Washington, DC

A circular, colonnaded structure in the classic style introduced in this country by Jefferson. The interior walls contain excerpts from his writings; the interior is dominated by a heroic statue of the great statesman sculpted by Rudulph Evans.

Jefferson National Expansion Memorial
11 North 4th Street
Saint Louis, Missouri 63102
(314) 425–4465

A 200-acre park on the Mississippi waterfront memorializes Jefferson and the others who directed westward expansion. The park is dominated by Eero Saarinen's graceful 630-foot high arch.

Lincoln Memorial
The National Mall
Washington, DC

A classical structure of exquisite beauty and dignity, the memorial contains a striking statue of the Great Emancipator, sculpted by Daniel Chester French.

Gettysburg National Cemetery
Gettysburg, Pennsylvania 17325

Site of Lincoln's famous address, November 19, 1863.

General Grant National Memorial
122nd Street and Riverside Drive
New York, New York 10027
(212) 666–1640

One of the most famous memorials in the world, Grant's Tomb is the resting place for President and Mrs. Grant.

Appomattox Court House National Historic Park
Box 218
Appomattox, Virginia 24522
(804) 352–8987

The place where General Robert E. Lee surrendered to General Grant, ending the Civil War. The tiny village has been reconstructed and includes the McLean house, where the actual signing ceremony took place.

John F. Kennedy Center for the Performing Arts
Washington, DC

A magnificent structure designed by Edward Durrell Stone, the Kennedy Center was authorized by Congress in 1958 as a National Cultural Center. It houses the Eisenhower Theater, a concert hall, an opera house, the American Film Institute Theater, the Terrace Theater, restaurants, and gift shops.

Mount Rushmore
Keystone, South Dakota
(605) 574–2523

Gutzon Borglum's incredible undertaking: the sculpting of colossal heads of Washington, Jefferson, Lincoln, and Theodore Roosevelt on the granite face of a mountain. It is one of the most striking and dramatic memorials ever conceived and produced.

The Smithsonian Institution
Washington, DC 20560
(202) 357–2700

The Smithsonian consists of fifteen museums, nine of which are located on the National Mall. There are many exhibits dealing with the Presidency and with individual Presidents and First Ladies, as well as with the history and progress of our constitutional system. One of the museums is the National Portrait Gallery, which features a Hall of Presidents containing portraits of every President, from Washington to Clinton.

Foundations

There are many foundations and other non-profit organizations devoted to the study of our Presidents, to the perpetuation of their heritage, the celebration of their contributions, and the maintenance of their homes, libraries, or museums. The following are membership groups that welcome newcomers, whose contributions and membership fees are tax-deductible. Almost all issue periodicals and conduct educational programs.

The AIA Foundation
The Octagon House
1799 New York Avenue, NW
Washington, DC 20006
(202) 626–7512

The Association for Preservation Technology International
PO Box 8178
Fredericksburg, Virginia 22404

The Colonial Williamsburg Foundation
Williamsburg, Virginia 23187
(804) 229–1000

Preservation Action
1350 Connecticut Avenue, NW, Suite 401
Washington, DC 20036
(202) 659–0915

Preserve our Presidential Sites
201 Bernhardt Drive
Buffalo, New York 14226
(716) 839–4494

The Smithsonian Institution
Office of Development
Washington, DC 20560
(202) 357–2359

National Parks and Conservation Association
1776 Massachusetts Avenue, NW
Washington, DC 20036
(202) 223–6722

National Park Trust
The Palisades
Box 40236
Washington, DC 20016
(202) 625–2268

The National Trust for Historic Preservation
1785 Massachusetts Avenue, NW
Washington, DC 20036
(202) 673–4242

Friends of Historic Mount Vernon
c/o Mount Vernon Ladies' Association
Mount Vernon, Virginia 22121
(703) 780–2000

Adams Memorial Society
Adams National Historic Site
1250 Hancock Street
Quincy, Massachusetts 02269
(617) 773–1177

Thomas Jefferson Memorial Foundation
Monticello
Box 217
Charlottesville, Virginia 22902
(804) 977–7380

Friends of Thomas Jefferson's Poplar Forest
Box 419
Forest, Virginia 24551–0419
(804) 525–1806

James Madison Memorial Foundation
129 Caroline Street
Orange, Virginia 22960
(703) 672–1776

Friends of Ash Lawn-Highland
Route 6, Box 37
Charlottesville, Virginia 22902–8722
(804) 293–9539

James Monroe Memorial Foundation
c/o Hon. Helen Taylor
Meadowfarm
16823 Monrovia Road
Orange, Virginia 22960
(703) 672–5588

Friends of The Hermitage
Ladies' Hermitage Association
4580 Rachel's Lane
Hermitage, Tennessee 37076–1331
(615) 889–2941

Friends of Lindenwald
Box 545
Kinderhook, New York, New York 12106
(518) 758–9689

James K. Polk Memorial Association
Box 741
Columbia, Tennessee 38402
(615) 388–2354

The Pierce Brigade
Box 425
Concord, New Hampshire 03302–0425
(603) 224–7668

The James Buchanan Foundation
1120 Marietta Avenue
Lancaster, Pennsylvania 17603
(717) 392–8721

New Salem Lincoln League
Box 272
Petersburg, Illinois 62675
(217) 632–4000

The Lincoln Memorial Association
The Lincoln Shrine
125 W. Vine Street
Redlands, California 92373
(714) 798–7632

Abraham Lincoln Association
Old State Capitol
Springfield, Illinois 62701
(217) 782–4836

Friends of the Lincoln Museum
Abraham Lincoln Museum
Lincoln Memorial University
Harrogate, Tennessee 37752
(615) 869–6237

Capital Area Preservation, Inc.
Andrew Johnson Birthplace
Mordecai Historic Park
1 Mimosa Street
Raleigh, North Carolina 27601
(919) 834–4844

The Friends of the Ulysses S. Grant Cottage
Box 990
Saratoga Springs, New York 12866
(518) 584–4768

The Ulysses S. Grant Association
Morris Library, Southern Illinois University
Carbondale, Illinois 62901
(618) 453–2773

Ohio Historical Society
(Harding Home, Hayes Center)
1982 Velma Avenue
Columbus, Ohio 43211
(800) 686–1541

Western Reserve Historical Society
(Lawnfield)
10825 East Boulevard
Cleveland, Ohio 44106
(216) 721-5722

President Benjamin Harrison Foundation
1230 North Delaware Street
Indianapolis, Indiana 46202
(317) 631-1898

McKinley Museum
Stark County Historical Society
Box 20070
Canton, Ohio 44701
(216) 455-7043

Theodore Roosevelt Association
Box 519
Oyster Bay, New York 11771
(516) 921-6319

Friends of the William Howard Taft Birthplace
2058 Auburn Avenue, Apt. 1
Cincinnati, Ohio 45219-3050
(513) 684-3262

Friends of Wilson House
2340 S Street, NW
Washington, DC 20008
(202) 387-4062

Historic Augusta, Inc.
Wilson Boyhood Home
111 10th Street, PO Box 37
Augusta, Georgia 30903
(706) 724-0436

Richland County Preservation Commission
Boyhood Home of President Woodrow Wilson
1616 Blanding Street
Columbia, South Carolina 29201
(803) 252-7742

The Woodrow Wilson Birthplace Foundation
1824 Coalter Street
Staunton, Virginia 24401
(703) 885–0897

Calvin Coolidge Memorial Foundation
Plymouth, Vermont 05056
(802) 672–3389

Herbert Hoover Presidential Library Association
Box 696
West Branch, Iowa 52358–0696
(319) 643–5327

Franklin and Eleanor Roosevelt Institute
511 Albany Post Road
Hyde Park, New York 12538
(914) 229–8114

Harry S. Truman Institute
US Highway 24 and Delaware
Independence, Missouri 64050
(816) 833–1400

Eisenhower Foundation
The Eisenhower Center
Abilene, Kansas 67410
(913) 263–4751

The John F. Kennedy Library Foundation
Columbia Point
Boston, Massachusetts 02125
(617) 929–4523

LBJ Foundation
LBJ Library and Museum
2313 Red River Street
Austin, Texas 78705
(512) 482–5279

The Nixon Library Associates' Club
The Nixon Library
18001 Yorba Linda Boulevard
Yorba Linda, California 92686
(714) 993–5075

The Gerald Ford Foundation
Gerald R. Ford Library
1000 Beal Avenue
Ann Arbor, Michigan 48109
(313) 741–2218

Carter Presidential Center
One Copenhill Avenue
Atlanta, Georgia 30307
(404) 331–3900

The Ronald Reagan Foundation
The Reagan Presidential Library
40 Presidential Drive
Simi Valley, California 93065
(805) 522–8511

Ronald Reagan Home Preservation Foundation
Box 816
Dixon, Illinois 61021
(815) 288–3404

George Bush Presidential Library Foundation
c/o Texas A&M University
Mail Stop 1145
College Station, Texas 77843–1145
(409) 862–2251

Publications

General

DeGregorio. William A. 1984. The Complete Book of US Presidents. New York: Dembner Books.

Gleason, David K. 1989. Virginia Plantation Homes. Baton Rouge: Louisiana State University Press.

Haas, Irvin. 1991. Historic Homes of the American Presidents, 2nd rev. ed. New York: Dover Publications.

Kochmann, Rachel M., and Helen Swenson. 1976. Presidential Burial Sites. Park Rapids: Haas Printing.

Schick, Frank L., et al. 1989. Records of the Presidency: Presidential Papers and Libraries from Washington to Reagan. Phoenix: Oryx Press

For significant buildings under the aegis of The National Park Service, the Library of Congress has the following documents:

    Historic American Building Survey (HABS)
    Historic Structures Report
    Historic Furnishings Report
    Historic Collection Management Report

To locate these publications, contact closest depository library.

A Presidential Libraries briefing book is available from the Office of Presidential Libraries. Address inquiries to:

Office of Presidential Libraries
National Archives and Records Administration
Washington, DC 20408

Biographies

Ammon, Harry. 1991. James Monroe: The Quest for National Identity. Charlottesville: University Press of Virginia.

Ambrose, Stephen E. 1990. Eisenhower: Soldier and President. New York: Simon and Schuster.

Ambrose, Stephen E. 1987. Nixon, 3 volumes. New York: Simon and Schuster.

Anderson, Judith Icke. 1981. William Howard Taft: An Intimate History. New York: Norton.

Bauer, K. Jack. 1985. Zachary Taylor: Soldier, Planter, Statesman of the Old Southwest. Baton Rouge and London: Louisiana State University Press.

Boas, Norman S. 1983. The Pierce-Aiken Papers. Stonington: Seaport Autographs.

Bragdon, Henry. 1967. Woodrow Wilson: the Academic Years. Cambridge: Belknap Press of Harvard University Press.

Brant, Irving. 1942–1962. James Madison, 6 volumes. Indianapolis: the Bobbs-Merrill Company, Inc.

Brant, Irving. 1970. The Fourth President. Indianapolis and New York: The Bobbs-Merrill Company, Inc.

Cannon, Lou. 1991. President Reagan: The Role of a Lifetime. New York: Simon and Schuster.

Carter, Jimmy. 1975. Why Not the Best? Nashville: Broadman Press.

Carter, Jimmy. 1992. Turning Point. New York: Times Books, Division of Random House.

Chitwood, O. P. 1990. John Tyler: Champion of the Old South. American Political Biography Press.

Cleaves, Freeman. 1990. Old Tippecanoe: William Henry Harrison and His Time. American Political Biography Press.

Coolidge, Calvin. 1929. The Autobiography of Calvin Coolidge. New York: Cosmopolitan Book Corporation. (Reprinted by the Calvin Coolidge Memorial Foundation, Plymouth, Vermont, 1989.)

Daniels, Jonathan. 1950. The Man of Independence. Philadelphia: J. B. Lippincott Company.

Downes, Randolph. 1970. The Rise of Warren Gamaliel Harding, 1865–1920. Ohio State University Press.

Edwards, Anne. 1987. Early Reagan. New York: Morrow.

Freeman, Douglas Southall. 1948–1952. Goerge Washington, 6 volumes. New York: Charles Scribner's Sons. (Volume 7 edited posthumously by J. A. Carroll and M. W. Ashworth.)

Ford, Gerald R. 1979. A Time to Heal. New York: Harper & Row.

Gara, Larry. 1991. The Presidency of Franklin Pierce. Lawrence: University Press of Kansas.

Grant, U. S. 1885. Personam Memoirs of U. S. Grant, 2 volumes. New York: Charles L. Webster and Company.

Green, Fitzhugh. 1989. George Bush: An Intimate Portrait. New York: Hippocrene Books.

Greer, Emily A. 1984. First Lady: The Life of Lucy Webb Hayes. Kent State University Press and The Rutherford B. Hayes Presidential Center.

Hargrove, Edwin C. 1988. Jimmy Carter as President: Leadership and Public Good. Baton Rouge: Louisiana State University Press.

Hecht, Marie B. 1972. John Quincy Adams. New York: The Macmillan Company.

Heckscher, August. 1991. Woodrow Wilson. New York: Maxwell Macmillan International.

Hoogenboom, Ari. 1988. The Presidency of Rutherford B. Hayes. Lawrence: University Press of Kansas.

Hoover, Herbert. 1951–1952. The Memoirs of Herbert Hoover, 3 volumes. New York: The Macmillan Company.

Howe, George Frederick. 1934. Chester A. Arthur: A Quarter Century of Machine Politics. New York: Dodd, Mead and Company.

King, Nicolas. 1980. George Bush: A Biography. New York: Dodd, Mead.

Klein, Philip Shriver. 1962. President James Buchanan. Lancaster: The James Buchanan Foundation.

Lash, Joseph P. 1971. Eleanor and Franklin. New York: W. W. Norton and Co.

Malone, Dumas. 1948–1981. Jefferson and His Time, 6 vols. Boston: Little, Brown, and Co.

McCoy, Donald R. 1967. Calvin Coolidge: The Quiet President. New York. (Reprinted by University Press of Kansas, Lawrence, Kansas, 1988.)

McCullough, David. 1992. Truman. New York: Simon and Schuster.

McFeely, William S. 1981. Grant: A Biography. New York: Norton.

Merk, Frederick. 1971. Fruits of Propaganda in the Tyler Administration. Cambridge: Harvard University Press.

Monroe, James. 1959. The Autobiography of James Monroe. Syracuse: Syracuse University Press.

Morgan, H. Wayne. 1963. William McKinley and His America. Syracuse: Syracuse University Press.

Morgan, Ted. 1986. FDR: A Biography. New York: Simon and Schuster.

Morris, Edmund. 1979. The Rise of Theodore Roosevelt. New York: Coward, McCann and Geoghegan.

Murray, Robert K. 1969. The Harding Era. Minneapolis: University of Minnesota Press.

Niven, John. 1983. Martin Van Buren, The Romantic Age of American Politics. New York: Oxford University Press.

Nixon, Richard. 1978. The Memoirs of Richard Nixon. New York. Gosset and Dunlap.

Nixon, Richard. 1990. Richard Nixon in the Arena: A Memoir of Victory, Defeat, and Renewal. New York: Simon and Schuster.

Peskin, Allan. 1978. Garfield. The Kent State University Press.

Pringle, Henry Fowles. 1939. The Life and Times of William Howard Taft. New York: Farrar and Rinehart.

Rayback, Robert J. 1959. Millard Fillmore. Buffalo: Buffalo Historical Society.

Reagan, Ronald. An American Life. New York: Simon and Schuster.

Roosevelt, Theodore. 1913. The Autobiography of Theodore Roosevelt. New York: Charles Scribner's Sons.

Ross, Ishbel. 1964. An American Family: the Tafts. Cleveland: World Publishing.

Schlesinger, Arthur M. Jr. 1965. A Thousand Days: John F. Kennedy in the White House. Cambridge: Houghton Mifflin, Riverside Press.

Sievers, Harry J., S. J. 1952. Benjamin Harrison, Hoosier Warrior.1833–1865. Chicago: Henry Regnery Company.

Smith, Elbert B. 1988. The Presidencies of Zachary Taylor and Millard Fillmore. Lawrence: University Press of Kansas.

Socolofsky, Homer E., and Allan B. Spetter. 1987. Presidency of Benjamin Harrison. Lawrence: University Press of Kansas.

Trefousse, Hans L. Andrew Johnson. New York: W. W. Norton and Company.

Truman, Harry, and Merle Miller. 1973, 1974. Plain Speaking. New York: Berkeley.

Truman, Harry S. 1955–1956. Memoirs. Doubleday: Garden City. (Reprinted in 1986 by Da Capo Press, Inc., subsidiary of Plenum Publishing Corp., New York.)

Truman, Harry S. 1960. Mr. Citizen. New York: Bernard Geis Associates.

Truman, Margaret. 1972. Harry S. Truman. New York: William Morrow and Company.

Welch, Richard E. 1988. The Presidencies of Grover Cleveland. Lawrence: University Press of Kansas. (American Presidency Series).

Williams, Harry T. 1965. Hayes of the Twenty-Third: The Civil War Officer. New York: Alfred A. Knopf.

Wiseman, Carter. 1990. I. M. Pei: A Profile in American Architecture. New York: Harry N. Abrams, Inc. [Chapter on the JFK Library, "The John F. Kennedy Library (196–479): Gateway to Fame," 92–119.]

Supplementary Readings on Specific Sites

Antiques Magazine. February 1989. (This issue is devoted to Mount Vernon.)

Antiques Magazine. July 1993. (The entire issue is devoted to Jefferson, Monticello, and Poplar Forest.)

Catalog of the Ernest Hemingway Collection at the John F. Kennedy Library, 2 volumes. 1982. Boston: G. K. Hall

Davenport, Don. 1991. In Lincoln's Footsteps: A Historic Guide to the Lincoln Sites in Illinois, Indiana and Kentucky. Madison: Prairie Oak Press.

"Design for a President: The Carter Presidential Center." Interior Design. May 1987.

Hanson, Robert F. "The Carter Presidential Center and Library." Georgia Journal. Summer 1988.

Schewe, Donald B. "Establishing a Presidential Library: The Jimmy Carter Experience." Prologue. Summer 1989.

Seale, William. 1992. The White House: The History of an American Idea. Washington, D. C.: The American Institute of Architects.

Other Works Consulted

ALA Handbook of Organization. 1991. Chicago: American Library Association.

American Automobile Association Tour Books

Historic Houses of America. 1980. New York: Simon and Schuster.

Bartlett's Familiar Quotations, 15th ed. 1980. Boston: Little, Brown and Company.

Bergere, Richard, and Thea Bergere. 1962. Homes of the Presidents. New York: Dodd, Mead and Company.

Boller, Paul F., Jr. 1988. Presidential Wives. Oxford University Press.

Bowling, Kenneth R. 1988. Creating the Federal City, 1774–1800: Potomac Fever. Washington, DC: AIA Press.

Cooke, Alistair. 1973. Alistair Cooke's America. New York: Alfred A. Knopf.

Current Biography Yearbook. 1988. H.W. Wilson Company.

Durant, John, and Alice Durant. 1955. Pictorial History of American Presidents. A. S. Barnes and Company.

Gardiner, Stephen. 1983. Inside Architecture. Englewood Cliffs: Prentice-Hall, Inc.

Harris, John, and Jill Lever. 1966. Illustrated Glossary of Architecture, 850–1830. New York: Clarkson N. Potter.

Information, Please Almanac. 1992.

Jefferies, Ona. 1960. In and Out of the White House. Wilfred Funk.

Jones, Cranston. 1962. Homes of the American Presidents. New York: McGraw-Hill.

Kern, Ellyn R. 1982. Where the American Presidents Lived. Indianapolis: Cottontail Publications.

Kochman, Rachel. 1991. Presidents' Birthplaces, Homes and Burial Places, rev. Osage: Osage Publications.

Kruh, David, and Louis Kruh. 1992. Presidential Landmarks. New York: Hippocrene Books, Inc.

Leech, Margaret. 1941. Reveille in Washington. New York: Harper and Brothers.

Katz, Herbert, and Marjorie Katz. 1965. Museums, USA: a History and Guide. New York: Doubleday.

McAlester, Virginia, and Lee McAlester. 1984. A Field Guide to American Homes. New York: Knopf.

McCullough, David. 1992. Brave Companions. New York: Prentice-Hall.

Myers, Elizabeth P. Presidential series volumes on Hayes, Cleveland, Van Buren, Andrew Johnson, McKinley, Buchanan, and Monroe. Chicago: Reilly and Lee Company.

National Park Service, Department of the Interior, Visitor Guides and Site Brochures.

National Park Service, Department of the Interior. 1985. The Complete Guide to America's National Parks (1884–1985), New York: Viking Press.

Nisensen and Parker. 1931. Minute Biographies, New York: Grosset and Dunlap.

The Official Museum Directory. 1989. New York: Macmillan.

Phillips, Steven J. 1989. Old House Dictionary. Lakewood: American Source Book.

Pratt, Dorothy, and Richard Pratt. 1956. A Guide to Early American Homes, North. New York: McGraw-Hill.

Pratt, Dorothy, and Richard Pratt. 1956. A Guide to Early American Homes, South. New York: McGraw-Hill.

Sale, Edith. 1927. Interiors of Virginia Houses of Colonial Times. Richmond: Wm. Byrd Press, Inc.

Schlesinger, Arthur M. 1953. The Age of Jackson. Boston: Little, Brown and Company.

Seager, Robert. 1963. And Tyler Too. New York: McGraw-Hill.

Steinberg, Alfred. 1967. The First Ten. New York: Doubleday.

Summerson, John. 1946. Georgian London. New York: Charles Scribner's Sons.

Tallmadge, Thomas E. 1927. The Story of Architecture in America, New York: W. W. Norton and Company, Inc.

Thane, Elswyth. 1966. Mount Vernon is Ours. New York: Duell, Sloan and Pearce.

Whiffen, Marcus. 1969. American Architecture Since 1780. Cambridge: The MIT Press.

White, Norval. 1976. The Architecture Book. New York: Knopf.

Whitney, David C. 1990. The American Presidents. New York: Prentice Hall.

Who's Who in America, 1991–1992. New York: Macmillan.

Who's Who in American Politics, 1991–1992. New York: W. W. Bowker Company.

Wills, Garry. Reagan's America: Innocents at Home. New York: Doubleday.

Juvenile

Encyclopedia of Presidents. 1987–1988. Chicago: Children's Press.

Presidents of the United States. 1989–1990. Ada: Garrett Educational Corporation.

World Leaders, Past and Present. 1987–1990. New York: Chelsea Publishers.

Fritz, Jean. 1989. The Great Little Madison. New York: Putnam.

Hoover, Herbert. 1962. On Growing Up: Letters to American Boys and Girls. New York: William Morrow and Co.

Lomask, Milton. 1965. John Quincy Adams: Son of the American Revolution. New York: Farrar, New York.

Tunis, Edward. 1969. The Young United States, 1783–1830. New York: Thomas Y. Crowell.

Index

331

333

334

336